Cambridge Imperial and Post-Colonial Studies Series

General Editors: **Megan Vaughan**, King's College, Cambridge, and **Richard Drayton**, King's College, London

This informative series covers the broad span of modern imperial history while also exploring the recent developments in former colonial states where residues of empire can still be found. The books provide in-depth examinations of empires as competing and complementary power structures encouraging the reader to reconsider their understanding of international and world history during recent centuries.

Titles include:

Miguel Bandeira Jerónimo
THE "CIVILISING MISSION" OF PORTUGUESE COLONIALISM, 1870–1930

Miguel Bandeira Jerónimo and António Costa Pinto
THE ENDS OF EUROPEAN COLONIAL EMPIRES
Cases and Comparisons

Gregory A. Barton
INFORMAL EMPIRE AND THE RISE OF ONE WORLD CULTURE

Rachel Berger
AYURVEDA MADE MODERN
Political Histories of Indigenous Medicine in North India, 1900–1955

Rachel Bright
CHINESE LABOUR IN SOUTH AFRICA, 1902–10
Race, Violence, and Global Spectacle

Larry Butler and Sarah Stockwell
THE WIND OF CHANGE
Harold Macmillan and British Decolonization

Esme Cleall
MISSIONARY DISCOURSE
Negotiating Difference in the British Empire, c.1840–95

T. J. Cribb (*editor*)
IMAGINED COMMONWEALTH
Cambridge Essays on Commonwealth and International Literature in English

Bronwen Everill
ABOLITION AND EMPIRE IN SIERRA LEONE AND LIBERIA

Anna Greenwood and Harshad Topiwala
INDIAN DOCTORS IN KENYA, 1890–1940

Róisín Healy and Enrico Dal Lago (*editors*)
THE SHADOW OF COLONIALISM IN EUROPE'S MODERN PAST

Leslie James
GEORGE PADMORE AND DECOLONIZATION FROM BELOW
Pan-Africanism, the Cold War, and the End of Empire

Robin Jeffrey
POLITICS, WOMEN AND WELL-BEING
How Kerala Became a 'Model'

Gerold Krozewski
MONEY AND THE END OF EMPIRE
British International Economic Policy and the Colonies, 1947–58

Zoë Laidlaw and Alan Lester (*editors*)
INDIGENOUS COMMUNITIES AND SETTLER COLONIALISM
Land Holding, Loss and Survival in an Interconnected World

Sophus Reinert and Pernille Røge
THE POLITICAL ECONOMY OF EMPIRE IN THE EARLY MODERN WORLD

Jonathan Saha
LAW, DISORDER AND THE COLONIAL STATE
Corruption in Burma c.1900

John Singleton and Paul Robertson
ECONOMIC RELATIONS BETWEEN BRITAIN AND AUSTRALASIA, 1945–1970

Leonard Smith
INSANITY, RACE AND COLONIALISM
Managing Mental Disorder in the Post-Emancipation British
Caribbean, 1838–1914

Miguel Suárez Bosa
ATLANTIC PORTS AND THE FIRST GLOBALISATION C. 1850–1930

Alex Sutton
THE POLITICAL ECONOMY OF IMPERIAL RELATIONS
Britain, the Sterling Area, and Malaya 1945–1960

Jerome Teelucksingh
LABOUR AND THE DECOLONIZATION STRUGGLE IN TRINIDAD AND TOBAGO

Julia Tischler
LIGHT AND POWER FOR A MULTIRACIAL NATION
The Kariba Dam Scheme in the Central African Federation

Erica Wald
VICE IN THE BARRACKS
Medicine, the Military and the Making of Colonial India, 1780–1868

Cambridge Imperial and Post-Colonial Studies Series
Series Standing Order ISBN 978–0–333–91908–8 (Hardback)
978–0–333–91909–5 (Paperback)
(*outside North America only*)

You can receive future titles in this series as they are published by placing a standing order. Please contact your bookseller or, in case of difficulty, write to us at the address below with your name and address, the title of the series and the ISBN quoted above.

Customer Services Department, Macmillan Distribution Ltd, Houndmills, Basingstoke, Hampshire RG21 6XS, England

---

The Political Economy of Imperial Relations

Britain, the Sterling Area, and Malaya 1945–1960

Alex Sutton
Lecturer in International Relations at the University of St Andrews

First published 2015 by
PALGRAVE MACMILLAN

Palgrave Macmillan in the UK is an imprint of Macmillan Publishers Limited,
registered in England, company number 785998, of Houndmills, Basingstoke,
Hampshire RG21 6XS.

Palgrave Macmillan in the US is a division of St Martin's Press LLC,
175 Fifth Avenue, New York, NY 10010.

Palgrave Macmillan is the global academic imprint of the above companies
and has companies and representatives throughout the world.

Palgrave® and Macmillan® are registered trademarks in the United States,
the United Kingdom, Europe and other countries.

ISBN 978–1–137–37397–7

This book is printed on paper suitable for recycling and made from fully
managed and sustained forest sources. Logging, pulping and manufacturing
processes are expected to conform to the environmental regulations of the
country of origin.

A catalogue record for this book is available from the British Library.

Library of Congress Cataloging-in-Publication Data
Sutton, Alex, 1984–
   The political economy of imperial relations : Britain, the sterling area, and Malaya,
   1945–1960 / Alex Sutton (Lecturer in International Relations at the University
   of St Andrews).
      pages   cm. — (Cambridge imperial and post-colonial studies series)
      Summary: "The Political Economy of Imperial Relations considers the relationship
      between Britain and Malaya after World War Two in theoretical and historical
      terms. It develops a new approach to imperialism, situating an understanding of
      the state in terms of the global economy. This approach challenges existing
      accounts of the relationship between Britain and Malaya by positing that it can
      best be characterized in terms of continuity rather than discontinuity. By
      analyzing the period from 1945 to 1960, the book charts Britain's commitment to
      Malaya, as well as Malaya's value to Britain, as part of the Sterling Area and
      in terms of the difficulties facing both the British and global economy at the
      time" — Provided by publisher.
      ISBN 978–1–137–37397–7 (hardback)
      1. Great Britain—Foreign economic relations—Malaysia—Malaya.   2. Malaya—
      Foreign economic relations—Great Britain.   3. Sterling area—History—
      20th century.   4. Malaya—Economic conditions—20th century.   5. Malaya—
      Colonial influence.   6. Imperialism—Economic aspects—Malaysia—Malaya—
      History—20th century.   7. Imperialism—Economic aspects—Great Britain—
      History—20th century.   8. Great Britain—Economic policy—1945–1964.
      9. Economic history—1945–1971.   I. Title.
      HF1533.Z4M47 2015
      337.410595′109045—dc23   2015014193

Contents

Figures and Tables

Figures

Tables

Acknowledgements

I am grateful to Steven Kettell, Peter Burnham, Ben Clift, Jim Tomlinson and Chris Clarke for all their help in the development of this manuscript. Their comments and advice have been invaluable and always appreciatively received. I would also like to thank both Jenny McCall and Jade Moulds at Palgrave Macmillan for all their support and guidance throughout the process of publication.

On a personal note, my parents, Paul and Maggie, have supported all my endeavours with love and understanding. I will be forever grateful. Finally, I owe an eternal debt to Sarah Branthwaite for her friendship, love and patience. I take great delight in dedicating this book to her.

Abbreviations

AAFA	Anglo-American Financial Agreement
BE	The Bank of England Archives
CD&W	Commonwealth Development and Welfare
CDFC	Colonial Development and Finance Corporation
DLF	(Malayan) Development Loan Fund
ECA	European Cooperation Administration
ECGD	Export Credit Guarantee Department
EPU	European Payments Union
ERP	European Recovery Program
GDP	Gross Domestic Product
IBRD	International Bank for Reconstruction and Development
IFC	International Finance Corporation
IMF	International Monetary Fund
MCP	Malayan Communist Party
OEEC	Organisation for European Economic Cooperation
OGL	Open General Licence
POSB	Post Office and Savings Bank (of Malaya)
RSA	Rest of the Sterling Area
SA	Sterling Area
TNA	The National Archives

Introduction

Why should we care about imperialism?

The study of imperialism often confronts us as a purely historical exercise. The prevailing discourse of our time is that imperialism has become an historical relic, a phenomenon that does not intrude into the workings of contemporary politics. With the formal process of European decolonisation in the 20th century, there is every reason to think that this is the case. Indeed, there is a substantial literature on the End of Empire across the disciplines.[1] It would seem quite reasonable then to imagine that imperialism has been consigned to the dustbin of history; however, recent developments in International Relations and International Political Economy contend that a new phenomenon has emerged, that of the "New Imperialism".

The New Imperialism, while a contentious term itself, refers to the US' imperial adventures at the end of the 20th and beginning of the 21st centuries. In other words, this development in scholarship identifies a resurgence of imperialism in the contemporary world. Indeed, the return to imperialism as an explanatory concept is something noteworthy itself, having been largely neglected for the second half of the 20th century (Harvey 2007; Kettell and Sutton 2013). While this development is a welcome one, it accepts the view that imperialism did, for a time, recede from global politics and return in a different and novel form, hence the prefix "new".

The "New Imperialism" is, ironically, a rather old term, and has previously been used to describe European imperial expansion at the end of the 19th century (Macqueen 2007; Gilmartin 2009). This irony directs me quite neatly to my point. The study of imperialism has been characterised throughout its existence by caesuras and neglect. Not only

1

has the study itself been neglected, but it has sought to explain this neglect with reference to the phenomenon itself: that there had simply been no imperialism. Hence, the first "New Imperialism" offers an anomaly. It is generally understood to refer to the Scramble for Africa, as if the acquisition of new land is the only imperialism, and ignores the maintenance of current imperial territory. The more recent "New Imperialism" assumes that formal annexation of territory was the "old" imperialism, and so seeks to explain contemporary imperialism as a new form: one without the state, or the occupation of territory (Kettell and Sutton 2013; Sutton 2013).

The more relevant moment for this text, however, is the end of empire. Fundamental to this idea of imperialism is that empire ended with a specific event, usually the granting of formal independence to a former colonial territory. This book seeks to explore this assumption, and to offer a more credible alternative to the apparent end of empire, one that can reconcile a series of imperialisms into a more coherent framework through a historical approach.

To highlight the value of a historical approach, Karl Marx offers a helpful metaphor. Marx (1971:536–537) invokes the story of the giant Cacus, son of Vulcan, who stole cattle from Hercules one night. Trying to cover his crime and avoid retribution, Cacus forced the cattle to walk backwards to his cave, so it would appear that the cattle had actually come from that direction, into the field, and disappeared: their location now a mystery. The problem Marx is highlighting here is that reality is more than appearance or perception. Bertell Ollman (2003:13) also highlights the significance of this passage, arguing that, in order to discover what really happened to the cattle, one needs to discover what happened the night before and to find out what is happening in the cave just out of view.

The caesuras commonly presented in the story of imperialism then are as the footprints of the cattle: it appears as if empire has ended but if we are to understand empire, then we must understand its history and its origins. Indeed, as Ollman (ibid.) points out, history is not simply a matter of discovering enough information but also how events and experiences can be incorporated into a broader understanding of social context. With imperialism, this is about understanding the historical origins of the phenomenon but also the processes through which it came into existence.

The field of History has dominated the study of British imperialism; however, it stretches out across a number of disciplines and literatures, from British foreign policy to Political Geography. The historical study of the British Empire, however, has recently seen the development of yet another new set of approaches, New Imperial Histories (Howe 2009). This development revolves around an ideational turn, which features two trends. First, what might be called "mainstream" Cultural History.[2] This broad approach can best be understood as trying to understand the British Empire and imperialism with a view to appreciating these phenomena in terms of culture, both the culture of Britain and the cultures that empire came to dominate. As such, this is very much an intersubjective approach to culture and imperialism.

The second trend offers a more radical understanding of empire characterised by the use of postcolonial theory.[3] This approach, contrary to the former, understands empire *as* a cultural phenomenon. To clarify, this approach emphasises imperialism not as a phenomenon with an attendant culture but as a cultural artefact itself. While Cultural History has broadly followed the trend of Imperial History in seeking to periodise imperialism, postcolonial literature has done the opposite and argued, given its understanding of imperialism as a cultural artefact, that imperialism has continued by virtue of its existence as a cultural phenomenon.

Cain and Hopkins (1980:465), however, make the point that British overseas expansion also needs to be appreciated in terms of the economic conditions, broadly understood, within which state managers make decisions. This has been a very successful means of understanding the basis behind major decisions in the history of the British state, which, of course, is the key factor in imperialism.[4] More recent scholarship has returned to this appreciation of political and economic history.[5] Indeed, this book's focus is British imperial economic relations, which lies in the overlap between Political Economy and Economic History. The value brought to the study of British imperialism by these fields has been the incredible detail offered by close analysis of state documents, mainly from the National Archives at Kew, which has allowed a variety of Political Economists and Economic Historians to chart the apparent ebb and flow of the British Empire during the 20th century.

As Burnham (2006:81) notes, and bearing in mind Ollman's earlier point, the close analysis of state documents is only one aspect of charting the political economy of imperial relations. The state itself needs to be abstracted and understood within a broader social context. This is not difficult in itself, as all theories of the state are also theories of society; however, the difficulty lies in determining what that theory is (Miliband 1973a:3–4).

Methodology

As the book seeks to understand the behaviour of British state managers, the most valuable source of information on the daily activity of running the state lies in government archives. The argument for this text used archival documents from the National Archives at Kew, London and the Bank of England Archives at Threadneedle Street, London. This work seeks to understand how Malaya was understood and treated by British state managers within the context of post-war reconstruction. In looking at Britain's relationship with Malaya, one has to consider the role, views and decisions of state managers – that is to say, the core executive.[6] This is best found in the archives at Kew and the Bank of England.

Given that the argument takes as an assumption that imperial and domestic economic policy are tools for achieving the same strategic goals, this book has focused on the role of state managers involved in the management of both domestic and imperial economic policy. Of particular importance were documents held within the Colonial Office, the Treasury and the Bank of England. However, also of relevance are documents from the Foreign Office, Cabinet and prime minister's collections. However, CAB and PREM can be somewhat incomplete as they provide only correspondence and papers handled by the Cabinet or the Prime Minister. As such, relying on these exclusively can minimise the debate that occurs around policy decisions and emphasise the conclusions reached by the Cabinet and prime minister – which can then also mislead about how important the Cabinet and prime minister are in decision making.

There are four basic advantages to documentary analysis from archival sources beyond both CAB and PREM series (Burnham et al. 2008).

- The documents contain the widest possible information upon which policy is based.
- One can find the history or lineage of policy decisions: how decisions made by the core executive are acknowledged, refined and considered.
- It is possible to find the clearly stated views of ministers and senior civil servants, which may not necessarily be found elsewhere or as authentically represented in other sources.
- It is possible to identify departmental divisions on policy, which transcend the individual official or ministerial views.

The thesis uses the dates 1945–1960 as the chronological boundaries for the empirical focus. These dates allowed the thesis to analyse a particularly acute episode of the dollar crisis in the late 1940s, as well as the still chronic but less acute 1950s. The thesis ends in 1960 as the point in which the Malayan Emergency is declared as ended, allowing for analysis of three years of Malayan independence from Britain and to provide some comparison between Malaya as a colony of the British Empire and as an independent member of the Sterling Area, to further highlight continuity in the relationship between Malaya and Britain.

Argument

The central argument of this book is to identify the continuity of the Britain–Malaya relationship between 1945 and 1960. Situating itself in the existing scholarship on imperial economic relations, I argue that prior texts have emphasised discontinuity in the Britain–Malaya relationship. With close documentary analysis from archival sources, and the application of a Marxist understanding of imperialism, this book seeks to show the Britain–Malaya relationship is better understood through continuity than discontinuity, even after Malaya had declared formal independence from Britain.

The value of an open Marxist account of imperialism lies in the approach's broader analysis of social relations. First, open Marxism rejects a dichotomising position on key concepts. As such, it views dichotomies such as foreign and domestic, and political and economic, as false, instead arguing for the inherent unity of these concepts. Therefore it avoids separating concepts such as the state and the market from another, acknowledging that one can only be understood in terms of the other and so permitting a more complete and sophisticated analysis of social relations.

Second, and building upon the first point, the approach offers a critique of the orthodox understanding of imperialism, that one state can exploit another. The understanding of capitalism as an inherently global social form, and of states as processing "nodes" for the global circuit of capital, allows the conception of an imperialism that is ontologically prior to more orthodox accounts of imperialism; this conception of imperialism requires no bridging concepts such as the reification of a state as an extant "thing" that can actually be exploited. The idea of states as "processing nodes", or "moments", within global capitalist social relations allows the thesis to conceive of imperial relations then as the international expression of capitalist social relations. One node effectively co-opts the capacity of another node in order to better improve its own processing potential, to stress the metaphor; though this is not necessarily detrimental to the co-opted node.

Third, by situating itself in terms of a broader understanding of social relations, the approach avoids the periodisation of history, as is particularly common in accounts of imperialism (Clarke 1992; Sutton 2013).

Structure

The structure of the book is outlined as follows. Chapter 1 builds upon the critique of existing accounts of British imperial economic relations in the Introduction, developing an approach that provides an understanding of the organisation and function of the state within capitalist social relations. The chapter develops a theory of imperialism from open Marxism, which understands the state as a form of social relations, and argues that imperialism is fundamentally the domination of one state by another to improve conditions for capital accumulation within its own territory, and to benefit the interests of capital-in-general.

Chapter 2 provides a historical background to Malaya, the Sterling Area and the British pre-war economy. It argues that the inter-war period saw Britain's continued relative economic decline, and the emergence of a global overproduction crisis. The Sterling Area grew out of these conditions, slowly, as a trading preference bloc and gradually took on the functions that characterise its use in the post-war period. The chapter then provides an account of Malaya's history within the British Empire and shows that its role as a top dollar earner within the Sterling Area is historically based and is seen to be particularly important immediately prior to the end of the Second World War.

Chapters 3–5 feature a close analysis of archival documents over the period 1945–1960. Chapter 3 details the immediate post-war crisis and the effect it had on Malaya, from 1945 to 1950, providing accounts of the Dollar Drain, colonial import policy to staunch the dollar deficit, as well as efforts by the British government to make European Recovery Program (ERP) loans available for colonial development, and the devaluation of sterling. This chapter argues that Malaya was a key bulwark in maintaining the Sterling Area and characterises the imperial relationship between Britain and Malaya. Britain strictly limits Malaya's imports, sequesters the dollar earnings from Malaya's rubber and tin industries and attempts to use ERP dollar aid for use in the development of Malaya's economy. The purpose of this direction was to alleviate the acute phase of the Dollar Drain on the Sterling Area and the British economy, to sustain the domestic reforms initiated by the post-war British government and to maintain international capital vitality.

Particularly noteworthy in this period is the lack of "specific" communication between Britain and its colonies. What instead exists are "to all colonies" communiqués. This, I argue, stems from the particularly severe nature of the crisis but exists neither before nor after this period, and is likely to have severely influenced the way British imperial history has been recorded – that "Empire" was seen as a "one size fits all" and, hence, has obfuscated our current understanding of British imperial relations.

Chapter 4 focuses on the period 1950–1955: the dollar deficit, seemingly diminished by the injection of US capital through ERP dollar aid, becomes acute once more. This chapter also sees one moment stressed in the literature on British imperial relations as a moment of discontinuity: *de facto* convertibility in 1953; however, this moment does not present itself as a disruption to British–Malayan relations. British state managers, once again, emphasise the great value of Malaya in supporting the Sterling Area and the British economy during this trade imbalance, and currency shortage. The chapter stresses continuity with the preceding chapter by arguing that the fundamental relationship has not changed: Britain continues to pool Malaya's dollars in the Sterling Area dollar pool to support sterling and the Area; Britain's commitment to Malaya is also realised through its efforts to find capital for the development of the Malayan economy, claiming that independence was not far away. Furthermore, the Malayan Emergency becomes particularly intense in this period, and Britain's resolve in prosecuting the campaign against the communist insurgents is clear.

Chapter 5 provides an account of the negotiations for and lead-up to Malayan independence, as well as the consequences of Malaya's independence to the relationship between Britain and Malaya from 1955 to 1960. A further event that is emphasised as a discontinuity in the literature on British imperial relations is *de jure* convertibility in 1958. The chapter argues, again, that there is strong continuity in this relationship due to the Sterling Area's role in managing this relationship, and Malaya's particular value to Britain and the Area. Despite the intuitive notion that independence, and also *de jure* convertibility, would provide a "watershed" event and cause a substantial and noticeable schism in British–Malayan relations, nothing profoundly alters in the relationship between Malaya and Britain. Malaya's assumption of "full membership" of the Sterling Area does not fundamentally change the relationship with Britain and this remains an imperial relationship: Britain still maintains control of Malaya's foreign exchange, for the most part; its very basic role within the Area does not alter either (as holding a deficit with

Britain, and a surplus with the US – so its sterling balances do not rise greatly while it generates large dollar surpluses for the Area).

The conclusion of the project summarises the arguments made within the main chapters and highlights some key implications of the project's argument and theoretical framework. This leads the Conclusion to highlight possibilities for future research on relevant themes and issues, particularly the importance of further research in other bilateral relationships within the Sterling Area as well as the possibility of considering the role of agency in terms of those relationships.

1
Conceptualising British Imperialism

This chapter establishes the theoretical framework for the analysis of Britain's relationship with Malaya. It accomplishes this by first providing an assessment of the current scholarship on British imperial economic relations. These accounts are argued to be problematic and an alternative, open Marxist approach is developed. This approach argues that imperialism is a relationship between two states, undertaken as part of a strategy designed by state managers of the dominant state with a view to achieving adequate conditions for the reproduction of capitalist social relations.

British imperial economic relations

The literature on British imperial economic relations can be categorised according to focus, as well as approach. This section distinguishes between the literature on the Sterling Area, the British Empire and on Malaya. However, these literature groups suffer from similar problems.

The literature on the Sterling Area summarises the operations of the Area in a discrete or continuous historical moment.[1] Accounts of the Area take the operation of the trading bloc as a whole unit, examining the behaviours of the institutions and practices within the Area, rather than by looking at specific bilateral relations within the Area.[2] As such, while they do provide excellent analyses of the Sterling Area from an institutional perspective, there is little theoretical scope beyond this and certainly none that applies to any of the specific relationships Britain maintained within the Sterling Area.

The general consensus of this literature has been that the Sterling Area was partly responsible for continued British relative economic decline (Schenk 1994:6–7). While there are notable exceptions to this consensus, this literature is characterised by that view.[3] Schenk's argument (ibid.:136) runs counter to the majority of literature on the Sterling Area in that it rejects the notion that the Sterling Area was responsible for the myriad of economic problems that plagued Britain from the end of the Second World War until 1960. Indeed, while the majority of scholars argue that the only purpose of the Sterling Area was to generate a sense of international prestige for Britain and sterling, she dismisses this claim. Schenk (ibid.) points out, citing archival evidence, that both the Treasury and the Bank of England knew that the Sterling Area "did not always generate prestige for the British economy and that the controls on the use of sterling which defined the system often brought sterling into disrepute" (ibid.:136).

Schenk (1994:7) recognises the value of approaches that analyse in specific detail bilateral relationships within the Sterling Area. Further, while acknowledging it as beyond the scope of her book, Schenk recognises "research into the experiences of the [Sterling Area] members will provide some interesting insights into the functioning of the sterling area in this period" (ibid.:135).[4] She remarks that the general consensus within the Sterling Area literature is that the Sterling Area was a net burden on the British economy; however, this consensus has been maintained despite the lack of substantial scholarship on the relationships within the Sterling Area. That is, the Sterling Area, in the literature on the topic, is taken as a unit and the complex of relationships within it are neglected to favour the notion of the bloc itself. Schenk (1994) does make the point that specific bilateral relationships between Britain and the members of the Sterling Area have not been provided any scholarly attention.[5]

The literature on the Sterling Area then can be understood as providing an overview of the workings of the Area as a trading mechanism and means of implementing British international monetary policy. While most literature on the Sterling Area was written during the 1950s and 1960s, some modern scholarship has tended to reject the tendency of these earlier authors to condemn the Area as a British folly. However, modern scholarship too is generally limited in scope. The literature's focus on the broader nature of the Sterling Area means that specific bilateral relationships within the Area are neglected. While accounts of specific relationships within the Area do exist, they provide no archival evidence that might elucidate these relationships in any great depth; they are in fact used to describe the workings of the Sterling Area as a currency area rather than to understand the relationships themselves. Indeed, notable authors in this field make clear that analysis of bilateral relationships within the Sterling Area is specifically lacking in the literature and is necessary in order to fully understand British post-war external economic policy.[6] Finally, these accounts also lack explicit theoretical engagement and tend to understand the Sterling Area in terms of its own particular institutional arrangements and mechanisms. There is, again, no theorisation of imperialism and no specific relationship within the literature upon which to apply it.

The literature to date on the economic and financial relations within the British Empire has followed a similar pattern to that of the literature on the Sterling Area, focusing on the empire as an institution for the management of these relations. This is a valuable and important focus for research, the principal feature of which is the institutional nature of the British Empire and the Sterling Area as a means of regulating British international financial and economic policy. However, what these authors do not provide is an analysis of the particular contours of specific relationships within the British Empire, and, furthermore, they provide only limited theoretical analysis of the nature of imperial relations.

The two major works on British post-war imperial economic relations were published at the same time and largely overlap, providing very similar approaches, analysis and conclusions: Hinds (2001) and Krozewski (2001). This is an amusing coincidence also pointed out by Darwin (2002:1177).

Krozewski (2001:191–193) identifies four stages of the post-war British Empire. Firstly, a juncture in 1947 with a shift towards the empire away from liberalisation due to the Convertibility Crisis. Secondly, in 1949, with the devaluation of Sterling and the Korean War, Britain became even closer to the empire. Thirdly, 1953 saw "the economic relationship between Britain and the empire diverge". And, finally, 1957 saw the end of any meaningful relationship between Britain and its empire (ibid.:194). Indeed, as Krozewski (ibid.:196) notes, "British policy forged an imperial protectionist bloc between 1947 and 1953 as an alternative to a closer association with the United States or Europe. From the early 1950s, Britain moved deliberately towards convertibility and a liberalised Sterling Area."[7] However, what Krozewski's analysis fails to identify is that the British state had no easy alternative, due to its choices in the pre-war years, but to rely on an imperial strategy following convertibility. Actual alternatives that were considered, such as ROBOT, were believed so radical as to be not worth serious consideration.

Krozewski's (2001:209) central point is that economic and financial relationships between Britain and its empire are "placed at the centre of studies of the international relations of the end of empire". His central argument is that the financial relationship between Britain and its empire, based upon sterling, first led to strengthening of ties and then to their rejection, and ultimately to the end of the British Empire (Krozewski 2001:186). Certainly, Krozewski's point is a laudable one: the role of political economy is essential in understanding international relations. However, Schenk (1996:869) makes two criticisms of Krozewski's (1996a) analysis of British imperial monetary policy in the 1950s, which are both present in his later work. Firstly, she points out that Krozewski conflates the issue of the sterling balances with Britain's commitment to convertibility and the liberalisation of trade, arguing that the sterling balances posed a serious constraint on the policy of liberalisation undertaken in the 1950s (Schenk 1996:869).[8] However, the convertibility to which Krozewski refers is not "full convertibility" but only the convertibility of current account transactions. "Full convertibility", total freedom of payments and for movement of capital to outside of the Sterling Area, was not considered by the British state (ibid.). Convertibility also referred to extra-Area convertibility (i.e. "external convertibility") – available for those outside of the Sterling Area but not those within it (ibid.).

Schenk's second criticism of Krozewski lies in his characterisation that this conception of convertibility actually occurred in 1958, pointing out that controls on sterling were gradually removed between 1953 and 1955, leading to a *de facto* convertibility in 1955 (Schenk 1994:128; Schenk 1996:870). *De jure* convertibility, as Schenk refers to the move towards official convertibility in unison with European states in late 1958, merely "formalised the status quo" (ibid.).

To Schenk, these two confusions about the nature and timing of convertibility crucially undermine Krozewski's argument that the issue of the sterling balances had a significant impact upon the policy and process of trade and payments liberalisation in the Sterling Area. Schenk (ibid.) points out that if the freedom to convert sterling balances was not affected by the gradual shift to convertibility in 1955, then how was it possible that the liberalisation of trade in the 1950s rested on the reduction of the sterling balances? To Schenk, these create neither a contradiction nor a dilemma for British state managers.

Schenk raises one further problem with Krozewski's article, noting that there is an implicit assumption in his work that Britain forced the Sterling Area countries to act against their own interests by requiring them to maintain their sterling balances, and to keep their link with sterling. However, as Schenk (ibid.:871) adroitly points out, independent countries within the Sterling Area had limited choices: either stay with the Sterling Area or shift to another reserve currency, the only alternative being the US dollar. However, shifting allegiance was by no means a reasonable alternative since US investment in colonial markets was not forthcoming; thus the only viable choice was to maintain reserves in sterling because investment and capital were only likely to come from the UK and Europe.

Krozewski (1997:850), in direct response to Schenk's criticisms, identifies a cleavage in the literature between two separate explanatory aims. Both Krozewski and Hinds seek to understand post-war inter-state relations, while Schenk's work belongs to a desire to understand British economic performance. This cleavage, he proffers, explains why he places such importance upon the 1958 date, and Schenk on the 1955 date (ibid.). It seems particularly unusual that these two explanatory goals are separated in the literature, given the obvious relevance of one to the other. It is crucial that these two explanatory aims be unified. Britain's relations with other states cannot be understood without also understanding Britain's economic performance, nor can Britain's economic performance be understood without understanding Britain's relations with other states, particularly the Sterling Area, an imperial institution intended to manage the external economic policies of its constituent states to the benefit of the British economy. The acceptance of this distinction broadly maps on to the dichotomy between states and markets, politics and economics. From this distinction derives a capacity to accept at face value cleavages and discontinuities in economic relations and political relations, and indeed Krozewski and Hinds argue that a number of cleavages occur in the relationship between Britain and its empire.

Hinds' argument is perhaps even stronger than Krozewski's in that he disregards the continuity provided by the Sterling Area with regard to Malayan independence.

> By 1954 it was clear that Britain had become resigned to the independence of Ghana, Nigeria and Malaya. These were still its three most important dollar-earning colonies. As a result, Britain accepted the destruction of a critical part of the structure upon which it had built its economic relations with its colonial territories in the postwar era. The economic questions governing colonial preparedness for independence were now totally irrelevant to political reform. However, without Ghana, Malaya and Nigeria, the colonial surplus in transactions with the Dollar Area was not very substantial. The

independence of these states therefore was going to leave Britain with an empire devoid of its most valuable assets.

(Hinds 2001:200)

Factually speaking, Malaya's independence had no impact whatsoever on its contribution to the Sterling Area dollar pool, to which it continued to contribute even after 1957. Where Krozewski, Hinds and Schenk all agree is that there is a distinct moment of change in British imperial relations in the Sterling Area. While Schenk states that this is in 1955, *de facto* convertibility, Krozewski (2001:186) and Hinds (2001:200) argue that this occurs throughout the 1950s and particularly in 1958, with *de jure* convertibility. This approach is best understood in terms of historical contingency; while this literature provides an excellent historical basis for understanding how and when this occurred, it does not provide an account of why this occurred. To elaborate, while this literature explains, delineates and analyses the events of themes of imperial relations and the Sterling Area in this period, it does not provide an account of these relations in terms of a theoretical understanding of the state, the market or imperialism. Certainly, these themes are implied in their work but they are not made explicit and their analysis suffers as a result. In making these themes explicit, we can question whether these apparent discontinuities in British imperial relations are just that, or is there, in fact, a stronger continuity running beneath them to which these cleavages are mere contingency and, therefore, not to be given analytical precedence?

Krozewski and Hinds' understanding of the state and imperialism seems broadly similar. However, where Hinds' understanding of the state, empire and imperialism is not given any explicit critical analysis, Krozewski's conception of empire undergoes limited theorisation. Indeed, he argues in support of his broad approach that "imperial relationships hinged on the nature of the imperial state... The British empire... showed remarkable coherence in terms of economic institutions" (Krozewski 2001:7). There is a level of homogeneity to Krozewski's argument concerning his understanding of imperialism; this is also apparent in his characterisation of Britain and its colonies according to "core" and "periphery" positions in the international economy (ibid.:8). Certainly, this characterisation of imperialism is evident in his analysis of British imperial relations as featuring moments of holistic discontinuity, which is to say that discontinuity affected the whole empire simultaneously and that Britain had a broad and all-encompassing understanding and approach to its entire empire.

While Krozewski does analyse the relationship Britain had with its empire, his analysis seems peculiar in some regards. While he argues that a discontinuity occurs in 1957, with the move to sterling convertibility, and this marks a genuine caesura in imperial economic relations, he also notes how Britain continued to rely on its former empire to support its external economic policy, and the viability of sterling as an international currency. Particularly, he makes mention of how Britain continued to rely on the allegiance of the political elites in newly independent territories, such as Malaya and Ghana, to support British international economic policy (ibid.:201). However, this then raises the question: what is the fundamental difference in a relationship prior to and then after 1957, when both states seek to perform in the same fashion relative to each other, to the same end? Certainly, the imperial relationship needs to be analysed and theorised before an adequate assessment of such a relationship can occur, for which Krozewski provides no account. Furthermore, Krozewski's point about the role of elites in the relationship between Britain and Malaya is problematic. This obfuscates the historically developed relationship between Britain and Malaya and leaves neglected an analysis of the social conditions within which this relationship existed, and instead invokes an idea that the state is a mere instrument of an elite with a specific agenda and ignores other structural considerations.

Indeed, analysis of Britain's economic and financial relations with its empire is very much a "political economic" analysis. There is little sense of the interaction and relationship between Britain and its colonies in any specific sense, and as such Schenk, Hinds and Krozewski reify the broader relationship and tend to ignore the fact that the empire itself was not an institution in any meaningful sense but a term used to describe an aggregate of relationships between Britain and a number of other states. This literature then, while extremely valuable in characterising the key moments and events of British post-war imperial economic policy, provides little scope towards understanding the relationships between Britain and its imperial possessions as fundamentally and essentially relationships between *states*.

Given the nature of this analysis, the conclusions they reach tend to be ones that favour periodisation and disjunctions in British imperial policy. Hence, Krozewski and Hinds, and, to a lesser extent, Schenk also, argue that British imperial economic policy alters substantially after the Second World War. They both argue that the immediate pre-war period sees discontinuity from after the war, and discontinuity after 1958 (convertibility) – though Schenk disputes the importance of this *de jure* convertibility. Hinds (2001:200) also finds a discrepancy after 1953, when Britain no longer found its dollar-earning colonies as valuable as previously; though, he too marks most particularly 1958 as the moment we see a clear disjuncture in British imperial policy.

This view is clearly falsifiable and depends on how much changes in the relationship between Britain and its specific colonies after this point. This book makes the argument that, even after 1958, we see a clear continuity in British imperial relations with Malaya from the Second World War and therefore we have clear reason to question the prevailing discourse on British imperial policy after the war.

While these approaches to British imperial economic and monetary policy are not without their advantages and explanatory value, particularly their ability to contextualise British economic policy and relate it to the relations with the British Empire and the Sterling Area, their capacity to explain British imperial relations remains limited. Furthermore, while each approach has its own specific limitations, there is a broader methodological critique that can be commonly levelled against them, that is, their understanding of social form. Kettell (2004:14) makes a similar point in regard to the literature on British exchange rate policy-making that can also be levelled towards approaches to British imperial economic policy.

> This concerns their failure to address the question of "social form", namely that of why society itself should assume the specific pattern of organisation that it does. Instead, existing approaches treat the present form of society and its associated "components", such as its division into separate public and private spheres, political and economic structures, and sectoral interest groups, in an unquestioned, ahistorical, and taken-for-granted manner, as prima facie given facts of social life.[9]
>
> (Ibid.)

This failure is also true for the more specific literature on the political economy of Britain's relationship with Malaya. The literature on this subject tends to focus on links between state and business in both Britain and Malaya. This literature, then, tends to be dominated by the "Gentlemanly Capitalist" approach,[10] or equivalents.[11]

Nicholas White's (1996) analysis utilises significant archival sources. He focuses on government–business relations in Malaya before, during and after the Second World War, specifically the period 1942–1957.[12] White characterises this as beginning with an era of pre-war planning, through the occupation of Malaya by Japanese forces, to the independence of the colony as the Federation of Malaya. White's study is a rejection of neocolonialist and instrumentalist approaches to the British–Malaya relationship. White criticises both approaches on the basis that the requisite cooperation between state and business on which these two arguments rely simply did not occur. As such, his argument maintains that the interests of imperial and colonial governments and business interests coincided more through luck than judgement. White's purpose is to analyse the relationship between business and government. His focus is principally on British business and investments in Malaya during this period, and he argues that these investments decrease in importance from the mid-1950s and shows a policy of British disengagement with Malaya rather than neocolonialism. However, White's analysis only covers up to 1957 and it does not feature the important role Malaya played in supporting Britain's post-war economic policy, even up until 1960.

While White is correct that instrumentalist and neocolonialist approaches, with their strong focus on the role of agency to perform the task of maintaining the circuit of capital, require evidence to support their premises of active agential cooperation between state managers and business elites, and he does indeed show that the evidence for such strong cooperation is lacking within the National Archives, he does not attempt to explain why the state acted in the interests of capital-in-general. Effectively, in dismissing an instrumentalist approach, White has entirely neglected an opportunity for an alternative explanation. His approach then is simply a negation of one possible theoretical explanation among many.

White (1996:266), despite rejecting the "gentlemanly capitalist" approach, does not consider alternative approaches explaining government–business links (or their absence) during this period. In essence, White argues that if there was no direct collusion between British and colonial governments and the business interests within the Malayan peninsula, then any notion of a state acting in the interests of capital must be rejected in its entirety. Indeed, White (ibid.:275) goes so far as to say that "colonialism and capitalism were never married", arguing instead that British policy towards Malaya was simply concerned with disengagement.[13] White (2004:16) rejects the neocolonialist view of post-independence Malaya as mere fantasy, arguing instead that we see a considerable level of disengagement between metropole and periphery. White's view of neocolonialism is still based on the gentlemanly capitalist approach, of which even Hack (2000:305) might be considered to be guilty in characterising Britain's "pragmatic approach" as one of establishing favourable successor elites; however, imperialism does not have to rely on conspiring business elites in order to exist.

This brief review of the literature on British imperial economic relations has identified four key problems: first, a general lack of consideration for specific bilateral relationships within the British Empire, and an urge to aggregate relationships into a single relationship with a monolithic institution; second, a tendency towards the historical periodisation of post-war imperial economic relations; third, a reticence to utilise a theoretical framework to consider the concepts at play in explaining imperial economic relations; and finally, a lack of desire to explain imperialism and its specific manifestations in terms of society more broadly and profoundly.

Conceptualising imperialism

It would be valuable then to understand the nature of the Britain–Malaya relationship in terms of the characteristics of the society in which it existed. In the literature on the topic, as it stands, this is not available. Indeed, within social theory, only Marxism provides an approach that avoids the problem of accepting the foreign–domestic, as well as the political–economic, dichotomies. It rejects the reification of the state and avoids treating it as something exogenous to society. Furthermore, a theory of imperialism is necessary if we are to fully understand Britain's relationship with one of its colonies, and theories of imperialism find their most numerous expression and most concrete analytical grounding in Marxist thought.

Marx (1992c:956) said, as a critique of vulgar economics, "all science would be superfluous if the form of appearance of things directly coincided with their essence." The chapter will begin with an introduction to the most basic elements of Marx's analysis of the capitalist mode of production, also exploring the role of crisis in relation to Marx's conception of capitalism, particularly focusing on the crisis of overproduction. The next section will engage with the Marxist literature on state theory, providing a basis for a critique and arguing for an open Marxist account of the state, as a form of social relations. Finally, drawing on the open Marxist understanding of the state, the chapter will provide a critique of the literature on imperialism, and then offer its own account of imperialism.

Capitalist society

Capitalist society, as with all prior societies, is a class society (Marx 2005:6). Class is not to be seen as a social category, indicated by an income threshold or social background, but a relation between people. It is the manner in which production is organised that is the defining characteristic of the organisation of society (Marx 1992c:721). As such, it is the acquisition and conservation of control over the means of production that organises society along class lines. In capitalism, the particular social organisation of production is between those who own the means of production and those who only have their labour to sell. Exploitation occurs between the owners of the means of production, the bourgeoisie, and the working class through the unremunerated extraction of surplus value from the latter by the former.

For Marx (1992a:252), capital can be quickly characterised as perpetual movement. It is value constantly in motion to become greater value. It is, in its most abstract form, "self-valorising value". Capitalist social relations can be further characterised by the distinction between use value, the social utility of a given commodity, and exchange value, the value that commodity can be exchanged for. Further, in capitalism, the latter subordinates the former (Clarke 1994:171).

Capital increases its value through the exploitation of labour in the production process, since labour is the only means by which new value can be created. Marx represents this in Volume II of *Capital* through the circuit of capital:

$$M - C \ldots P \ldots C' - M'$$

where M is Money Capital, and is transformed into Commodity Capital (C). This then undergoes the Production process (P) and is transformed into Commodities of a *greater value* (C') which are then sold and transformed into Money (M') once more (though now of a greater quantity). This process can be broken down further, as follows:

$$M - C(lp + mp) \ldots P \ldots C' - M'(M + m)$$

Here the initial Commodities (C) which the Money Capital (M) originally purchases can be broken down into the commodities of Labour Power (lp) and Means of Production (mp), which are then set to work in the form of Productive Capital (P). The cycle then enters the phase of Commodity Capital and is transformed back into Money Capital to be put back into the circuit again. It is the productive phase of the cycle in which surplus value is extracted through the exploitation of labour power.[14]

It is only when capital has completed the whole circuit, having been transformed into its various forms that it increases its own value (Marx 1992b:133; Burnham 2006:78). This circuit, once complete, is then undertaken repeatedly on ever larger scales to accumulate surplus value of ever greater levels. The expansion of capital is necessitated through the inherently competitive nature of capitalist production; for example, by seeking to reduce the cost of labour power or the time required for the production process, capital is able to generate a greater level of surplus value than it would otherwise and thus expand greater than it would otherwise. This dynamic is transmitted to all other capitals through the means of the value-form: the increase in productive capacity leads to changes in the exchange value of the commodity, thus forcing other capitals to imitate. If this is not possible for a competing capital, then its relative decline in productivity will result in a decline of surplus value extraction, thus leading eventually to the destruction of capital.

The circuit of capital is both abstract and particular. The circuit exists as a general process of capital production and self-valorisation as well as a multitude of individual circuits throughout society. Coexistence of these phases of capital is only a result of the completion of the circuit in its entirety (Marx 1992b:183). Furthermore, capital exists in and only through the forms it takes – capital only exists in perpetual movement.

A crucial aspect of the circuit is the variety of problems that may affect the reproduction of this process – it is crisis prone (Burnham 2006:77). As Marx (1992b:183) points out, "every delay in the succession brings the coexistence into disarray, every delay in one stage causes a greater or lesser delay in the entire circuit, not only that of the portion of the capital that is delayed, but also that of the entire individual capital." If a delay occurs in one phase of the circuit, then the entire circuit is brought to a halt. For example, a halt in the first phase (M–C) would lead to a hoarding of money capital with no productive application; in the productive phase, labour and the means of production cease to be employed; and in the final phase, produced commodities form unsaleable stockpiles. Each of these delays has the potential to be a crisis.

As John Holloway (Bonefeld 1992b:145–147) notes, the notion of crisis focuses attention on dissonant moments in time as instances in which transformation can occur, and emphasises that society is neither predictable nor a steady progress towards a specific point. For Holloway, Marxism is a theory of social instability. Crisis arises from the fact that capitalism is an inherently unstable social form, and that it is unstable because of its class antagonisms. It is the antagonistic relationship between producers and the owners of the means of production that provides the foundation for the conflict within capitalist society (Marx 1992c:791). Indeed, as Holloway notes (1992b:149), this is the fundamental arrangement of capitalist social relations: if the owners of the means of production ceased exploitation, then society would disintegrate.

Further, crisis should not simply be seen as *economic* – this is merely the manner in which it is immediately apparent. Rather, rejecting the political–economic dichotomy, crisis "expresses the structural instability of capitalist social relations, the instability of the basic relations between capital and labour on which the society is based" (ibid.:159). As Simon Clarke (1994:79) also notes, it is within the notion of surplus value that the implications for the understanding of the tendencies of capitalist accumulation towards crisis are revealed, as it leads us "to identify the driving force of capitalism as the insatiable appetite of capital for surplus value". An element of the instability inherent to capitalism, as Clarke (1992:135) argues, is not only that the "driving force of accumulation, imposed on individual capitals by the pressure of competition, is the tendency for capital to develop their productive forces without limit" but also that the compulsion for the extraction of ever more surplus value leads to the removal of barriers to accumulation wherever they exist, and so leads to the expansion of the capacity of production without limit, in turn leading to the crisis of overproduction.[15]

The circuit of capital is fraught with the possibility of crisis at each stage. Each stage is prone to a variety of crises that will cease the process of self-valorisation, ranging from crises affecting the money form of capital (manifest as inflation), to labour discontent (this could take the form of strikes or disputes over working conditions), and overproduction crises (Burnham 2006:78).[16] The overproduction crisis as "the fundamental tendency of the capitalist mode of production" embodies capitalism's most basic contradiction (Clarke 1999:71). Continued accumulation relies on the continuing capacity for the market to purchase the commodities produced while providing a sufficient rate of profit; however, this capacity is limited by the purchasing power of the working class, which generates more surplus value than it receives in wages, and so "the inherent trajectory of the capitalist system is to therefore generate a large mass of commodities in excess of the consumptive limits of the market", so causing a crisis of commodity overproduction (Kettell 2006:26).[17]

The disproportionalities,[18] or crises, of the circuit of capital can manifest themselves fetishistically. An example of relevance to this book would be in the manifestation of an overproduction crisis as a currency shortage. As Simon Clarke (1994:136) explains about the overproduction crisis, "the crisis itself arises when the commodity capital which emerges from the process of production cannot be transformed into money. This happens because elsewhere somebody is holding money, which they do not immediately transform into commodities, so it is the existence of money which makes crises possible." Indeed, it is only through the separation of production and circulation inherent to capitalism that this crisis can occur. This is often seen as a trade disequilibrium, and was the fundamental cause of the Dollar Drain, which Clarke (1999:71) also terms a disproportionality. During the post-war period, where the productive power of the US led to a world shortage of dollars, since US goods were in great demand while non-US goods were not competitive enough to be sold in the US, therefore few dollars were exchanged for non-US goods. As such, while there were plenty of goods to be purchased, there was no money with which to purchase them, thus leading to a global crisis that, as ever, could be only be mitigated through the intervention of the state.

The state is often established as a pre-ordained object within the greater number of political theories; frequently, it seems a theory may start *in media res*, with the state pre-defined according to some unknown criteria. Indeed, as John Holloway (1994:24) remarks:

> In the tradition of political science, the state is taken as a basic, and largely unquestioned category. The state's existence is taken for granted before any discussion begins... In the study of contemporary politics, the determinants of state action, the relations between states, the changing forms of government, and so on, are analysed, but all on the basis of an assumed starting point, the "state".

As such, we must ask the questions, "What is the state?" and, perhaps more pertinently, "Why does it exist?". Fortunately, and famously, these questions have been asked before by Evgeny Pashukanis (1978:139):

> Why does class rule not remain what it is, the factual subjugation of one section of the population by the other? Why does it assume the form of official state rule, or – which is the same thing – why does the machinery of state coercion not come into being as the private machinery of the ruling class?; why does it detach itself from the

ruling class and take on the form of an impersonal apparatus of public power, separate from society?

Pashukanis, therefore, is asking why society appears to us in a form different to one we might intuitively imagine: as a distinct political entity, the state. The question of form and the state will be dealt with in the next section, on open Marxism.

Open Marxism

Bieler and Morton, who are otherwise critical of open Marxism, characterise it as a "critical theoretical questioning of taken-for-granted assumptions about the social world and the practical conditions of dominance and subordination in capitalism" (Bieler and Morton 2003:468).[19] While it seems likely that all varieties of Marxism would make claim to the same critical credentials, open Marxism's value lies in its starting point and its critical reappraisal of the class antagonisms between capital and labour. Open Marxism's greatest contribution to the discussion of capitalist social relations is its conceptualisation of the state, providing an account of the state that is more sophisticated and more reliable than either instrumentalist or structuralist accounts of the state (Tsolakis 2010:390).

As Marx (1992a:170) noted, a peculiarity about capitalist social relations is that they "assume a fantastic form different from their reality". Holloway continues with this logic. The state as a form of social relations also follows this pattern:

> it is a relation between people which does not appear to be a relation between people, a social relation which exists in the form of something external to social relations... This is the starting point for understanding the unity between states: all are rigidified, apparently autonomous forms of social relations.
>
> (Holloway 1994:27)

It is necessary to understand states not as separate political entities but through their essential unity; the state is a form of social relations within the capitalist social form, which is itself an inherently global phenomenon (ibid.:26).

Open Marxism returns to the position of Marx that, by analysing the relationship between capital, the state and labour, the distinction between political and economic is exposed as an illusion. This conclusion enables critiques of positivistic approaches; theories that reify the state, and consider the market an external phenomenon: both exogenous to "society" and a thing-in-itself (Bieler and Morton 2003:470). Open Marxism therefore deems it necessary to take the social relations of production as a starting point.

The term "open Marxism", first coined by Ernest Mandel and Johannes Agnoli (1980) though with intellectual origins preceding the term by some years, characterises the approach in opposition to an analytical "closure", by which two things are meant (Bonefeld et al. 1992a:xvi). Firstly, closure can refer to an acceptance of the boundaries of a "given world" as its own theoretical boundaries. Secondly, it can also refer to a determinism, in either a causalist or a teleological sense of the word. These two faces of closure are interconnected because "acceptance of horizons amounts to acceptance of their inevitability and because determinist theory becomes complicit in the foreclosing of possibilities which a contradictory world entails" (ibid.).

Form is an important issue for definition in open Marxism, in this instance, due to its relevance to the concept of the state. More often than not, form is understood as a type, or genus, of a thing; for example, a pear is a form of fruit. Or, more pertinently, a state can be seen as a fascist state, or a Fordist state and so forth. However, the concept of form, as understood by open Marxism, is seen as the "mode of existence: something or other exists only in and through the form(s) it takes" (ibid.:xvii). The concept of species form requires intermediary concepts in order to bridge the gap between the abstract and the particular; for example, how does "*the* state" become "*a* fascist state"?, etc. However, form as a mode of existence avoids this analytical trap as it "makes it possible to see the generic as inherent in the specific, and the abstract as inherent in the concrete, because if form is existence then the concrete can be abstract (and vice versa)" (ibid.).

Open Marxism has been criticised on the basis that it undertakes exactly that which it criticises in this instance, in that it abstracts the state and posits its substance to be "capital", "declaring differences in state form to be inessential and irrelevant" (Bieler et al. 2010:34). This critique has basis in Marx's response to the use of what he terms "speculative philosophy":

> My finite understanding supported by my senses does of course distinguish an apple from a pear and a pear from an almond, but my speculative reason declares these sensuous differences inessential and irrelevant. It sees in the apple the same as in the pear, and in the

pear the same as in the almond, namely "Fruit". Particular real fruits
are no more than semblances whose true essence is "the substance" –
"Fruit". By this method one attains no particular wealth of definition.
The mineralogist whose whole science was limited to the statement
that all minerals are really "the Mineral" would be a mineralogist
only in his imagination. For every mineral the speculative mineralogist says "the Mineral", and his science is reduced to repeating this
word as many times as there are real minerals.

(Marx and Engels 1975:68)

However, this critique neglects that the ideas of, for example, the Fordist
state and even the state itself are abstractions. Even the concept of the
pear is an abstraction to which we compare every – what we term –
pear we sensually encounter. The intuitive point that Marx raises, that
the essence of an apple is to be an apple, is only true in the abstract
sense and not the concrete. Indeed, the only account of the differences
between different states, allowed by the logic of this critique,[20] would
be simply to describe them in every detail, avoiding the relation of sim-
ilarities to each other due to the abstraction and fetishisation that this
requires.

This returns us to the fundamental starting point of an open Marxist
analysis of capitalism, which is class struggle; as such, unlike other
accounts of the state, the open Marxist account requires no "bridging
concepts" and remains parsimonious in its account of the state as a
form of social relations, that is a manifestation of capitalist social relations. Furthermore, the critique that it is "capital" which remains the
substance of the state is false and represents a misunderstanding, or at
the most an uncharitable interpretation, of the concept of form as used
by open Marxism. Social relations are manifest as the state – a mode of
existence of social relations which is capitalist – that is not to argue a
deterministic account of the state that it is inherently and inextricably a
manifestation of "capital". However, Marx develops this critique of form
in his attack on speculative philosophy as well. Marx characterises the
retort as such:

The diversity of the ordinary fruits is significant not only for my sen-
suous understanding, but also for "the Fruit" itself and for speculative
reason. The different ordinary fruits are different manifestations of
the life of the "one Fruit"; they are crystallisations of "the Fruit"
itself. Thus in the apple "the Fruit" gives itself an apple like existence, in the pear a pear-like existence. We must therefore no longer

say, as one might from the standpoint of the Substance: a pear is "the Fruit", an apple is "the Fruit", an almond is "the Fruit", but rather "the Fruit" presents itself as a pear, "the Fruit" presents itself as an apple, "the Fruit" presents itself as an almond; and the differences which distinguish apples, pears and almonds from one another are the self-differentiations of "the Fruit" and make the particular fruits different members of the life-process of "the Fruit". Thus "the Fruit" is no longer an empty undifferentiated unity; it is oneness as allness, as "totality" of fruits, which constitute an "organically linked series of members".

(Ibid.:69)

His critique of the above characterisation is that the speculative philosopher "on the one hand apparently freely creates its object a priori out of itself and, on the other hand, precisely because it wishes to get rid by sophistry of the rational and natural dependence on the object, falls into the most irrational and unnatural bondage to the object, whose most accidental and most individual attributes it is obliged to construe as absolutely necessary and general" (ibid.:72).

However, Marx's point here applies more readily to the critics of open Marxism than to open Marxism itself. By adopting species-form instead of form-as-existence, one necessarily becomes tasked with construing the characteristics of "a state" as characteristic of a species of states. This retains the problem pointed out above – that all thought requires abstraction to some degree but the point of "over-abstraction" is not made clear and, indeed, this critique can be levelled against all forms of abstraction whether it is against "mystery", "fruit", "mineral", "apples", "human beings" or anything that does not exist solely in the realm of the senses. Adopting a "golden mean" approach is as fallacious as adopting an approach from either extreme.

It is not "capital" which remains the substance of the state but rather that the state is a form of social relations, a manifestation of how, specifically in capitalism, people interact with each other and how society is constituted. While it may seem almost redundant to point this out, this is a basic point of open Marxism that the national form of the state is a mode of existence of (global) capitalist social relations. Furthermore, the account given by Bieler et al. (2010) provides a functionalist approach to the state (focusing on the specific capacity and purpose of the state) rather than the organisation and constitution of the state as a form of social relations (Burnham 1994).[21]

A further retort to this problem is the emphasis on the dialectical approach of open Marxism, in that it actually seeks to synthesise the abstract and the concrete. What Bieler et al. (2010:34) consider "epistemological austerity" is actually an attempt to avoid the extreme fluctuation between abstract and concrete, which characterises other accounts of social relations. By rejecting the superficial differences between states, or at least leaving these accounts to area specialists, open Marxism avoids the trap of reifying and fetishising these differences.

As Burnham (2001:106) argues, the nature of the state, as a capitalist state, needs to be understood in the context of the intrinsic contradictions of the global economy, namely the capitalist mode of production. To understand the state in terms of the "traditional" theories of international relations would simply reify the fetishised and fantastical social relations that the state propagates (such as the political–economic or internal–external dichotomies); the state must be seen in terms of its unity with other states, as "political nodes" within the global capitalist economy (Kettell 2004:22). Thus, as Holloway (1994:36) argues, "[u]nderstanding the development of the state cannot be a question of examining internal and external determinants, but of trying to see what it means to say that the national state is a moment of the global capital relation."

The state, for open Marxism, is understood of as a form of capitalist social relations. It is a manifestation of the class-based, crisis-prone nature of capitalism. The form and existence of the state are necessarily intertwined with the reproduction of the capitalist system. The state is, in essence, a means for society to manage and sustain itself. Class antagonism is inseparable from the reproduction of capitalist social relations. However, "the maintenance and reproduction of capitalist relations, then, is not something that is automatically ensured, but involves continual action by the state in order to regulate class struggle and to address the various crises that emerge as a result of the instability of the capitalist social form" (Kettell 2004:22). So, capitalism is a fractious and unstable social form, with many specific capitals ostensibly competing among themselves, yet the state's role is to regulate this fractiousness and act on behalf of capital-in-general; this is the only method through which capital expansion can occur generally (ibid.). Indeed, as Holloway and Picciotto (1977:80) observe:

the survival of the political institutions and hence of capital depends on the success of that struggle in maintaining this separation, by channelling the conflicts arising from the real nature of capitalist society into the fetishised forms of the bourgeois political processes. Thus the very separation of economics and politics, the very autonomisation of the state form is part of the struggle of the ruling classes to maintain its domination.

The nature of the state then is not to act on behalf of specific capitals, or fractions of capital, but rather on behalf of capital-in-general, as Burnham (2001:110) notes:

> As political nodes in the global flow of capital, states are essentially regulative agencies implicated in its reproduction but unable to control this reproduction or represent unambiguously the interests of "national capital". Rather, state managers seek to remove barriers to the capital which flows in and through their territories. The fundamental tasks of state managers (from welfare to the management of money, labour and trade, etc.) therefore relate directly to ensuring the successful rotation of capital both nationally and internationally.

The state itself can be further fetishised in theory. As discussed earlier, typologies of state are one instance of the fetishisation of the state form. Another instance of this is the historical periodisation of the state, which can be a manifestation of a causal or teleological determinism. That is, it can reify the particular and alienate the abstract, thus creating a conceptual void between the two. A quote from another dialectical thinker, Francis Herbert Bradley, although ostensibly nothing to do with open Marxism, is a good way to describe this problem.[22]

> Say that the present state of the world is the cause of that total state which follows next on it. Here, again, is ... self-contradiction. For how can one state A become a different state B? It must either do this without a reason, and that seems absurd; or else the reason, being additional, forthwith constitutes a new A, and so on forever. We have the differences of cause and effect, with their relation of time, and we have no way in which it is possible to hold these together. Thus we are drawn to the view that causation is but partial, and that we have but changes of mere elements within a complex whole.
>
> (Bradley 1930:194)

As such, following on from Bradley's point, that state A and state B are entirely illusory and the distinction between the two is fantastical, there is a fundamental unity between all historical periods: distinctions between historical periods are false. Indeed, as Clarke (1992:149) notes, "the basis of comparison of successive epochs is the permanence of their contradictory foundations, in the contradictory form of the social relations of capitalist production"; in essence, periodisation is, at best, a historical contingency and therefore capitalism can only be understood as a complex totality (ibid.).

The next section of the chapter will analyse one of the traditionally held "stages" of capitalism not as a historical period, or species, of capitalism but rather as a strategy undertaken by the state to resolve crisis conditions. The importance of analysing imperialism is to ensure that the relationship between Britain and Malaya is properly characterised. It must not simply be declared an imperial relationship – it must be understood in a manner consonant with the analysis of the state previously undertaken in this chapter.

Imperialism

Theories of imperialism can be categorised into three distinct waves.[23] Firstly, what might be termed the "classical" theorists of imperialism. These authors followed a very similar pattern and, thus, tended to be prone to similar problems. While, for example, Hobson (1902 (1968):81) might stress that underconsumption drove imperial expansion, and Hilferding (1981:256) would argue that overproduction drove imperialism, both theorists, and their successors,[24] argued two key things: firstly, they offer an instrumentalist account of the state, that it was enthralled to the power of a small group of capitalists; and secondly, that imperialism marked a specific and distinct historical period of capitalist development.

The "second wave" of theories of imperialism occurred in the 1970s and is generally synonymous with Dependency Theory and World Systems Theory (Brewer 1990:161), and developed from Leninist ideas of uneven development.[25] These theories characterised the world economy according to zones of development: core, semi-periphery and periphery, with surplus value being channelled from periphery to core states. The value of these approaches lies in their conceptualisation of capitalism as an inherently global social form and the emphasis upon understanding the state as a part of this system; however, it is the system that finds the focus within second-wave theories of imperialism, with the state analytically subordinate to the structure of international capital. This conceptualisation of the state and the teleological/determinist notion of development accept a species-form understanding of the state.

The most recent wave of thought on imperialism has occurred within the last 20 years. The "New Imperialism",[26] as it has been termed, focuses solely on developments within the current configuration of the international state system, particularly the actions of the US. While there are a variety of approaches within this new wave of imperialism, they tend to agree that imperialism as it exists today is qualitatively different to the imperialism of the 19th and early 20th centuries and that there now exists a new stage of imperialism, historically distinct from those that preceded it – one that eschews conquest and the seizure of territory traditionally associated with imperialism in favour of soft power and the adherence to shared values.[27] Unusually with this new wave of study on the topic, there are divided normative approaches to imperialism. While classical imperialism and dependency theories both viewed imperialism as immoral, there exists division in "New Imperialism" as to whether this is the case.[28] Such approaches tend to overemphasise the ideological factors of imperialism and so ignore, or at least diminish, the economic factors of imperialism.

The literature on the nature of inter-state competition within open Marxism does not explicitly discuss imperialism, other than to dismiss traditional approaches as indulgences in historical periodisation (Clarke 1992:149). For example, Lenin's conception of imperialism as the "highest stage" of capitalism is considered and critiqued on this basis. As with the state, the issue between form-species and form as mode-of-existence can be applied to the concept of imperialism. As other Marxist authors have used the concept of imperialism, they have often understood imperialism as a "species" of capitalism, thus turning it into a "stage" of capitalism, or even into a "type" of state. Open Marxism, in its application of form as mode-of-existence, avoids this dilemma:

> Once the relation between structure and struggle is seen in terms of form as mode-of-existence one can never return to ideas of the development of capitalism on the basis of distinct stages...(as in Lenin)...Dialectics comes into its own as the critique of, precisely, such a division into stages. Critique comes into its own dialectically, as inherent in the movement of contradiction and, so, an open Marxism is able to demystify the notion of times in a forceful way.
>
> (Bonefeld et al. 1992a:xvii)

However, the language, logic and argument are present within the literature to easily draw out an idea of imperialism that is very much in keeping with open Marxist theory. It is necessary to understand the relations between states in order to typify and understand the phenomenon of imperialism as it is to be used within this book.

Imperialism is manifest through the international behaviour of the state and its competition with other states. If we take the state to be a form of capitalist social relations, then we can conclude that its survival requires the continuation of these relations: "it is therefore not just a state in a capitalist society, but a capitalist state, since its own continued existence is tied to the promotion of the reproduction of capitalist social relations as a whole" (Holloway 1994:28). However, it is not the case that a national state can exist simply on the reproduction of global capital: capital reproduction must occur within its territory (ibid.:34). The emphasis in this regard must be placed on the relation of capital to the national state, as Holloway (ibid.:33) observes, this "is a relation of a nationally fixed state to a globally mobile capital". Since capital is inherently mobile, states must seek it out in order to immobilise it – they must actively promote conditions favouring the reproduction of capital. This is the basis for the phenomenon of imperialism.

Certain notions of imperialism conceived of states exploiting each other, thus creating "classes" of states: core and periphery states.[29] This is a conclusion that stems from an analysis that takes the superficial view of states as political entities exogenous to capitalist social relations – the state in capitalist society; in essence, this divorces the political from the economic and denies the logic of the state as a *capitalist state*.[30] Through understanding the essential unity of the capitalist social form, and the state as a political moment within the capitalist mode of production, it becomes clear, as Holloway (ibid.:34) notes, that the competition between the specific, national forms of the state is not, as previous theories of imperialism have characterised them, as competitions between "national capitals" but rather it is a contest to attract and then immobilise capital within their territories so as to retain a share of global surplus value. This can take the form of acting to develop conditions that favour the reproduction of capital within the boundaries of a state but, also, "capital may accumulate in the territory of one national state as the result of the exploitation of labour in the territory of another state – as in the case of colonial or neo-colonial situations" (ibid.:35). Ultimately, this is how relative positions within the inter-state system are formed; relationships of supremacy and subordination are founded upon a state's ability to attract and immobilise capital within its territory (by whatever means).

Imperialism then is the action of one state to dominate another to its own advantage. It is neither a historical period of capitalism, nor a type of state, nor, as Gallagher and Robinson (1953:1) have shown, is it something that can be constituted only as a formal "empire". The origin of imperialism lies in the crisis-prone nature of capitalism, as an attempt by one state to improve conditions for accumulation within its own territory, as a means of removing barriers to accumulation by "foreign adventure", whether this is through the extraction of raw materials, access to cheap labour, as a means of controlling markets, or to open markets for domestic goods. Its use in this book is to explain the relationship between Britain and Malaya, to explain how Britain used Malaya to limit, if not resolve, the effects of a global economic crisis manifest as a currency shortage.

The postcolonial critique of Marxist grand narrative

An alternative understanding of the postcolonial world has become prominent in recent years with the development of postcolonial theory. Developing from a critique of Marxist grand narrative and with origins in Foucauldian thought, postcolonial cultural analysis, and especially Subaltern Studies, has focused on marginality, rather than exploitation, with textual analysis being adopted as a dominant method of analysis.

While some Cultural Historians might admit to being baffled by postcolonial theory, this branch of scholarship on the subject of the persistence of empire deserves close enquiry (Porter 2005:xv). Indeed, the origins of postcolonial theory lie in the "cultural turn" in the discipline of History, which has seen postcolonial theory come to dominate Cultural Studies also (Eagleton 2003; Chibber 2013:4).

This approach crucially saw imperialism as a form of cultural expression rather than culture being an expression of imperialism, and principally developed from a critique of Marxism. The focus for postcolonial theory was not the material basis and social relations of production but rather the ideational and cultural. This critique of Marxist thought is developed further by an argument that historical materialism offers a universalising and totalising grand narrative, subsuming difference and annihilating cultural dissimilarities to the totalising logic of capitalism. Chakrabarty (1989) argues that agency is different in the postcolonial world due to socially developed psychology – workers do not operate in India as in the West with a utilitarian calculation but by other factors. Chakrabarty declares this the difference between bourgeois and non-bourgeois culture (Chibber 2013:18). This leads to a shift in focus towards social "fragments" – parts of social life that cannot be easily subsumed within bourgeois social theory, particularly Marxism, and thus ignored by it as not worth of analysis. As such, this is both a marker of resistance and an analytical strategy for postcolonial theory (ibid.:19).

The postcolonial approach, then, seeks to understand the marginalised without incorporating them into a grand narrative; rather, the attempt is made to understand them in their own terms or, at least, terms other than those provided by Western social theory.

Vivek Chibber (2013:12–19), in an extensive critique of postcolonial theory, identifies six main theses of the approach:

1. Colonial capitalism had no hegemonic bourgeoisie able, or willing, to tackle the *ancien régime* of landed overlords.
2. Since there was no revolutionary aspect to the colonial bourgeoisie, capital abandoned its universalising drive. As such, since social development was different from that in Europe, European theories are not appropriate for studying the East, and so it needs its own specific theories.
3. Due to the above difference, and the continued existence of alternative forms of domination, power and capital are no longer synonymous as in European theories and societies, and therefore European theories are inadequate in theorising colonial societies.
4. The plurality of sources of power in colonial societies (e.g. caste, ethnicity, religion) shows that Marxists are wrong in providing a teleological view of capitalist development.
5. Colonial nationalism is spurious in itself, since the two spheres of politics persisted (popular and elite) due to the lack of a hegemonic, universalising bourgeoisie, and so is the historiography that legitimised it. It is not a means of emancipation, or change necessarily.
6. Imperialist and postcolonial societies cannot be understood in the same analytical framework since they diverge in both structure and trajectory.

Chibber's (ibid.:248) conclusions about the postcolonial approach orbit around a fundamental misunderstanding of historical materialism by postcolonial theorists. Rather than treating Marxism as a totalising paradigm, it should be seen as a means of understanding the historical development of capitalist social relations as a global social form. Indeed, for Marx, the historically developed and observable material conditions of production were the key to understanding social relations. Marx and Engels (1998 [1845]:43) elucidate the historical materialist method in *The German Ideology* quite clearly:

> Its premises are men, not in any fantastic isolation and fixity, but in their actual, empirically perceptible process of development under definite conditions. As soon as this active life-process is described, history ceases to be a collection of dead facts.

Where postcolonial theory has taken consciousness, or culture, as the principal determining element of social life, Marx (1971 [1859]:20–21) took the exact opposite view:

> It is not the consciousness of men that determines their existence, but their social existence that determines their consciousness...Just as one does not judge an individual by what he thinks about himself, so one cannot judge such a period of transformation by its consciousness, but, on the contrary, this consciousness must be explained from the contradictions of material life, from the conflict existing between the social forces of production and the relations of production.

For historical materialism, the goal is not to dismiss difference but to understand that difference in terms of the historically conditioned social relations that underpin global society. As such, postcolonial theory, in its efforts to divorce itself from Marxism, has also divorced itself from a comprehensive understanding of how the social relations of production and the material basis of production condition and create social existence. Indeed, this manifests as a total rejection of any desire to understand commonality or similarity, which, returning to Holloway's (1992b:150) point, is how society appears to us: fragmented and dissonant. Postcolonial theory, then, is, at worst, a reformulation of bourgeois theorising and, at best, a fundamental misunderstanding of Marx's method.

Conclusion

This chapter has assessed the literature on British imperial economic relations, and particularly those with Malaya. It has found them prone to a number of problems: an emphasis on discontinuity; a preference for historical periodisation; a lack of theoretical rigour, which has led to the first two problems; and finally, a tendency to avoid questions of social form. The chapter then sought to develop an account of imperialism consonant with an "open Marxist" methodology, situating this theory in terms of capitalist social relations and the state as a form of these relations The chapter then responded to the postcolonial critique of Marxist theory, arguing that this critique, firstly, misunderstands the Marxist approach and, secondly, deliberately avoids questions of social form.

The chapter ultimately sought to characterise a theory of imperialism as a strategy undertaken by a state intended to resolve crises emerging from the unstable and fractious nature of capitalism. This strategy manifests as a specific and historically conditioned relationship between two states, further conditioned by those states' relationships with the global economy. As such, the requirement to study imperialism is to understand both the relations between those states, and how those states relate to the global economy.

The following chapter offers a concise historical overview of British relative economic decline, the Sterling Area and Britain's historically developed relationship with Malaya.

2
British Relative Economic Decline

The chapter will provide an overview of the political economy of Britain during the first half of the 20th century, focusing on Britain's position in the global capitalist economy and its continued relative economic decline. The chapter will also provide historical accounts of both the Sterling Area and Malaya. This chapter intends to provide a historical background to, and so contextualise, the thesis' main narrative in the subsequent chapters. In so doing, it is the intention of this chapter to avoid the periodisation of history, as well as to illustrate that the nature of the post-war relationship between Britain and Malaya finds its origins in Britain's relative economic decline.

The chapter will begin with an overview of Britain's relative economic decline since the end of the 19th century. The chapter will then provide a summary of the Sterling Area, its origins in Britain's economic problems and as an attempt to remedy them in the inter- and post-war periods. This will include elaboration of the Sterling Area as a discriminatory trading block, the existence of the "dollar pool" within the Area, and Britain's position as "treasurer" within this organisation.

The final section of the chapter will give a summary of the historic relationship between Malaya and Britain from Malaya's incorporation into the British Empire in the 19th century. This portion of the chapter will focus on Malaya's place in the Sterling Area, the role of Malaya as an exporter of high-value commodities and, principally, Malaya's status as the principal net dollar contributor to the Sterling Area dollar pool and its subsequent importance during the global dollar shortage.

Relative economic decline

Britain's economic problems after the Second World War were the continuation of a pre-war trend, a fundamental capitalist crisis; an overproduction crisis within the global economy. In the immediate post-war period, this began to manifest as disequilibrium in production and trade between Western and Eastern hemispheres, and then taking the form of a currency shortage, particularly of US dollars. Britain sought dollars through US aid, and also from the Sterling Area. Specifically, the dollars from the Sterling Area were earned mainly through the sale of Malayan rubber and tin to dollar markets. As such, Malaya was crucial not to solving Britain's currency shortage but, rather, to ameliorating it until a more durable means of resolving the global crisis could be put into place.

However, Britain itself was suffering from a more long-standing economic problem than the broader global crisis: one that had, in fact, characterised the British economy since the end of the 19th century. Britain was suffering from relative economic decline due to a reliance on heavy industry and a lack of global competitiveness in those industries.[1] While the dollar shortage that characterised the immediate post-war period was one of Britain's foremost economic concerns at the time, it would be improper to exclude from this chapter an overview of the chronic economic ailment from which Britain suffered during the late 19th century and onwards which provided the conditions for the post-war currency crisis.

The economic situation Britain suffered after the Second World War can be traced back to the relative economic decline of Britain, beginning in the late 19th century. David Coates (1994:249) acknowledges three features of British economic decline: "the dwindling competitiveness in world markets of UK-based manufacturing industry; the diminished capacity of many of those industries for technological and organisational dynamism and innovation; and the resulting loss of manufacturing employment of a 'negative' kind".[2]

Kettell (2004:5), emphasising the role of the state and labour discontent, contends that British relative economic decline can be best characterised by "a growing dependency on industries of diminishing international importance, and a progressive rise in labour dissatisfaction and radicalism". Furthermore, he argues that these problems were exacerbated by the First World War, leading to "a politicisation of economic conditions and policy-making, and which raised the expectations of capital and labour as to what the post-war state could be expected to achieve" (ibid.).

Hobsbawm (1999), while noting that relative decline was inevitable as a statistical phenomenon, argues that the ensuing loss of impetus and efficiency was not inevitable. Britain failed to adapt to new conditions, not because it was unable to but because there was no desire to do so. Indeed, as Hobsbawm (ibid.:156) argues, while there may have been innovation and entrepreneurial drive in other industrialising countries, "however strongly the winds of change blew elsewhere, as soon as they crossed the Channel to Britain they grew sluggish". How and why this economic malaise occurred is a significant question in British economic history and, while it is possible to characterise the relative decline, explanations of the phenomenon remain generally unsatisfactory.[3]

The conservatism of British capital has been attributed to the peculiar character of the English "bourgeois revolution" or, as Nairn (1964:20) has declared it, the revolution "which did not happen" in England. The Nairn–Anderson thesis argues that, due to this "incomplete revolution" and a subsequent amalgamation between feudal aristocracy and capitalist bourgeoisie, the "English capitalist class...was conservative from the outset" (Nairn 1964:21). Dintenfass (1992) provides the statistic that in 1904, 88% of newly registered companies in Britain were privately (not publicly) registered while between 1911 and 1913 the figure was 83%, providing about 80% of economic output by 1914. As such, he suggests that the lack of close links between financial and industrial capital as existed in Europe was indicative of an absence of entrepreneurial spirit in the British bourgeoisie. This anti-entrepreneurialism can also be attributed to the aristocratic values adopted by the bourgeoisie. However, this also tends towards an argument for British exceptionalism that goes beyond that of the "first starter" problem, which led E.P. Thompson (1965:312) to accuse both Nairn and Anderson of "inverted Podsnappery".[4] However, a charitable interpretation of the Nairn–Anderson thesis would be that it offers an account of how capitalism developed in Britain, rather than arguing that Britain is characterised by a peculiar species of capitalism.[5] Bearing that in mind, Perry Anderson (1987:71) emphasises Britain's problems as a first-starter:

> The fundamental origin of the decline of British capitalism lay in its initial priority. As the historical first-comer, British industrialisation arrived without deliberate design, and triumphed without comparable competitors. British manufacturing acquired its shape unawares, from modest immediate constituents: just as it won world hegemony with no strategic plan, but simply from the spontaneous force of its own chronological lead – within the framework of an English commercial imperialism which preceded it. The easy dominance that British industry achieved in the first half of the 19th century laid down certain durable lines of development... [which] ... once

set...became progressively greater handicaps in competition with later industrial economies.

Nairn and Anderson's arguments also served to explain the alleged corporatist ideology of the working class. Due to the amalgamation of aristocracy and bourgeoisie, the emergent working class had no distinct class or rival ideology to "oppose" and so had never developed a comprehensive ideology of its own. As such, Britain's working class had remained disunited and limited to craft–trade unionism. However, Thompson responded that this was false: working-class consciousness had actually found expression through the election of Labour governments. Indeed, Poulantzas (1967:74) goes some way towards agreeing with Thompson in this regard by suggesting that anybody wishing to study the British working class would be better off looking towards an analysis of the Labour party rather than any conception of a dominant class consciousness.

With a commitment to the liberal state model still dominating political discourse in Britain, and therefore with state intervention extremely limited, unemployment became a serious concern with the rate not dropping below 10% from 1921 to 1939 and reaching a peak of 22.1% in 1932, at almost 3 million workers (HMSO 1940). A report by Edward Hilton-Young, the Financial Secretary to the Treasury, to the Cabinet in 1921 identified the global nature of the economic problems at the time, but also noted the specific problems that affected the UK.

> The most important immediate influence in Great Britain is the relatively high cost of production caused mainly by the higher rate of wages. There is no short cut for avoiding the necessary process of adjusting costs to those of our competitors. Readjustment however may be expedited by more widespread understanding of the economic situation, and it is of fundamental importance that no scheme of relief should hinder this process.
>
> (TNA CAB23/27, Cabinet Meeting
> Conclusions, 6 October 1921)

Labour dissatisfaction and a lack of international competitiveness in British industry were key factors in the relative decline of the British economy. By the beginning of the 20th century, Britain's share of global manufacturing had fallen from around a third to only a sixth, its share of world trade had gone from 25% to 14%, and it was rated 9th in the world for economic growth and 10th for productivity (Kettell 2004:42).

Labour unrest reached a peak of 160 million working days in 1926, during the General Strike of that year, with 90% of that from work stoppages in the coal industry alone (British Labour Statistics Historical Abstract 1886–1968; HMSO 1940). Furthermore, between 1918 and 1921 GDP per capita fell by 24% and in 1926 this was lower than it had been in 1906 (HMSO 1940). However, British decline was also manifest in an area that had previously seen Britain maintaining an absolute advantage over other countries: international finance. While Britain's financial system was investing in the industries of competitor countries, competition for Britain's financial dominance was also emerging. By 1870 Britain's annual investments has begun to exceed her net capital formation at home: the City was making more money from the UK's industrial competitors than from the UK itself. Furthermore, Marcello de Cecco (1974:103) notes that the late 19th and early 20th centuries saw Britain's hegemonic financial role diminishing and, despite London's unchallenged dominance in the international financial system prior to this, "the general characteristic of the period is the cumulative loss of importance on the part of Britain" to emergent financial centres such as Paris, Berlin and New York.

Coates (1994) and Elbaum and Lazonick (1984;1987) emphasise the problem of cumulative causation with regard to British relative economic decline – that the origins of weakness and strength lie at some earlier point – and so, while it is necessary to understand the origins of relative decline, it is also necessary to emphasise change. Coates (1994:266) uses this to invoke a Marxist analysis of British relative economic decline: by stressing the contradictions within capitalism, he argues, in a similar fashion to Anderson (1987), that it was within Britain's own early successes as a first-starter that led to its relative economic decline.

The dominance of the liberal state model prevented the state from intervening in the processes of capital to resolve the barriers to accumulation that had occurred. However, this began to change between the two world wars. The immediate post-war response by British state managers was to reassert the liberal state model. By bringing Britain back onto the gold standard in 1925 at the deliberately overvalued pre-war rate of $4.86, state managers sought to impose deflationary discipline on Britain's economy and thus "put pressure on capital and labour engaged in the staple trades to reduce wage costs, adopt more efficient methods of production, and to move into newer and higher quality lines of production more attuned to the changing demands of the world market", or so was the intention (Kettell 2004:77–80).[6]

However, the purpose of the return to the gold standard was not just to place competitive rigour on the British economy, but also to maintain a level of governing autonomy and for state managers to insulate themselves from the effects of adjustment. Even after the final collapse of the gold standard, British state managers sought to return to the liberal model, characterised by desires to "contain class unrest within politically safe limits, to provide favourable conditions for capital accumulation while sustaining pressure for improved competitiveness and economic adjustment, and to minimise the state's directly visible involvement with the economy" (ibid.:117).

The inter-war period was characterised by "the most fundamental tendency of the capitalist mode of production": commodity overproduction (Clarke 1999:71). As Burnham (1990:26) notes, the relative lack of productivity in Western Europe, the vast productive capacity and growth of North America and the subsequent demand for US goods led to a trade and a monetary crisis. Indeed, as Burnham also notes, this was not a shortage of foreign currency reserves per se, but rather a manifestation of disequilibrium in global production and trade.[7]

The origins of the disequilibrium in global trade and production that precipitated the shortage of dollars lay not solely in the structure of the British economy, but cause also lay in the successful development of new production methods in the US. Before the war, it was clear that the UK and Western Europe were increasing their imports from the markets of North America, particularly the US. This is in part due to the development of Fordism.[8] Characterised by extremely efficient mass production techniques, the realisation of the relationship between mass production and mass consumption (through the increase in workers' wages), and attempts to homogenise the workforce to ensure an increase in the rate of labour exploitation, the Fordist model (in a massive internal market full of eager consumers) permitted enormous productivity growth.

Compared with the prevailing production techniques of European firms, whose, as Burnham (1990:24) notes, "growth in output encountered recurrent obstacles and increases in capital stock did not alter existing production techniques thereby resulting in low productivity growth", Fordist-style production meant that the US had "an enormous advantage in most fields of industrial production" (ibid.). This was one of the key factors in the change in the global supply of dollars.

In the inter-war period, the vast productive power of the US outcompeted other economies that wished to purchase US goods but were unable to sell their own to the US. This was exacerbated by the Second

World War, during which the US, isolated from mainland attack and deprived of many markets from which it imported, expanded its economy to substitute a number of goods that it had previously imported. Demand for US-manufactured goods (which accounted for one half of all US exports) had been stimulated since the US increased its competitiveness, in terms of both the quality of the goods and the cost of their manufacture, during the war.[9] This applied to a very wide range of goods and this advantage was self-sustaining, as when new products were developed they were brought into production more swiftly and more cheaply in the US (Table 2.1).

By the end of the 19th century, the US balance of payments had turned into surplus. From 1914, the balance of US trade had been in surplus every year, the smallest of which was $84m in 1936. Europe's share of US imports had fallen from 50% before 1914, to 30% in the inter-war period and to 15% by the end of the Second World War. The US' share, over the same period, had risen from 34% before 1914 to 58% after 1945. During the 1930s, the US' overall surplus (due to the current account surplus and the influx of capital investment) was financed mainly by gold sales to the US.[10] However, the net flow of gold to the US in the latter half of the 1930s actually exceeded world production, and did not resolve the underlying problem, and was therefore unsustainable (ibid.). Furthermore, with the beginning of the Second World War, sterling was fixed to the dollar and the UK started to liquidate its dollar assets to support the war effort; however, this too was unsustainable and the balance of payments was adverse until the commencement of the Lend-Lease programme (BE C43/31, "Central Reserves", 18 January 1951).

The most major development in the global dollar shortage was its geographical shift: the period since the end of the 19th century had

Table 2.1   World supply and use of dollars, 1925–1939 ($ million)

	Annual average		
Dollars supplied by the US	1925–1929	1932–1933	1935–1939
Imports	4,331	1,427	2,554
Public financial resources	11	7	16
TOTAL dollars supplied	6,951	2,030	3,345
TOTAL other funds	–558	455	1,077
TOTAL dollars used by other countries	6,393	2,485	4,422

Source: TNA T230/177, "World Supply of Dollars", 25 June 1952.

Table 2.2 Geographical distribution of US exports and imports, 1905–1950 (%)

	North America	South America	Europe	Asia
Imports				
1905–1914	22	12	50	15
1925–1929	24	13	30	30
1932–1937	24	14	30	29
1948–1950	36	22	15	19
Exports				
1905–1914	20	4	66	6
1925–1929	25	9	48	12
1932–1937	23	8	45	17
1948–1950	29	12	34	19

Source: TNA T230/177, "World Supply of Dollars", 25 June 1952.

seen Europe's share of the dollar supply dwindle while North and South America's share had increased. Mainly, this was due to the isolation of the Americas during the two world wars, leading to a large degree of self-sufficiency, but the US also found alternative sources of those primary goods in the Americas for which there still remained a large import demand in the US (e.g. petrol, aluminium, iron ore, coffee). Meanwhile, Europe and also the Sterling Area produced "goods for which home substitutes are developed in the United States or for which United States demand is weaker" (BE C43/31, "Central Reserves", 18 January 1951). The Sterling Area, however, also provided to Britain a degree of support in the global shortage of dollars, allowing the UK and Area members to substitute a large number of goods that had previously been imported from the US, as well as providing the collective benefit of pooling convertible currencies in the Exchange Equalisation Account (EEA) to be rationed out by the UK according to need.

The Sterling Area

The Sterling Area, as described by an unpublished Foreign Office paper written by Allen Christelow, under-secretary to the Treasury, on the "official history" of the area, was an institution comprising a group of countries with strong ties to the UK who found it "convenient to use the flexible financial mechanisms of the London capital market" (TNA FO371/82915, "The Sterling Area", 24 January 1950).[11] Of course, this brief definition ignores the historical basis behind the Sterling Area, as well as the specific dynamics of the currency bloc.

The traditional account of the origins of the Sterling Area in this official paper holds that they were concomitant with the extension of British sovereignty throughout the 19th century and the extension of the area within which sterling was used as a means of exchange, and within which UK banks operated. The development of the London Money Market further extended the geographical range and purposes of the Sterling Area. Furthermore, the position of Britain in international trade also meant that most world trade was conducted in sterling. Indeed, the official history of the Area maintained that the Sterling Area grew naturally as a result of Britain's political and economic expansion, and subsequent laws "setting up" the Sterling Area were merely official stamps of existence rather than the genuine inception of the Area (ibid.).

Certainly, there is an element of truth to this perspective, as Britain expanded so were other countries incorporated into Britain's political and economic influence. London banks established branches in foreign countries, mostly in British colonies. These branches tended to hold their reserves in London for a variety of reasons (e.g. limited investment opportunities or inadequate (or non-existent) central banking mechanisms). For similar reasons, smaller countries held their reserves in London also (these earned interest and were generally convertible on demand into gold at a fixed rate). In certain colonial cases, of which Malaya was one, this practice was formalised and regulated by currency authorities that held reserves in gold but increasingly in sterling (ibid.).

Before 1914, reserves in gold and convertible currencies were very small – they were simply an issue of maintaining essential working balances. Trade was largely conducted in sterling and it was only due to the UK's strong trading and creditor position, as well as the ability to alter the bank rate with its effect on the cost of lending and the money supply, that the UK could operate on such small reserves. If the balance of payments turned temporarily adverse (due to over-lending or seasonal fluctuations), a rise in the base rate was enough to draw foreign funds to London and reduce London lending. This would lead to funds coming to London and sterling appreciating above the outward gold point (BE C43/31, "Central Reserves", 18 January 1951).

Empire exporters generally asked for payment to be made in sterling from foreign transactions. Foreign exchange grew in London; however, traders were not particularly conscious of this fact. When foreign exchange was received, it was swiftly sold for sterling. Empire imports worked in a similar way: settlement was made through London in sterling, and London lost foreign exchange or gold.

> Colonial currencies are purely subsidiary currencies pegged to and fully backed by Sterling. The Colonies at present run no working balances of any particular size in currencies other than sterling and, except for marrying of buying and selling operations in other currencies, the banks have to clear transactions in non-sterling currencies through London.
>
> (BE OV65/4, "IMF – Malaya", 24 March 1952)

The First World War brought a *de facto* end to the gold standard and, with it, a suspension of the obligation of the Bank of England to exchange gold on demand to foreign creditors. This obligation resumed in 1925 when Britain returned to the gold standard. From 1925 to 1930 (during the gold standard), the UK's position became much weaker. A great deal of dollar investments had been disposed of, the unstable situation in Europe had led to an outflow of capital from Europe to America (through sterling) and social measures in the UK increased demand for food and other consumables – most of which had to be imported from the dollar area. Sterling was under pressure in this period and was often at the gold point despite much less lending abroad. It was still the rule to trade in sterling, however (BE C43/31, "Central Reserves", 18 January 1951).

Britain's participation in the gold standard was abandoned in 1931, with Britain adopting a variable exchange rate, and subsequently this saw the final collapse of the gold standard. The abandonment of these systems led to the EEA technique. The establishment of the EEA meant that the Bank of England acknowledged no obligation to keep sterling stable in terms of gold or any other foreign currency but would intervene to avoid violent fluctuations in the rate that sterling was quoted, which was around $3.50 (Kettell, 2004:115). However, sterling was still freely convertible, there was no exchange control, and settlements between central banks were still made in gold.

The decision of 1931 led to an ambiguous "sterling bloc". Sterling was fluctuating, as were many other currencies, and to avoid some of the more violent fluctuations, some countries opted to peg their currencies to sterling (at different times and rates). These countries could be divided into two groups: those that had a long association with sterling (the Empire and certain dominions, Egypt, Iraq), and countries which chose to do this for the sake of convenience (there is no clear distinction, though the first group tended to have large sterling reserves) (TNA FO371/82915, "The Sterling Area", 24 January 1950).[12]

In 1932, the British government passed the Import Duties Act, which imposed a flat rate tariff on all imports to the UK, except on raw materials and foodstuffs (McKay 1932). At the Imperial Economic Conference in Ottawa in 1932, Britain sought to introduce a formalised Imperial Preference System.[13] This resulted in a trading area approximating the British Empire and dominions, which would have low, reciprocal tariffs for internal trade and high tariffs for any external trade outside of the area, the purpose of which was to ensure access to markets for British produce and to stimulate Commonwealth trade (Eichengreen and Irwin 1995:2–7).[14] From 1932 until the start of the Second World War the monetary system remained unchanged, as did sterling's role as an international currency, but the store of value had shifted. This led to a general favouring of gold reserves rather than sterling, and unwillingness to commit to accumulation of sterling without limit. Variations in the rate of exchange were accepted as a method of avoiding the depletion of reserves and preventing excessive accumulation (this was generally incompatible with the gold standard). The ending of the gold standard also led to Britain being forced to bargain bilaterally due to the lack of automatic equilibrating force.

The Second World War led to a further change in definition, formalisation and restriction of the store of value, effectively creating what is now understood to be the Sterling Area. Britain had persistent budget deficits and so its position in the international economy changed significantly between 1914 and 1939. Due to the acceptance that Western hemisphere currencies would become increasingly vital and scarcer during the war, the first exchange controls were implemented in August 1939. These exchange controls were copied throughout the Sterling Area and resulted in the Treasury maintaining a monopoly of all gold and stipulated foreign reserve payments within the Sterling Area (this prohibited payments to all non-residents without permission of the Treasury, and allowed the Treasury "to exercise control over all securities marketable abroad and to compel their registration with a view to compulsory requisition by HMG"). This was the creation of the "dollar pool" and the exact nature of the Sterling Area after the Second World War until its demise in 1972 (TNA FO371/82915, "The Sterling Area", 24 January 1950).

The introduction of the Defence (Finance) Regulations saw the legal emergence of the Sterling Area as a further means of exchange control.[15] This gave the Sterling Area a formal geographic definition in law as

the UK, the Isle of Man, all dominions, colonies and mandated territories except Canada, Newfoundland and Hong Kong; it also included
Iraq, Egypt, Sudan and Iceland. However, strictly speaking, membership was kept vague as UK law applied only to UK residents. Generally,
members of the Sterling Area were expected to depreciate their currency against the dollar and maintain parity with sterling; maintain
foreign currency reserves as necessary; and to continue to buy and sell
their gold and foreign exchange reserves in London. This was a continuation of an older practice; however, the "dollar pool" was seen
as new and that it had now become an essential part of the Sterling
Area (ibid.).

There was freedom of payments within the Sterling Area and Area
members could also authorise the transfer of sterling to non-members.[16]
A willingness to accept "restricted-use" sterling (this was effectively a
readiness on behalf of the recipient to accumulate sterling) led to a
"Special Accounts" status for non-SA members (e.g. Argentina) and was
seen as a greater financial sacrifice than that of dollar deficit members
(who had fewer restrictions on their use of sterling). By the 1950s, the
"greatest problem of Sterling Area management" arose from the UK's
huge debts with the rest of the Area (ibid.). In 1938, London assets
held by Sterling Area members stood at £216m, offset by substantial UK
assets in members' territories. In 1945, sterling balances and short-term
assets held by Sterling Area members were £2,674m with much fewer
offsetting liabilities. Further sterling balances (to the tune of £600m)
were held by countries outside of the Sterling Area who held "Special
Accounts" status (ibid.).

Exchange controls were generally designed to manage how sterling
was transferred (across various exchanges) into dollars. Sterling Area
countries, however, maintained trading relations with numerous countries not in the dollar area and, as such, control agreements with these
countries were necessary if exchange control was to be maintained.[17]
These early monetary agreements attempted to unite several objectives:

- fixed rates of exchange, which could only be changed after mutual
  consultation;
- offered overdraft facilities for the financing of current account
  deficits;
- established freedom of payments within the currency area concerned;
- perhaps most importantly, creation of a mechanism for consultation
  on all technical questions, particularly with a view to preventing

large capital flows to the dollar area and increasing the area within which sterling could permissibly be used.

However, the "official account" of the Sterling Area, while generally accurate in empirical terms, contains certain elements of interpretation that skew the idea of the Sterling Area and, particularly, its origins. The traditional account makes the argument that the Sterling Area had existed for a long time, had served the allies well during the war and provided financial and monetary stability after the war. Furthermore, the paper argues, the Area should be "protected, strengthened and expanded" and that "its existence permits us to look forward to the time when sterling will again be the basis of exchange and we can do so because the machinery is there and well nigh intact" (TNA FO371/82915, "The Sterling Area", 24 January 1950).

Burnham (1990:8) notes: "the British state perceived its fundamental interests to lie primarily with the Sterling Area nations". As such, "whilst the major nations of Western Europe engaged in vigorous intra-European trade, Britain concentrated on renewing its traditional trading links with the Commonwealth" (ibid.:11). Strange (1971:75) regards this perception, and the maintenance of the Sterling Area, as an issue of status. Furthermore, she argues that the Sterling Area lulled Britain "into a false sense of immunity" to the unavoidable changes of the contemporary international system (ibid.). However, Schenk disagrees with this part of Strange's argument.[18]

Schenk (1994:136) shows, citing archival evidence, that the British government was aware that the Sterling Area did not consistently generate "prestige" for the economy, and that the systems of sterling management within the area in fact often lowered the standing of sterling. This is particularly evidenced by the constant search for means of sterling convertibility and by the incremental disposal of trade discrimination as a tool of Sterling Area policy. However, Schenk does agree with the broad consensus of work on the Sterling Area: that the role the Sterling Area played in Britain's post-war economic policy, agreeing with the general consensus that the Sterling Area had, in fact, hindered capital accumulation and external economic policy. In fact, Schenk (ibid.) argues that the Sterling Area can be viewed as a "mechanism through which large investment flows were sent abroad, large short-term liabilities were accumulated and trade discrimination was pursued".

Furthermore, the Sterling Area system after the war can be characterised by three features: "members pegged their exchange rates to sterling, maintained a common exchange control against the rest of the world while enjoying free current and capital transactions with the UK and, thirdly, maintained national reserves in sterling which required pooling foreign exchange earnings" (ibid.:8). The principal purpose of the exchange controls, however, should be seen in terms of the post-war dollar shortage: these controls were intended to restrict convertibility of sterling into dollars. Without these controls, British gold and currency reserves would have swiftly dwindled and Britain and the Sterling Area would have been unable to import any goods from the US, exacerbating the fundamental problem (the inability of British goods to compete with US exports). Furthermore, the post-war settlement required large-scale dollar imports to sustain itself (Holland 1984). In essence, the Sterling Area was essential to Britain's continued economic vitality and, without it, harsh austerity measures would have been necessary, bringing the entire post-war consensus into doubt.

Before the Second World War, Malaya was already earning a huge proportion of Sterling Area dollars. On average, over the period 1935–1938, Malaya earned US$157m net per year, which amounted to 31.8% of the total dollar earnings of the Sterling Area (BE OV65/3, "Malaya's Contribution to Sterling Area Dollar Income", 15 January 1947).[19] The average annual dollar deficit for the Sterling Area over this period stood at US$230m; however, without Malaya's dollar earnings, this table would have been US$380m. If the UK had not been included in that table, the Sterling Area would have been in surplus by US$87m (ibid.).

By the end of the Second World War, only a few colonies were consistent net dollar earners for the Sterling Area: Malaya, British West Africa and Ceylon. Malaya was the greatest dollar earner of these colonies, earning almost twice as many dollars as Gambia, the Gold Coast and Ceylon, the next three largest earners, combined (TNA FO371/76049, "Malaya as a Dollar Earner and Raw Material Supplier", 30 April 1949). The British used this money, as well as for other members of the Sterling Area, to pay for imports from the dollar area and to support the reserve position upon which the strains of UK economic policy was placed (TNA FO371/82915, "The Sterling Area", 24 January 1950). These primary-producing colonies were generally unable to benefit from the dollar pool as much as others since the purpose of the dollar pool was to act as a central reserve, providing collective support for those countries who required dollar goods but were unable to earn dollars through exporting to the dollar area. Certainly, by the end of the war, the British were in no hurry to dismantle one of the best methods of accumulating foreign reserves, of which Malaya was a key component.

British Malaya

The British interest in Malaya developed following the seizure of three strategic islands in the Straits of Malacca by the British East India Company over a period of almost a hundred years. This section of the chapter details that history from 1786 until the end of the Second World War.

The British East India Company seized control of the island of Penang in 1786, followed 14 years later by the ceding of territory on the Malay Peninsula itself by the Sultan of Kedah to the company for an annual fee.[20] The British East India Company subsequently sought to expand their interests in the region by acquiring the "uninhabited mangrove island" of Singapore in 1818, signing a series of treaties with the Sultan of Johore to build factories there until the Sultan concluded a treaty with the Company in 1824 that handed Singapore over to British control in perpetuity (Winstedt 1944:20). A further treaty with the Dutch ceded Malacca to the British in 1824.

However, with the abolition of the East India Company in 1858, the Straits Settlements (Penang, Singapore, Malacca) fell immediately under the authority of the India Office. This was not considered a "natural" arrangement and the India Office gradually came to the realisation that, not only did the Straits Settlements have very little geographical, ethnic or political relevance to India, but that they no longer required the surpluses from India to sustain themselves. As such, in 1867, the British government "yielded to local agitation" and the Straits Settlements came under the authority of the Colonial Office (ibid.).

By the end of the 19th century, Singapore had become part of the Straits Settlements along with Malacca and Penang; meanwhile, the nine Malay states were divided into the Federated Malay States,[21] within which the Sultans had much less power and the British had more influence, and the "unfederated" Malay states,[22] in which the Sultans retained a lot of their power but still had to accept a British "advisor". However, during this period, the British presence in Malaya, particularly in the Federated Malay States, gradually became more powerful and the British themselves were hopeful of achieving a central government for the whole region, though this period actually saw greater decentralisation in Malaya (TNA CAB24/234, "Visit to Malaya", 25 February 1933). By the 20th century, Malaya consisted of two British settlements: Penang and Malacca, as well as nine Malay states, which were ruled by Sultans who governed under a written constitution with advice from a council of state.[23] Malaya's excellent geographical position as a trade route through to the East substantially contributed to its rapid material development in the first half of the 20th century (ibid.; TNA CO967/84, "Notes on Development in Malaya", August 1950).

During the Second Word War, Malaya was occupied by Japan from 1942 for three and a half years, "during which time practically nothing came into the country and practically nothing went out. Industry languished and in most cases came to a standstill. Thus on the liberation of the country both Government and Industry were faced with an enormous rehabilitation programme" (ibid.). Rubber estates and tin mines had deteriorated significantly due to neglect, sabotage as a denial measure by anti-Japanese partisans, and appropriations by occupying Japanese forces (ibid.; BE OV65/3, "Malaya", 22 February 1943). It was also in 1942 that the then colonial under-Secretary, Harold Macmillan, famously reminded the Empire of the value of the relationship between Britain and its colonies and what they could look forward to after the war:

> The governing principle of the Colonial Empire should be the principle of partnership between the various elements composing it. Out of partnership comes understanding and friendship. Within the fabric of the Commonwealth lies the future of the Colonial territories.
>
> (cited in Horne 1988:82)

During the war, the British were already making plans for the future of the colony after the expulsion of the Japanese. Lucius McCausland, an advisor to the Governor of the Bank, in a letter to Cobbold, Fisher and Kershaw, identified that the high dollar earnings of Malayan rubber and tin exports made the future of these industries of great importance to Sterling Area Exchange Control. However, due to movements towards increased synthetic rubber production in the US, as a means of overcoming the wartime shortage of rubber, the US would be in the sole position of deciding the future of the world rubber industry, and therefore had to be appeased in some way in order to permit the natural rubber industry to flourish after the war. It was also problematic because there was a widespread belief in the US that the rubber industry in Malaya was inefficient due to the rush to set up rubber estates and plantations there, and the vested interests that maintained them. This was not far from the truth and it was believed that the mergers of certain contiguous large estates could overcome these inefficiencies (BE OV65/3, "The future of the Malayan Rubber Industry", 2 June 1942).

Certainly, decisive action needed to be taken, as the UK could not simply allow pre-war production methods and practices to continue if the US government was already very suspicious of UK rubber policy. It was then decided to investigate the organisation of the Malayan rubber industry, the companies that managed the estates and the London rubber market in the belief that "a reorganisation designed in the combined interests of the backward races who will produce the rubber and of the progressive Americans who will consume it would greatly strengthen our hands when the future of the industry comes to be considered" (ibid.).

However, even with considerations about the efficiency of future production, the priority was simply on restarting the rubber industry and Malaya's economy as quickly as possible (BE OV65/3, "Reoccupation Problems", 29 December 1942).

> It will be a prime consideration to recommence the production of rubber and tin without delay. Large imports of stores, equipment, etc. will be required. Import control over all goods from all sources will be necessary to give exchange priority to essential imports and at the same time eliminate remittances for dispensable goods.[24]
>
> (BE OV65/3, "Malaya and Hongkong: Reoccupation
> problems – Exchange Control", 20 August 1942)

As such, stockpiles were established in the Commonwealth for the immediate resumption of rubber and tin production (BE OV65/3, "Malaya", 22 February 1943).[25] The rubber and tin industries were instrumental for their dollar earnings and it was agreed in a Treasury Committee meeting that Malaya's reoccupation would lead to its immediate reinsertion into the Sterling Area system of exchange control.[26]

> Agreed in principle that the re-occupied part of Malaya would at once resume its position as part of the sterling area under Defence (Finance) Regulations; that transfers from other sterling area countries would be free... The policy should be to impose no ban on outward transfers to the sterling area or on dealings in sterling area currencies.[27]
>
> (BE OV65/3, "Treasury Committee Minutes of
> Meeting", 23 November 1943)

The Colonial Office informed the Bank that occupying Commonwealth soldiers were to be accompanied by a rubber mission who would co-opt liberated rubber planters who would then be immediately put to work on restarting rubber plantations – there was no consideration given to handing over the estates to their pre-war owners straight away as the intent was to purchase all the rubber produced to create large stockpiles. This was not intended to be long-term policy and the British government sought advice from the Rubber Growers Association; however, the government still believed that they would have to merge a number of estates and plantations in order to improve efficiency in the industry (BE OV65/3, "Rubber in Malaya", 13 April 1943; BE OV65/3, "Malaya – Reoccupation", 17 August 1943).

When the rubber and tin industries restarted, there was confidence that there would be significant demand for both of these products as long as price fluctuations were minimal. Indeed, Malayan tin was considered of the highest quality (BE OV65/3, "The Views of US Firms interested in trade with Malaya", 24 November 1943). However, with the reoccupation of the country, high unemployment, labour unrest and food shortages soon led to a high level of discontent among the population, which ultimately resulted in the growth in the strength of the Malayan Communist Party (MCP) (ibid.).

The MCP had split from the Kuomintang (KMT) in 1927 and there was an "underground war" between the two groups for many years, until the waning of the KMT in Malaya led to the MCP becoming the *de facto* political organisation for Chinese Malays (TNA CO537/7285, "Military Implications of the Emergency", 19 November 1951). There was a strong continuity between the strength of the MCP and the traditional Chinese "secret societies" (known as "Triads") that had existed throughout the Orient for many years. Indeed, the Triads in Malaya had been virtually the only authority within Malaya's migrant Chinese population – resolving all intra-Chinese disputes, holding criminal and civil courts and even conducting limited conflicts – until 1890 when they were declared illegal. As such, the MCP's importance to the Chinese population in Malaya was not simply as a political organisation that provided national, or even ideological, representation but was based on traditions of social organisation that were many hundreds of years old (ibid.). Indeed, Malaya's broader politics, and certainly party politics, were structured around racial, rather than class, lines and continued to be so for many years.

Conclusion

This chapter has given a background of the economic situation of Britain from the late 19th century until the end of the Second World War. Britain suffered from relative economic decline, characterised by a reliance on increasingly uncompetitive industry, a growth in labour unrest, high unemployment and an increasingly beleaguered state.

While this remained the broader political-economic context for much of the 20th century, acute economic crises beset Britain throughout.

Out of the recurrent crises of the early 20th century, British state managers sought to sustain international trade and the value of sterling and this was through the gradual and formal establishment of the Sterling Area. While it can be argued that the Sterling Area had existed for some time (and the orthodox account of the Area is that it had), the Area only came into existence after Britain's final withdrawal from the gold standard in 1931, the passing of the Import Duties Act in 1932 and finally with the exchange control acts enacted at the start of the Second World War. Britain's role in the Sterling Area was that of treasurer, pooling the Area's currencies in the EEA. This was, in essence, a means of supporting British currency reserves as a means of supporting the value of sterling, as shown by the rationing of the Area's own reserves to them as the situation dictated. While this role allowed Britain to manage the trading relations of the Sterling Area's members with considerable ease, it also allowed Britain to balance any trading disequilibria that it had developed itself. The EEA was a means through which sterling could be kept within a specific band of exchange with other countries, through the large-scale purchasing and selling of foreign currencies to maintain the value of sterling, and a tool by which Britain could sustain its own trade deficit.

The balance of payments problem, especially with the US, and the ensuing global dollar shortage, meant that the EEA was in a constant struggle to maintain the value of sterling. This is not to say that Britain was exploiting other states for the purpose of maintaining its own currency, but rather that the trading bloc that Britain had set up to favour its own markets, and to maintain its own currency, could only be sustained through the large-scale expenditure of its reserves. This meant that countries within the Sterling Area that had traditionally been high dollar earners became more important to the maintenance of the Area, and the chief dollar earner was Malaya.

Following Malaya's occupation during the war, the British were very eager to resume the rubber and tin trades in Malaya, going so far as to send rubber missions along with Commonwealth troops who were securing the country. Officials in both the Colonial Office and at the Bank stressed Malaya's importance, and Malaya was reinserted into the Sterling Area mechanism as soon as it was liberated, giving instruction that this was of the highest concern. As the next chapter will show, this is exactly what happened.

3
The Dollar Drain and Colonial Import Policy (1945–1950)

This chapter will examine British responses to the Dollar Drain and the Convertibility Crisis with respect to the Sterling Area and, and most particularly, the British relationship with Malaya. One aspect of this chapter, as with the other two empirical chapters, is to emphasise the reliance of the British state on the Sterling Area, which was the sole means of multilateral trade outside of the dollar area[1] and, as such, vital to the reconstruction of global trade after the Second World War, and to the reconstruction of the British economy.

This chapter, in concert with subsequent chapters, emphasises the continuity in the British relationship with Malaya and avoids truncating history according to perceived shifts in British governing strategy. While Schenk (1994:136) argues that the Sterling Area can be viewed simply as a "mechanism through which large investment flows were sent abroad, large short-term liabilities were accumulated and trade discrimination was pursued", this chapter will argue that the institutional arrangement described by Schenk, and the understanding of empire by both Krozewski (2001) and Hinds (2001), actually obfuscates the relationships between Britain and other states. The importance of Malaya in this context is as a crucial palliative component in this strategy to maintain the Sterling Area and to support Britain's economic position more broadly. The relationship between Britain and Malaya is not an explicitly imperial one and the archival documents certainly contain no evidence of British villains twirling their moustaches at the pooling of Malaya's dollars in the Sterling Area reserve. Rather British state managers clearly see the importance of Malaya in maintaining the Sterling Area due to its large-scale trade of rubber and tin with the US, providing a substantial injection of dollars into a trading bloc that was running a huge deficit with the dollar area. It is also clear from the archives that

British state managers are well aware that Malaya holds an importance directly to Britain, and that its dollar contribution is vital to Britain's post-war reconstruction also. This importance is also made clear through efforts by British state managers to develop Malaya's economy and, as Kaplan (1990) has argued, through British commitment to fighting the Malayan Emergency.

The chapter intends to provide the following context to the Britain–Malaya relationship. First, the Sterling Area is understood to be a crucial component of British post-war governing strategy, as well as being considered essential to the resurgence of global trade after the war, and so too to the health of the global economy. Secondly, the dollar deficit, or the Dollar Drain in this period, is characterised as a manifestation of a trade disequilibrium between the US and the rest of the world. This disequilibrium was a manifestation of a global overproduction crisis, an inherent tendency of capitalist social relations. Finally, the analysis of the relationship between Britain and Malaya is intended to highlight its enduring importance to Britain. The value of Malaya to the maintenance of the Sterling Area derives from its status as a large net-exporter of rubber and tin to the US, thus earning substantial dollar surpluses from this trade. The status of the highest dollar earner within the Sterling Area made Malaya extremely important to British international economic policy, and broader governing strategy.

The purpose of the Sterling Area was to act as a preferential trading bloc but also to provide a payment mechanism for all extra-Sterling Area trade. As such, all external currency was pooled under the control of the British government. The British government was thus able to make demands on the trade practices of the member countries of the Sterling Area as it was legally permitted to ration foreign reserves, and thus limit how much each country was able to spend on extra-Area imports. The structure of the Sterling Area allowed the UK to manage the trade policies of the member countries generally, and so to alter the nature of the global economy to its own ends. Whether this worked to the specific advantage of the UK in each case is important but is not the totality of the relationship. While this may have been the intent of the British government, it is also important to understand the nuance of the relationship. Malaya benefited from this relationship through the very nature of the Sterling Area: providing Malaya with access to a very large market and the use of a single currency for all trade transactions. Furthermore, Britain also sought to provide Malaya with a significant level of aid in order to develop its economy; admittedly, this was for improving civil order and Malaya's capacity for dollar income, but nevertheless, this was a clear benefit from the relationship with Britain.

This period marks a particularly acute crisis for the British economy and, therefore, for the Sterling Area. While we find that the particular and historically developed relationship between Britain and Malaya retains its pre-war character, and fulfils a specific role within the Sterling Area, this period is characterised by the marshalling of the whole Area. All states within the Empire and Britain's trading bloc are ordered to support sterling, to make austere cuts to dollar spending and to make substitutions to dollar goods where possible, as well as trying to maximise dollar earning

In this period, ironically, it is particularly difficult to identify Malaya's role in the Sterling Area. Indeed, it is practically indistinguishable from the rest of the relationships Britain has with its other colonies. This moment actually obfuscates the fact that these are unique, particular and historically developed relationships between Britain and its colonies by virtue of the fact that the acute nature of this crisis is so severe that the whole Sterling Area is called upon to undertake the same task.

Malaya after the Second World War

The war and occupation had left the rubber and tin industries in a parlous state: 10% of rubber trees had been lost due to cutting out and neglect, and weeds covered sizeable areas of the large rubber estates, requiring a great deal of clearance work. The tin industry had suffered severe equipment damage due to scorched earth policies, Japanese requisitions and also looting. A great deal of infrastructure had been damaged and food was in short supply (TNA CO1045/177, Visit of Labour Adviser to Federation of Malaya, 13 December 1947).

Malayan recovery was seen as essential to the expansion of Sterling Area trade with the dollar area due to its rubber and tin trade with the US (TNA T236/3995, "Rest of Sterling Area v. USA", 29 October 1945). In 1946, Malaya's dollar earnings amounted to a net surplus of some US$100 million, while the first half of 1947 saw that increase to US$140 million, and the whole of 1948 saw Malaya earn a surplus of $117 million with the US alone and with her total net surplus with the dollar area standing at around US$172 million (TNA FO371/76049, "Malaya as a Dollar Earner and Raw Material Supplier", 30 April 1949; TNA CAB129/20, "Cabinet Paper 227(47)", 5 August 1947). This was despite the fact that rubber prices had fallen consistently since the end of the war, from 18 p/lb in 1945 to 12.91 p/lb in 1948 (Lim 1967:323).

Indeed, the rubber mission sent along with Allied troops during the liberation of Malaya made the process of reconstructing Malaya's econ-omy much more rapid. Certainly, the imperatives given to the rubber mission, and the sentiment in London at the time, about the former and future value of the Malayan economy to the Sterling Area and the British economy, remained true. While, in 1945, Malaya's dollar earn-ings accounted for only 7% of the Sterling Area total, in 1946 this had grown to 30% (BE OV65/3, "Malaya's Contribution to Sterling Area Dol-lar Income", 15 January 1947). In a letter to the Colonial Office, the Bank underlined how important colonial development was in terms of its impact upon the balance of payments of the UK and the Sterling Area.

> The pre-war dollar earning capacity of tin would be invaluable to us at this time and it does not seem to me that the statistical position of the metal or its prospects over a period of years are such that, even during the present scarcity, an investment in tin mining machinery paid for in dollars would not yield a handsome dividend in dollars also.
>
> (BE OV65/3, "Letter to Colonial Office", 12 May 1947)

The rubber industry too required significant rehabilitation. However, a cautious policy was necessary since the synthetic rubber industry in America was now competing with the natural rubber industry for the same market, and at lower costs. Nevertheless, significant effort was undertaken to improve the output of Malayan rubber and was realised only shortly after Malaya's liberation with the rapid expansion of dollar area trade (TNA CO1045/177, Visit of Labour Adviser to Federation of Malaya, 13 December 1947).

The lead-up to convertibility

Immediately after the war, the newly returned Labour government engaged in a massive reconstruction programme, which also included substantial domestic reforms. This required considerable government expenditure and high volumes of imports of vital goods. Burnham (1990:vii) remarks, during the Attlee government, that the Cabinet was convinced of "the necessity to restore international capitalist viability to the British economy". As such, in order to pursue this policy of domestic reconstruction "the state required rapid accumulation which could only

be achieved if Britain could reconstruct an adequate international payments system to facilitate trade and secure regular imports of essential
commodities and raw materials" (ibid.:9). However, this was easier said
than done, as Burnham details:

> The British state was facing a severe economic crisis. The origins of
> this crisis, however, did not lie with the convertibility obligation or in
> industrial stagnation. The crisis was one of foreign currency reserves
> which had dwindled because of the expansionist programme pursued
> by the government.
>
> (ibid.:10)

In 1946, however, there seemed to be cause for optimism. Britain sur-
passed pre-war export levels in May of that year and, by the final quarter,
they were 10% *above* pre-war levels. Simultaneously, imports had been
reduced to 72.2% of their pre-war level. This resulted in a balance of
payments deficit less than half that which was being discussed at the
Washington Loan talks for the American Association of Finance and
Accounting (AAFA) (Kaplan 1990:5). Hugh Dalton, the Chancellor of
the Exchequer, was more than sanguine about the future prospects for
the economy:

> I have been able, as Chancellor, to meet all the demands on the public
> purse literally with a song my heart. If we keep together as we have
> since V-J Day, the shortages and frustrations which still afflict us will
> disappear like the snows of winter, and give place to the full promise
> of springtime.
>
> (Quoted in ibid.:6)

However, these figures were misleading. The markets to which Britain
was exporting were not the same as those from which Britain was
importing. Indeed, the trade deficit *was* lower than expected; however, Britain was drawing on the line of dollar credit (extended by
the AAFA) at the anticipated rate. In 1946, Britain received 42% of its
imports from the dollar area, but only sent 17% of its exports there;
the share of imports grew in 1947 to 46% (ibid.:6). In late 1946, however, Stafford Cripps told *The Times* of "the double balance of payments
problem", referring to both the trade deficit and the dollar deficit (ibid.).
In 1946, the overall trade deficit stood at £344m, with the dollar deficit
at $1,330 million, and 1947 saw the overall trade deficit at £343 mil-
lion, with the deficit with the dollar area standing at $2,301 million

(HMSO 1950). However, the overall trade balance turned into surplus in 1949, while the dollar deficit remained both large and persistent until the 1960s.

This deficit was inevitable. As David Eccles, MP remarked: "It is no use saying that the goods can come from the Sterling Area; they are simply not there" (quoted in Burnham 1990:43). Indeed, as Burnham (ibid.:44) observes, the US held a *de facto* monopoly on the most important commodities: "the attractiveness of the dollar rendered any alternative based solely on the Sterling Area as likely to be unworkable and highly unpopular". Thus, the imbalance in global production and trade (between the Western and Eastern hemispheres) manifested itself as a balance of payments crisis, principally in finding US dollars to pay for imports (ibid.:14). As such, Burnham (ibid.) concludes: "the need to maximise accumulation was thus translated into the need to accumulate world currency". The key means of accumulating world currency at the time was by cutting down the quantity of dollar imports, through the imposition of trading restrictions.

In 1945, after negotiating the AAFA, Britain was extended a \$3.75bn line of credit by the United States, and \$1.25bn by Canada. However, this generosity was premised on four major concessions: the dissolution of the Sterling Area dollar pool, an obligation to non-discriminatory trade, the repayment of British war debts and the instigation of general convertibility of Sterling within a year (ibid.:51). However, this line of credit was being rapidly exhausted: in the first half of 1947 alone, \$1.45bn had been spent. However, as was noted by the Cabinet, the crisis in dollar reserves was not principally due to an issue of productivity or infrastructure but "because we cannot sell our goods in the market from which our supplies alone can come" (quoted in ibid.).

On 3 July 1946, Lucius Thompson-McCausland, an adviser to the Governor of the Bank of England, wrote to the British delegation at the AAFA negotiations (BE 3A38/1 "Footnote to memo on American Loan", 3 July 1946). He identified to them certain prejudices that the US had concerning the nature of the Sterling Area and how this might affect negotiations over the loan, particularly the dollar pool. He made clear the British government's position on the dollar pool. While the dollar pool had only been "official" since 1939, it had been a well-established practice of the Sterling Area whereby Area members made most transactions for external payments in sterling and then left London to manage any consequent foreign exchange. By the end of the Second World War, the practice of pooling foreign exchange in such a fashion was at least a century old; however, the particular idea conveyed by the term "dollar pool" only become relevant with wartime exchange controls and the concentration of purchases from North America (ibid.; TNA FO371/82915, "The Sterling Area", 24 January 1950).

Thompson-McCausland understood that the Americans believed the Sterling Area dollar pool as a "wartime innovation", which required members of the Sterling Area to hand over their dollars to London who could then strictly control the Sterling Area's dollar expenditure. Indeed, he reiterated to the delegates that this was not close to the "facts" but was widely believed by the US negotiators (BE 3A38/1 "Footnote to memo on American Loan", 3 July 1946). Furthermore, and perhaps most importantly, the Sterling Area had nowhere near the amount of dollars for the amount of goods the US wished to sell, meaning that while the US might seek to dissolve the Sterling Area's dollar pool as an obstacle to free trade, the repercussions of that dissolution would potentially lead to disaster for the Sterling Area. Indeed, while dollar reserves in July 1946 were at their highest since December 1945, at £121m, this still represented a very low level of foreign exchange indeed for the EEA. However, the US still held the idea throughout negotiations and so it remained a source of friction (ibid.).

With the date of the convertibility obligation fast approaching, the Colonial Office intended to make clear to the Sterling Area that the upcoming convertibility of Sterling would have no impact on colonial import policy whatsoever. As such, a telegram was sent to all colonies five days before convertibility, which initially stated outright that general convertibility would have no repercussions for the colonies' ability to convert sterling, since "convertibility was purely a financial matter" and that "the Colonies have always had full convertibility of their current earnings of sterling for approved imports from dollar sources" (BE OV44/82, "Circular No.75", 10 July 1947).

While Arthur Creech-Jones, the Colonial Secretary, was broadly correct and the convertibility of the sterling held by Sterling Area members was not in serious doubt, it is the second part of the quotation that is revealing. The Dollar Drain prior to this telegram had already led to strictures on import policy and this telegram also reiterates this position. While discussions with the US were ongoing with regards to the specifics of import restrictions, the Colonial Secretary emphasised the continued importance of limiting imports.

Pending receipt of the revised directions please maintain close limitation of imports from the United States and other dollar sources, continuing to restrict them to the barest essentials for the running of your economy. The drain upon the reserves of the United Kingdom and the Colonies is at present much larger than had been expected and severe restrictions will continue to be required.

(Ibid.)

Therefore the enquiries made by Sterling Area members regarding the question of continued convertibility of their sterling had become an irrelevance. Their ability to convert sterling had been *de facto* limited by the severe import restrictions imposed on them by the UK. As such, while the colonies' ability to convert sterling remained undiminished during this period, the Dollar Drain led to import restrictions that severely curtailed their ability to spend dollars.

Sir George Bolton, an adviser at the Bank at that time, was strongly against the Convertibility Clause and, prior to 15 July, had argued vociferously against its implementation, circulating a note entitled "Economic and Industrial Crisis" to Bank officials:

When the inevitable monetary crisis develops we shall find ourselves hamstrung without means to take measures to save Sterling and the British Commonwealth from collapse. The effect of convertibility will be to add substantially to the drawings on the US dollar credit without giving us any offsetting advantages of any kind. The effect of non-discrimination in monetary and trade policy will largely prevent us from taking any kind of trading measures to enable us temporarily to acquire goods and services from those countries who owe us money and/or are willing to hold sterling.

(Bolton quoted in Fforde 1992:143)

However, on 23 June 1947, Bolton, while warning that convertibility would be catastrophic, acknowledged that the suspension of convertibility before it had occurred would be more catastrophic yet and so the Bank would have to look beyond 15 July as convertibility was now a fait accompli (ibid.:59). Indeed, Bolton was originally opposed to the details of the AAFA prior to its signing; however, the details of the loan were supported by Keynes, Sir Wilfred Eady and the Chancellor and so it was approved (BE 3A38/1, "Bonavia from Rickatson-Hatt", 4 September 1947).

On 15 July 1947, the day of convertibility, an "off the record" Press Conference was arranged by Bernard Rickatson-Hatt, the Bank of England's Press Secretary, for Bolton to guide how the story played out in the press (BE 3A38/1, "Convertibility of Sterling", 15 July 1947). It was attended by the City editors of the major news agencies.[2] Bolton sought to reassure the media that sterling would not only be available for conversion but that it was inevitable; in effect, Bolton, while seeking to provide some background to the obligation, sought to bolster confidence in sterling.

He emphasised the importance placed on this event by the US government and claimed that more was being made of this date in the US than in the UK. He underscored the inevitability of convertibility by claiming that, while the obligation to convert rested with the AAFA, an extension of the "multilateral use of Sterling" was more than likely as the UK had to trade gold or dollars against the sterling balances accumulated by other countries (ibid.). He claimed the multilateral use of sterling had been developed since the end of the war and London had "recaptured" its position as the centre of world trade and was at the time financing more trade than could be supported by British resources. While a lot had been made of the current "dollar domination", British state managers regarded New York and the US banking system as unprepared to take over the financing of world trade (ibid.).

Bolton emphasised that the obligation was not to convert sterling but to make sterling available for current account transactions between countries, and as such the Bank preferred to use the term "transferability" rather than convertibility. The link between the transferable accounts area, the dollar area and the Sterling Area was the rate in New York, kept rigidly between \$4.02¾ and \$4.03¼ as a result of British intervention, which was through the support of sterling in New York money markets by the Bank of England. As a result of this, a large proportion of the £3.5bn of accumulated sterling balances would be segregated and unlikely to come back on the exchange market. A large number of countries would be short of sterling and sterling would become, outside of the dollar area, technically, a hard currency. In addition to this, an arrangement had been made whereby central banks of countries outside the Sterling Area could use their sterling anywhere in the world (ibid.). This shortage could then be balanced by an increase in British imports and so the future of world trade was closely linked to the position of sterling (ibid.). In essence, Bolton made a public case that sterling was well placed to benefit from convertibility while privately acknowledging that it would be a catastrophe.

On 15 July 1947, in accordance with the AAFA, sterling became convertible for current account transactions.

The fallout from convertibility

As Schenk (1994:59) notes, "the system of quantitative import restrictions devised by Britain and copied in the rest of the sterling area discriminated in varying degrees against non-sterling imports for the purpose of conserving the central foreign exchange reserves". This resulted in an increase in intra-Sterling Area trade, the main beneficiary of which was the UK. Since the principal trading relationship of Sterling Area members was with the UK, this policy resulted in an increase of British exports to the Sterling Area. Schenk (ibid.:54) identifies three principal goals that Britain hoped to achieve through coordinating trade within the Sterling Area: reducing the keenness of the dollar deficit by purchasing more goods with sterling, reducing Britain's debts with its colonies in the most manageable fashion, and providing a surplus to support Britain's traditional deficit with non-sterling countries.

A report on the Sterling Area by the Foreign Office makes reference to the stipulations in the Washington negotiations regarding the Sterling Area dollar pool, and reveals the US aversion to the Sterling Area's discriminatory practices:

> The Anglo-American Financial Agreement called for the break-up of the "so-called sterling area dollar pool", but as the negotiation parties neglected to define what this meant and as the British in this particular context were inclined to argue that no such institution existed, no changes have followed.
>
> (TNA FO371/82915, "The Sterling Area –
> A Background Paper", 24 January 1950)

Indeed, the Sterling Area was the one offsetting factor for the convertibility of sterling. As such, in June 1947, efforts were made to restrict the import of non-priority items from the dollar area. However, the situation continued to deteriorate and more severe import restrictions were imposed. These restrictions led to a specific limit on dollar imports equal to three-quarters of the period July 1948–June 1949 (Kaplan 1990:9; TNA T236/3995, "Outward (Secret) Telegram no.372 from Commonwealth Relations Office", 22 October 1949).

Before the commencement of convertibility, the UK had entered into agreement with a number of countries to ensure the transferability of sterling in all currency areas for current transactions. By the time of convertibility on 15 July 1947, practically the whole world was covered by these arrangements. The result of this was that countries with sterling accrued from current account transactions could be freely spent in any other currency area for current transactions (BE OV44/82, "Confidential Telegram no.935", 20 August 1947). This arrangement held a degree of risk for the significant loss of dollar reserves. However, the severity and rapid development of the world shortage of dollars, coupled with international anxiety of Britain's dollar reserves, led to foreign holders of sterling converting as much of their sterling into dollars as possible (ibid.).

Two weeks before the suspension of convertibility, Creech-Jones sent a telegram to all colonies providing a background to the financial and monetary position of the UK and the Sterling Area. He explained that the government was set to enforce "drastic economies on imports into the United Kingdom in view of the very grave shortage of external resources" (BE OV44/82, "Telegram no.84", 6 August 1947). Furthermore, by this time the adherence to the Convertibility Clause had caused the drastic deterioration of Britain's reserve position, leading the Colonial Secretary to characterise the British exchange position in a dim light:

> the United Kingdom balance of payments position has substantially deteriorated. The underlying shortage of the means of external purchasing power, particularly American dollars, has therefore become still more acute.
>
> (Ibid.)

This deterioration required the implementation of even more draconian import restrictions for the colonies and the Sterling Area. The Colonial Secretary then made clear that not only was he considering the adoption of the measures being undertaken in the UK now in the colonial Empire also but, in the meantime, new import guidelines would be imposed on the colonial Sterling Area as a whole:

> Each Colony should limit its overseas expenditure whether in dollars, sterling or any other currencies in such a way as to minimise the risk of drawing down of the total overseas assets standing to its credit, and, if possible, to build up those assets, which, of course, consist predominantly of sterling balances in London. In present circumstances it is imperative that Colonies should seek to live within the income which each is earning. Not only does a drawing down of accumulated funds mean that undue pressure is being put upon scarce supplies, but also that monetary resources are being dissipated

which might be of vital importance if prices or primary products become less remunerative than they are at present ... Briefly, it means of course continuing restriction of imports to minimum essentials, including imports from the Sterling Area.

(Ibid.)

Indeed, while no specific import policy was implemented regarding the discrimination of trade between the UK and other sources, it was made clear that "any economies in hard currency expenditure which can be effected without introducing discrimination should be immediately adopted" (ibid.). However, in a subsequent telegram, the Colonial Secretary informed the colonies of the specific measures announced by the prime minister in the House of Commons that day, which ranged from limiting the import of luxury goods to an increase in points for food on basic rations (BE OV44/82, "Telegram no.85", 6 August 1947).

Four days before the suspension of convertibility, a timetable had been drawn up for "Operation Gearcrash" – the sequence of action leading up to the suspension of convertibility. In a memo drawn up by the Bank regarding Gearcrash, the procedure for the Sterling Area makes clear that, due to the UK controlling the reserves and the gross dollar earnings of Sterling Area members, the only course of action available was a change in policy. Sterling Area countries would now be told that their expendable sterling would not "now in principle be freely transferable to American accounts; that in practice [Britain] shall allow transfers if we are satisfied that their dollar expenditure is being rigorously curtailed, and that for this purpose a target must be set after discussion" (BE OV44/16, "Operation Gearcrash", 16 August 1947).

Operation Gearcrash led to a number of concerns among "Agreement Countries"[3] that Britain appeared to have "trapped" them into freezing their sterling balances and then immediately restricted their use of their remaining free sterling. Indeed, Britain was very clear to emphasise to Sterling Area countries that "Sterling is not just a means of acquiring dollars and that our action in deciding to police the use of free Sterling throughout the world is the only way of under-pinning the whole edifice of transferability" (ibid.).

Even with non-agreement countries (such as New Zealand and Australia), the UK had made informal agreements that import controls would prevent balances from being depleted and that dollar imports in particular would be very strict and discriminate to the benefit of the UK and the Sterling Area (ibid.). However, the Bank suggested that a close examination was needed of how much Australia and New Zealand counted on the UK "for US dollars over and above their current earnings from the dollar area since this is the proper point of comparison with the cut which we shall be imposing on other countries who do not happen to enjoy the facilities of the Sterling Area dollar pool". Operation Gearcrash also identified that Whitehall would need to implement a plan to emphasise to the Sterling Area that discriminatory action would be necessary to mitigate the Dollar Drain, which was to occur only a few days later (ibid.).

Two days before the suspension of convertibility, a conversation took place between Hugh Dalton (the Chancellor), Sir Edward Bridges and Ernest Rowe-Dutton (the Permanent and Third Secretaries to the Treasury, respectively). This conversation revolved around the surprise felt by the Chancellor that certain monetary agreements remained which obligated the UK to convert sterling into gold in certain circumstances. The Chancellor insisted that these agreements be rescinded, but both Bridges and Rowe-Dutton underlined to the Chancellor that these agreements were not only reciprocal but that the UK had earned substantial quantities of gold from them, particularly from France (BE OV44/16, "Note of a conversation with the Chancellor", 18 August 1947).

They put forward two more points to the Chancellor concerning the abrogation of the agreements. First, that it would be difficult to expect European central banks to support sterling without indemnifying their purchases against a loss, and it would also put the Sterling Area into a tricky position as the reciprocal nature of the agreement meant that there would be no guarantee of convertibility of European currencies into sterling or gold. This led to their final and most convincing point:

> We also pointed out that the monetary agreements plus the Sterling Area system represented the sole remaining international monetary system and if this were damaged owing to imprudent and hasty action trade would practically come to an end.
>
> (Ibid.)

The Chancellor was compelled by this statement and agreed with Bridges and Rowe-Dutton that "apart from the...suspension of the convertibility clauses, every attempt should be made to maintain the monetary agreements" (ibid.). The Chancellor's about-turn then hinged on the point that the monetary agreements to which Britain was party were essential for the continued vitality of international trade. Considering the limited trade occurring between Eastern and Western hemispheres at this point, the Sterling Area and the ancillary monetary agreements to which Britain was then party represented the last bastion of international trade and so to rescind these agreements, or to damage them in some other way, might have brought short-term benefits to Britain but would have ultimately led to a cessation of a large part of international trade, and would certainly have exacerbated the global crisis, much to the detriment of the vitality of global capital.

On the eve of suspension, Ernest Bevin, the Foreign Secretary, tabled in note that the press should be told that although convertibility was being suspended, it was only a temporary expedient and that the value of sterling would be maintained internationally. Furthermore, he insisted that Britain was neither seen as "bankrupt nor down and out" (BE 3A38/1, "Convertibility Announcement", 19 August 1947).

A subsequent press conference held by George Bolton and Bernard Rickatson-Hatt at the Treasury underscored the themes that the government wished to put across, but principally to boost confidence in the UK's economic position. The run on the reserves had ensured that an atmosphere of crisis had existed within both the Treasury and the Bank well before the announcement on the suspension of convertibility (BE 3A38/1, "Press Conference at HM Treasury", 20 August 1947). As such, the decision of the government to cut off the American Account Area and Canada from the rest of the world was a "simple and not unexpected" action and was done in cooperation with the US government. While Bolton remained upbeat about the US–UK relationship, claiming that both governments were in accord over the actions taken, the US government froze the loan granted to the UK due to the suspension of convertibility (BE 3A38/1, "News Summary", 21 August 1947). However, Bolton maintained that it was impossible to refuse convertibility while America provided the funds but, since reserves were being used, it was possible to refuse this obligation (BE 3A38/1, "Press Conference at HM Treasury", 20 August 1947). Furthermore, subsequent to this conference, where Bolton's opinion seemed to contradict the one he adopted on the eve of convertibility, Bolton now underscored that he never misled, he claimed, the City editors – he never believed convertibility was sustainable but he did consider sterling a strong currency and that it was essential that it be maintained as an international currency (BE 3A38/1, "Bonavia from Rickatson-Hatt", 4 September 1947).

Treasury Order SR+O No.1785 temporarily suspended sterling conversion into dollars which, Dalton warned, would lead to disruption of trade and so too some supplies. Dalton revealed the reasoning behind the suspension of convertibility to the public: the Dollar Drain had become totally unsustainable and, in the five working days leading up to 15 August 1947, amounted to US$176m, and US$66m the Monday and Tuesday following. The decision was disappointing, Dalton testified, but these were considered "necessary precautions" to maintain sterling. Dalton emphasised that there was "no crisis" and, so the Bank understood, it was generally accepted that the suspension of convertibility was not an issue of policy but rather a recognition of the "reality" of the situation, and that the Treasury were not seeking to return immediately to convertibility and would not for some time (BE 3A38/1, "News Summary", 21 August 1947; BE, 3A38/1, "Bonavia from Rickatson-Hatt", 4 September 1947).

The government was still committed to maintaining sterling's official rate and so measures were taken to ensure that sterling was maintained at £4.03 to the dollar, as well as to maintain the gold rate (BE OV44/82, "Confidential Telegram no.94", 25 August 1947). Indeed, George Bolton made clear that the key issue, following suspension, was to maintain the value of sterling and that, unless significant action was taken, sterling could have been devalued to £2 to the dollar and £200/oz of gold (BE 3A38/1, "Bonavia from Rickatson-Hatt", 4 September 1947). Crucially, the monetary agreements and mechanisms extant before convertibility remained the same. The Sterling Area is specifically mentioned as remaining the same in its relations with the rest of the world. This meant that certain monetary discrimination would be a necessary consequence of suspension, which the US would simply have to accept (BE 3A38/1, "Press Conference at HM Treasury", 20 August 1947).[4]

At the press conference announcing the cessation of convertibility, George Bolton declared that rationing of dollars for the Sterling Area members might be necessary and so there would be interruption of normal trading. However, this did not manifest itself directly: in the Sterling Area, the British government committed itself to continue to meet all claims by Sterling Area countries for dollars though there were provisos made for India, Sudan, Egypt and Iraq (BE OV44/82, "Confidential Telegram no.94", 25 August 1947; TNA T230/177, Note from JM Fleming to L Helsey, 5 March 1948). Instead, trade restrictions found immediate realisation in a series of telegrams to the colonies (BE 3A38/1, "Press Conference at HM Treasury", 20 August 1947).

Colonial import policy

Creech-Jones, on the day of suspension, sent a number of telegrams to the colonies outlining the procedure for how to deal with the post-suspension situation. He characterised the situation as a major eco-nomic crisis and believed that the colonies would want to know how to return to a more stable and prosperous situation since "the Colonies are so closely linked with the United Kingdom in finance and trade that the economic stability of this country must always be of vital inter-est to them" (BE OV44/82, "Unnumbered Telegram to All Colonies", 20 August 1947).

Creech-Jones provided further background to the crisis by identify-ing the problem fundamental to the failure of convertibility. Before the Second World War, the UK had substantial foreign income but had lost this due to having realised most of its investments and incurred large debts in financing the war. It had therefore become difficult to pay for imports on current income (and it was impossible to do so without substantially increasing UK exports). These difficulties had been miti-gated to date "and their true character partly concealed" by UK imports being financed under lend-lease and mutual aid during the war, or by American and Canadian credits after the war (ibid.).

With the announcement of the suspension of convertibility to the colonies, Creech-Jones, confusingly, stated to the latter that they "are not directly involved by this action but it is of very great general sig-nificance [to them] and will have many repercussions" (BE OV44/82, "Confidential Telegram no.935", 20 August 1947).

The importance of the colonies to the UK is underscored in the first of these telegrams:

> That is why our present financial position is one of comparative, though we believe temporary, weakness. But against that weakness can be placed the underlying permanent strength which can be drawn, in the interests of both Britain and yourselves, from the nat-ural resources and people of this country and those of its overseas connections.
>
> (BE OV44/82, "Unnumbered Telegram to All Colonies", 20 August 1947)

The Colonial Secretary identified that the problem facing the UK was its balance of payments, particularly its adverse balance with the dollar area caused by Britain's inability to pay with exports for the goods it needed to import. Britain also had to balance with repairing war damage, deal-ing with arrears generated during the war, while "undertaking other necessary and desirable developments at home and overseas" (ibid.).

This had been exacerbated by the high global prices of primary products and the global shortage of dollars:

> This shortage is due to the need of countries all over the world to import from the United States more than they can pay for with their current exports. As we ourselves are not able to replace the US as a source of supply of goods, other countries have been driven, in order to acquire the necessary additional dollars to pay for these imports from America, to require the United Kingdom to pay directly or indirectly in dollars for the goods we buy from them. This additional drain on our dollar resources has led to the measures just announced limiting the spending in the dollar area of sterling held by certain foreign countries.
>
> (Ibid.)

In regard to this problem and its acute character, given the recent suspension of convertibility, Britain enacted domestic import controls: trying to reduce imports, increasing production either as a substitute for goods that would ordinarily be imported, or specifically for export. The government was aware that although these were not austerity measures, they certainly required an element of sacrifice from the British people and a marked increase in production (ibid.).

The Colonial Secretary recognised that the role the colonies would play was through Britain's ability to control their reserves and their import policy as members of the Sterling Area.

> The Colonial territories can help in several ways. They can ensure that they do not [sic] add to the United Kingdom's difficulties by themselves importing more than they can pay for with current earnings, since that would involve using up Colonial reserves and asking the United Kingdom to export goods without any return in imports.
>
> (Ibid.)

Not only was there a desire to balance trade generally within the Sterling Area, but also to actually reduce imports substantially below exports to boost the size of the reserves. Indeed, the British government believed that "local action for minimisation of dollar requirements is primarily a matter of control of imports" (BE OV44/82, "Telegram no.91", 20 August 1947). In the meantime, the British government suggested to the colonies that the granting of all new import licences be suspended.

Further, while there was there a drive to limit imports from the dollar area, there was also a drive to limit imports from the Sterling Area for goods that could be used for export to the dollar area.

> Secondly, [the Colonies] can help by confining their imports, wherever possible, to a level below that of the actual earnings of their exports, thereby adding to their financial balances and strengthening the general position of the sterling area. The restriction of imports for current consumption has the same practical importance in the Colonies as in the United Kingdom itself. It is particularly important that there should no unnecessary expenditure in American dollars, but it is also, in current conditions, necessary that there should be the greatest possible economy in imports from any part of the world, including the sterling area itself.
>
> (BE OV44/82, "Unnumbered Telegram to
> All Colonies", 20 August 1947)

The colonies, Creech-Jones impressed, could also help by finding substitutes for goods that came only from the dollar area (or for goods which could be exported and sold for dollars), but the principal help the colonies could bring to bear on the problem was through import restriction and increased production for export.

> As in the United Kingdom, only an increase in production can afford a satisfactory long-term solution of these difficulties. Restriction of consumption must be regarded as a temporary expedient which it would be most undesirable to continue as a permanent policy. The increase of Colonial production is therefore the major long-term contribution which Colonial territories can make.
>
> (Ibid.)

The general sentiment of the relationship between Britain and its colonies within the Sterling Area is summed up at the end of the telegram, and captures the dominant relationship Britain played in altering the markets of the colonies to suit the ends of international trade, the resolution of the acute phase of this crisis and, therefore, the interests of capital-in-general. It also reveals a symbiotic quality to the imperial relationship: not only is Britain reliant on the colonies, particularly Malaya, for its strategy in restoring world trade but the colonies themselves are also reliant on the relationship for development and economic growth.

The whole-hearted co-operation of the Governments and people of the Colonies is essential if Colonial production is to play its part in the rehabilitation of a world ravaged by war, in the restoration of economic stability in the United Kingdom, and in the development of the Colonies themselves.

(Ibid.)

The government had announced measures to suspend the rights of countries outside the Sterling Area to spend their sterling freely in the dollar area. These measures left "perfect freedom for the expenditure of sterling not merely in the Sterling Area itself but in all other countries outside the dollar area", and the government attempted to reassure the Sterling Area that the utmost would be done to maintain sterling as an international currency, even in that limited role (BE OV44/82, "Confidential Telegram no.935", 20 August 1947).

While the British government wanted to reassure Sterling Area members that they would always be able to convert their sterling into dollars and that the measures announced suspending the right of countries outside the Sterling Area from spending sterling in the dollar area

will not of course apply to [Colonial territories. Their] position, as also that of other members of the sterling area, is that on the one hand [they hold their] reserves in sterling and [surrender] to the general pool [their] gross dollar earnings and on the other [they have] dollars made available to them to meet all their dollar requirements subject to an understanding that their imports and other policies are such as to minimise their dollar needs.

(Ibid.)

On the one hand, while a caveat was made concerning measures for severe restrictions on all but the most necessary goods on sterling convertibility into dollars, Creech-Jones also makes clear that, while the British government did not want to disturb this arrangement, it had become even more important that the condition in regard to the minimisation of dollar needs was observed with the "greatest strictness" (ibid.).

The technical effect of the new arrangement meant that all members of the Transferable Account Area had their rights to transfer sterling to the dollar area suspended. It was hoped to maintain the Transferable Account Area and, in fact, to continue to expand this area so that Sterling on Transferable Account would be available over as large an area

as possible outside of the Sterling Area (and the dollar area) for current account transactions (BE OV44/82, "Confidential Telegram no.94",
25 August 1947). The gravity of the situation, according to Creech-
Jones, could "hardly be exaggerated, nor the reluctance of HMG to
adopt these measures". In keeping with the tone of stability and that
this was a planned measure, Creech-Jones emphasised to the colonies
that it was important to realise that the suspension of convertibility was
not simply a return to the circumstances before 15 July 1947, since the
British government still saw sterling as freely transferable throughout
the Sterling Area and also throughout the Transferable Account Area. He
further pleaded that the colonies themselves emphasise a sense of stability, proportion and continuity to their own banking and mercantile
communities (ibid.).

Some days after suspension, and after some negotiation and the
serious consideration of the various non-discrimination clauses of
the AAFA, a more fleshed-out import policy had been developed for
the colonial Sterling Area. The AAFA required the colonial governments
of the British Empire to avoid discriminating against imports from the
US or Canada. Since, according to the IMF, the UK and the colonial
Sterling Area counted as a single unit with common foreign exchange
reserves, any expenditure by one member of this group was a strain on
the whole group's foreign exchange reserves; therefore it was permitted
for them to discriminate in favour of other members of the group but
not in favour of those outside of the group. As such, the colonies could
not discriminate against the US or Canada unless in favour of the UK or
other colonial territories; likewise the UK could not discriminate other
than in favour of the colonial territories, thus giving the British government the opportunity to pursue trade discrimination through its import
policy (BE OV44/82, "Secret Telegram no.98", 5 September 1947).

The Colonial Secretary was insistent that "a regime of wartime austerity as regards imports must...be reinstituted and rigid standards of
essentiality be adhered to...and the cutting down of imports from all
sources must be regarded as of paramount importance" (ibid.). However, Creech-Jones acknowledged the difficulty that the Colonies would
have to contend with in applying these measures to individual commodities (BE OV44/82, "Secret Telegram no.99", 5 September 1947).
Creech-Jones also lifted the temporary ban on granting import licences,
though emphasised that most existing import licences would have to
be amended to take into account the new rules of non-discrimination.[5]
Practically, outstanding import licences were left to the consideration
of individual colonial governments but Creech-Jones suggested that all

licences should be reviewed, with a particular emphasis on considering only the "bona fide" licences (BE OV44/82, "Secret Telegram no.98", 5 September 1947),

Due to the near-catastrophic drain on the reserves, which by September stood at a total of £559m (their lowest post-war level), and with dollar reserves at only £21m, Britain had to go further than simply diminishing imports from the dollar area. Creech-Jones declared it had become inevitable that, wherever colonial governments found it possible to restrict imports, they must do so even if it were from other members of the group or the UK. As such, all colonial governments were to impose restrictions on goods from the UK, other colonies and foreign countries. This required a return to individual import licensing. Creech-Jones, invoking the strictures of the Second World War, required that a system would need to be implemented which was "at least as strict as that obtaining at the height of the last war" (ibid.). Licences for goods from the UK were, in general, not granted for inessential goods and only in restricted quantities for essential goods. Only where consumer goods were essential to maintaining production were licences granted (ibid.). Of course, imports from outside the Sterling Area were required to be even lower than imports from countries within the Area, as far as was practical, although exceptions were made for goods from "war shattered countries" with a slight preference for these goods even over goods from the UK. This was regarded by Creech-Jones "as justifiable and as in the United Kingdom interest on exchange grounds" (ibid.).

Preference was also placed upon goods needed for capital development, and a specific hierarchy of imports was created to use as a guideline for the import of such commodities.

> The question will arise how to treat goods only obtainable from hard currency sources and needed for capital development. Where such imports can be shown to be likely to lead to additional production of a dollar earning or dollar saving nature to an extent which will more than repay the cost of the imports within two years, licenses may be issued. Where such imports will not lead to substantial earning of dollar revenue or the saving of dollar expenditure, licenses should be refused. Where such imports will lead to dollar earning or dollar saving substantially in excess of the value of the imports but not likely to arise within two years, import licenses should not be issued without reference to me.
>
> (Ibid.)

Export policy, however, was not similarly constrained and Creech-Jones made sure that the colonies were well aware of their obligations regarding the direction of their exports.

> The urgent need to earn more foreign exchange makes it the common interest of the group to ensure that the maximum amount of goods available for export in any member country is guided not to destinations within the group but to hard currency destinations outside the group. The group as a whole is unable to earn foreign exchange sufficient to pay for its imports from the rest of the world and these imports will therefore have to be cut down far more drastically than has recently been contemplated.
>
> (Ibid.)

Subsequent to these guidelines on import policy, Creech-Jones made a request for estimated import and export balances with the Western hemisphere for 1948, including any expected payments for invisible earnings. He emphasised, once again, the vital importance of these figures and that "it is difficult to overstate the critical position which confronts the UK and Colonies as regards their dollar reserves, and every possible effort must be made in 1948 to cut dollar expenditure to the bone" (BE OV44/82, "Secret Telegram", 16 September 1947). This was seconded shortly after by the Dollar Drain committee, which requested from the Board of Trade a three-month forecast of payments on imports and returns of expenditure to and from "dollar countries proper", as well as from any other countries that presented payment difficulties. The request and supply of the information was considered essential due to the very tight margins that the British government was dealing with at that point: namely, the ever-dwindling gold and dollar reserves (TNA CO537/2009, Dollar Drain Committee, 17 November 1947). By this point in 1947, dollar reserves stood at only £27m, with gold reserves their lowest since March 1946 at £501m (Bank 1970:162).

However, come the beginning of 1948, little had developed to resolve the deficits that were draining the dollar reserves. The Dollar Drain Committee acknowledged that goods from the Western hemisphere were not only still very much in demand, they had now become absolutely vital. However, the Dollar Drain Committee felt that it was no longer possible to ask the colonies to undertake an import policy of self-denial of vital goods, and thus restoring the sources of pre-war supply to meet requirements was considered a priority. This led to the realisation that the British government was faced with altering the pattern of trade yet again after wartime distortions (TNA CO537/3095, Progress Report from Committee, 13 January 1948). This brief realisation by the Dollar Drain Committee highlights an interesting point about the nature of imperial relations: that Britain's relationship with its colonies had to be *sustainable*, and therefore could not be an entirely exploitative "one-way street". British imperial strategy then had to be carefully balanced to support the colonies while they also supported Britain.

The Committee itself recognised that there were four aspects to the nature of the problem that Britain currently faced. First, Britain needed to begin supplying many of the commodities to the colonies as it had before the Second World War. Second, trade connections were not good enough. This was especially problematic if production increased and there were no markets available to which to export goods. Third, coordination of policy throughout the Sterling Area was poor; there was little synergy between policies on production, export and import licences. Fourth, and perhaps most important, diversion of exports to the Colonies was not just more an avoidance of a dollar loss than a dollar save, but it also infringed upon Britain's capacity to earn dollars itself. This meant that it was vital to get the colonies to economise first and switch later, as it was their demand that remained the problem (ibid.).

The beginning of the European recovery program

The production/trade imbalance was ameliorated somewhat by the introduction of the European Recovery Program (ERP), the Marshall Plan. Marshall Aid, as C. S. S. Newton (1984:391) puts it, can be seen as a response to Europe's rapidly developing dollar shortage in 1947. The first countries to benefit from the ERP were Greece and Turkey in early 1947, but Britain received the most substantial share of the Marshall Aid. With ERP, Britain expected an end to its dollar deficit by 1951 and freedom from the US aid by 1952 (Kolko 1972:443). However, this expectation did not find purchase; Britain's dollar deficit rose to £157m in 1949 (ibid.:457). This occurred primarily because of a fall in exports due to the US recession in 1948–1949.

Of course, Marshall Aid did not manage to solve the problem of global disequilibrium either. Indeed, this was expressed by Dean Acheson in a memo to President Truman in 1950.

At the end of ERP, European production will have been restored and substantial recovery achieved. But the problem of payment for American goods and services will remain. The countries of the free world will still require from us a volume of exports which they will not be able to pay for if their exports to the United States remain at present levels. Put in its simplest terms, the problem is this: as ERP is reduced and after its termination in 1952, how can Europe and other areas of the world obtain the dollars necessary to pay for a high level of United States exports, which is essential both to their own basic needs and to the well-being of the United States economy.

(Quoted in Newton 1984:407)

Both Newton (1984) and Burnham (1990) disagree with the "lifeline" thesis of Marshall Aid, though in different fashions. Newton (1984:408) argues that Marshall Aid solved no problems at all for Europe, or the trade disequilibrium. Noting that even before the war, Europe had never directly balanced its trade with the US, he maintains that, following the cessation of Marshall Aid, the currency crisis would quickly resurface. However, rearmament programmes prevented this from actually happening.[6] Burnham (1990:112) argues that Marshall Aid was not a panacea since "no overall state of economic paralysis existed". What Marshall Aid did, he argues, was to ease the pressure on dollar reserves so that the British government could continue with its expansive domestic reconstruction programme, without significantly altering the quality of life of the British subject. The archival evidence supports Burnham's thesis. State managers ultimately considered the grants and loans from the ERP more as a support for the British economy and a tool for the development of the productive capacity, not just of Britain but also its colonies, than a means of resolving the crisis itself (BE OV46/6, "General Memorandum for OEEC: United Kingdom Position in 1950–1951", December 1949).

The US saw the UK and its colonies as a single economic unit, and the official feeling in Washington was that the Sterling Area also could not be restricted as it was making a "highly important contribution to world trade and ... it provides an effective, although limited, multilateralism" (BE OV46/5, "Sterling Area", 28 July 1948; BE OV46/5, Discussion between Governor and Sir Wilfred Eady, 1 April 1948). This was a recognition of the UK's own policy, stated by Thomas Catto, the Governor of the Bank of England, which accepted that it had an obligation to "look after the Colonies", and therefore it would have been "inconsistent with this policy and make no sense to refuse to allow the Colonies to buy essential good from here or, if we cannot supply them, to provide the necessary dollars" (ibid.). However, this also had some negative repercussions.

In general, we obviously wanted the Dominions and Colonies to economise in dollar expenditure as much as possible and it probably suited us for the Dominions to borrow some dollars if they could from IMF etc., though borrowing dollars and piling up sterling balances was obviously not a process which could continue indefinitely.

(Ibid.)

As such, given the definition of the UK in these talks, that it also included all colonies, dependent territories and protectorates, the US and UK agreed to

adopt such financial and monetary measures as may be necessary to stabilise its currency, establish or maintain a valid rate of exchange, balance its governmental budget as soon as practicable, create or maintain internal financial stability (including the adoption or maintenance of appropriate credit policies), and generally restore or maintain confidence in its monetary system.

(BE OV46/5, "Economic Co-operation Agreement between the USA and the UK", 12 May 1948)

Given the great reliance on a broad imperial strategy during this period, action was required, then, to be taken in support of colonial development. For Malaya this also meant ensuring the successful prosecution of the emergency that had been declared on 16 June 1948. Indeed, in a Cabinet paper on 1 July 1948, Malaya, prior to the outbreak of the Emergency, was described as

the most peaceful country in South-East Asia and had taken long strides towards the re-establishment of stable, prosperous conditions...It is by far the most important source of dollars in the Colonial Empire and it would gravely worsen the whole dollar balance of the sterling area if there were serious interference with Malayan exports.

(TNA CAB129/28, CP (48)171, 1 July 1948)[7]

Certainly then, here we see in Cabinet documents that the pre-war relationship between Britain and Malaya remains the same in this post-war crisis. Indeed, the historically developed and unique relationship between Malaya, Britain and the global economy is not only well understood by British state managers but clearly distinct from other imperial relationships.

In a letter from Sydney Caine, the Third Secretary to the Treasury to Henry Wilson-Smith, the Second Secretary to the Treasury, Caine informed Wilson-Smith that he had been informed by William Gorell-Barnes, the Assistant under-Secretary of State for the Colonies, of discussions by the London Committee on European Economic Co-operation about the possibility of ERP and International Bank loans for the colonies. According to Caine, the Treasury ideally wanted Britain and its colonies to take all ERP loan dollars on offer and to borrow from the International Bank also. However, due to problems in negotiating this with both the International Bank and the US, the Treasury sought for the UK to take up the ERP loans, while the colonies would take up the International Bank loans.[8] Due to considerable differences in interest rates, this raised certain difficulties. Pressure had to be brought on the colonies to accept this agreement, which would not have been made easier if they were denied the benefits provided through the cheaper ERP rate. Indeed, it would have been very difficult to persuade the colonies that they would have to be left out of the ERP (because they had enough dollars for their own needs) while simultaneously being asked to borrow dollars from the most expensive lender. (TNA T232/154, "Caine to Wilson-Smith", 2 July 1948).

The Treasury then sought to make this offer reasonable either by working to allow the colonies access to ERP loans or, if possible, by making an internal adjustment within the colonial Sterling Area to equalise interest rates. The letter from Caine ends by emphasising that the Colonial Office required the Treasury's agreement on the principle of allowing access to ERP loans or making internal adjustments to equalise rates on International Bank loans so as to strengthen the case for colonies signing the agreement over American aid before 6 July 1948. (TNA T232/154, "Caine to Wilson-Smith", 2 July 1948).

By 6 July 1948, the Treasury had come to the conclusion that the issue of bringing the colonies into the ERP itself was not even to be contemplated; however, there remained a possibility that the Colonies might receive a proportion of the first quarter loan received from the ERP. Indeed, the Treasury were happy "for the Colonies to receive some of the loan, or to borrow from the International Bank and have an equalisation of those interest rates, but they would be brought in to that degree only "for the purposes of the supply of raw materials" (TNA T232/154, "ERP loans for Colonies", 6 July 1948).[9] Arthur Creech-Jones telegrammed the colonies to inform them that the British government would not ask the colonies to seek International Bank loans since they were of a high rate of interest that was not offset by the potential advantages;

furthermore, there was the additional problem in colonies such as Malaya, which was a net dollar earner, in asking them to borrow dollars at uneconomic rates when they earned significant quantities by themselves (TNA T232/154, "Circular Despatch to all Colonies from Arthur Creech-Jones", 20 September 1948).[10]

Sir Oliver Franks, the British Ambassador to Washington, wrote to the Foreign Office that the European Cooperation Administration (ECA) had reached an agreement on the initial loan to the UK, $300m from April to December 1948, with the possibility of increasing the loan for the subsequent three months to April 1949. While it was claimed by the ECA that there would be no specific percentage link between grants and loans from the programme, the ECA make clear that their intention was to make the British government take up the loan obligation of $300m as the price for obtaining grant assistance to the ratio of 3:1 (i.e. grant:loan) over the whole period. As such, the ECA were accepting the percentage link but avoiding admitting that. Franks admitted that while this was not ideal, it was difficult to provide an argument that the British government was happy to accept free money but not money that curtailed consumption when the whole package is necessary for economic recovery. Furthermore, as Franks pointed out, the ECA position was a point of policy and likely immovable. The grant:loan ratio was inevitable (TNA T232/154, "Telegram no.3312", 7 July 1948).

Stafford Cripps, now the Chancellor of the Exchequer, in discussion of Franks' telegram, was very concerned that the grant:loan ratio could no longer be opposed and, more importantly, that the US could not see the restriction on the use of the loan purely for the purchase of capital goods as valid, though he was hopeful that a compromise could be sought on this issue, especially since Cripps had recently claimed in the House of Commons that the government would use the American loan on capital items (TNA T232/154, "Discussion of telegram no.3312", 8 July 1948). In the following telegram from Franks, he urged the Foreign Office to authorise him to accept the existing terms of the agreement and move towards the final negotiation of the loan itself, as he felt it was as good a deal as they were likely to get (TNA T232/154, "Telegram no.3370", 9 July 1948). The American Aid and European Payments (Financial Provisions) Bill, published on 14 December 1948, authorised payment of UK contributions to the Paris Agreement. It also provided statutory authority to and provided the permission for an audit and report to Parliament on the "Special Account" and the Intra-European Payments Account. By the 20 November 1948, the total received from the ERP was $453m. $348m was Grant Aid and the equivalent in sterling was paid into the Special Account (BE 3A38/1, "EC Aid Accounting Arrangement", 15 December 1948).

The aid system of the ERP worked according to a system of need, established by a forecast of dollar deficits (which were very difficult to predict accurately). An intra-European payments system was also established in which debtor states received drawing rights from creditor states, according to a need determined by dollar deficit forecasts. Aid was also given, in certain instances, in the form of commodities (BE OV46/6, "Future of ERP", 30 September 1949). A Bank of England memo on the future of the ERP described the negotiations behind this system as a "sordid wrangle" and was similarly scathing about the principles of dollar allocation.

> [They] have highly damaging effects. They penalise countries for doing well. Every country's interest lies in proving that it cannot increase its dollar earnings or reduce its dollar expenditure and that it cannot balance its intra-European position. If a country does well, it loses aid. The better it does, the more its aid is cut. There is no incentive for a country to take the difficult decisions which are needed to make it viable.
>
> (Ibid.)

However, the initial dollar aid was extremely helpful and Stafford Cripps defended this aid to the House of Commons.

> We must underline once more the extent of our dependence at the present time on this very American aid. I must remind the House of the extract from the Board of Trade Journal of 16th October last, which said that without American aid, the present position in Britain would be that there would be less meat and eggs, there would be cuts in butter, sugar, cheese and even bacon, cotton goods would have disappeared from the home market, tobacco consumption would have been cut by three-quarters and house building reduced perhaps to 50,000 a year. Unemployment, as we have been told by Ministers, basing themselves upon this document, might well have risen to one and a half million or more and there would have been a lower standard of living resulting in a diminished productive effort.
>
> (Hansard Vol.460 cc1111–1230, HC
> Debate 27 January 1949)

The chancellor was keen to emphasise the value of the ERP to the reconstruction and restructuring of Britain's economy. However, Cripps, in the same debate, made sure also to emphasise the Sterling Area and the colonies as vital pillars of Britain's economy. Indeed, he urged that yet more could be expected from the colonies to support the Sterling Area's dollar deficit.

> We must maintain and increase the very valuable contribution made by the Colonies through the sale of materials to the dollar area. This means continued development of Colonial resources – a development which has in the past unfortunately been gravely neglected. It also means that we have to export goods to the Colonies in increasing quantity, both in return for the goods they export and in order that these new developments can take place.
>
> (Ibid.)

Thus, while ERP was one measure of supporting post-war reconstruction, so too was the imperial strategy of wide-scale dollar rationing throughout the Sterling Area. Particular within this strategy, and among these relationships, was the scale of Malaya's dollar contribution, standing over and above all other colonies by some measure. Throughout 1948, Malaya was estimated to have provided $172m towards the colonial dollar surplus, which stood at, bearing Malaya's contribution in mind, $178m, while the Sterling Area's dollar deficit stood at $1,800m for the same period. However, Malaya's actual contribution was closer to $230m, including Singapore's entrepôt earnings (TNA FO371/76049, "Malaya as a dollar earner", 30 April 1949).

However, concerns were raised that Malaya could become "another Burma", in terms of its civil unrest, and so disrupt the pattern of Western economic recovery. As Malaya was overwhelmingly the greatest dollar earner in the colonies and the Sterling Area, there was serious concern that any further development of the insurgency in Malaya could affect the rubber and tin industries, diminishing exports to the dollar area and thus threatening its dollar contribution to the Sterling Area and, therefore, severely hinder the resurgence of global trade (TNA FO371/76049, "Malaya as a dollar earner", 30 April 1949). Furthermore, while Malaya's importance as a dollar earner for economic recovery was much appreciated by the British government, so too was its role as a vital supplier of raw materials necessary for ERP, as well as for the American economy (TNA FO371/76049, "Letter to UK delegation to UN", 2 April 1949). However, almost a year later, in a letter from Thomas Lloyd, Permanent under-Secretary to the Colonial Office, to John Paskin, the Assistant Secretary, the situation in Malaya was still unstable and renewed commitment was required in order to maintain the Malayan contribution to the dollar pool (TNA CO537/5996, "Lloyd to Paskin", 28 March 1950; PREM8/1126, "Suggestion by Ministry of Defence", 19 April 1950). In early 1950, the prime minister set up a "Malaya Committee" to oversee the stability of Malaya and the prosecution of the Malayan Emergency (PREM8/1126, "Terms for the creation of the Malaya Committee", 22 April 1950).

The relationship between Britain and Malaya required a careful balancing act of ensuring that Malaya was providing and saving as many dollars as possible but, in order to do this, it needed substantial investment to maintain dollar earnings and savings. This required the development of the Malayan economy and the spending of dollars to achieve that. The dynamic (which is to say not-entirely "one-way") nature of imperial strategy is manifest here in the fact that Britain's relationship with Malaya had a particular character and purpose that, while managed by the institutional framework and mechanisms of the Sterling Area and the British Empire more broadly, can only be understood as a bilateral relationship that had developed historically with both Britain and the global economy.

By this point the Sterling Area still represented the largest multilateral trading organisation in the world after the war. By 1948, £5bn of $13.8bn (36%) visible world trade conducted was in sterling. Considering invisible earnings, this figure came closer to 50% of international payments that were conducted in sterling. The Foreign Office felt that "these facts stem partly from the ramifications of the sterling area itself and partly from the world shortage of dollars", but nevertheless it was the *de facto* principal trading and monetary organisation in the immediate post-war period (TNA FO371/82915; Sterling balances in South East Asia', 28 March 1950). Indeed, Sir Sidney Caine, the Head of the UK Treasury and Supply Delegation to Washington, in discussion with US Treasury officials, diagnosed the fundamental division existing in world trade.

> The world was divided into two broad areas. The dollar area where more was being produced than consumed; and the non-dollar area where consumption was greater than production. Our thinking should be in the direction of determining whether any measure proposed would bring about a better balance between the two areas.
>
> (TNA T230/177, "Note of meeting with
> US Treasury", 8 June 1949)

Sidney Caine's characterisation of the problem affecting the global economy is an exact description of an overproduction crisis, albeit geographically represented as a trade imbalance between two hemispheres. Caine's statement was in response to George Bolton's suggestion that an open general licence import policy was required since, he argued, global trade would only revive from large-scale voluntary capital investment flows (ibid.). If trading restrictions were eased in the non-dollar area, it would lead to a greater willingness in the US to invest in foreign capital. This sentiment was echoed by Sir Henry Wilson-Smith, Second Secretary to the Treasury, who felt it would also inject competitive rigor into the non-dollar area, thus leading to lower prices and improved productivity in the UK and Sterling Area. However, this suggestion was not pursued and instead the UK moved closer to devaluing sterling, while maintaining Britain's important imperial relations.

Devaluation

A Treasury memo in 1948 discussed the advantages and disadvantages of fixed and floating exchange rates (TNA T230/177, "The Dollar-Sterling Rate", 30 August 1948). The memo identified that, with US inflation rising and primary goods production at a low, US goods and raw material prices would continue to rise, and hopefully improve the UK's deficit with the dollar area. However, this did not occur since UK prices increased at a greater rate and, despite consistent increases in production and export growth, it was clear by early 1949 that exports were not growing as quickly as imports, and as such were in relative decline (Burnham 1990:127). Given the trading of sterling for dollars at a much lower value than the official rate, it seemed as if one of the only options was a devaluation of sterling (Kolko 1972:458).

There was significant speculation in the press about the strength of sterling. A piece in the *Economist* on 3 September 1949 (517) summed up Britain's position very well, emphasising that Britain was no longer facing "business as usual":

> The old banker of the Sterling Area is certainly playing his traditional part, but today he is playing it on a scale beyond all pre-war precedent and doing so without the substance which enabled him both to play the part and to thrive on it.

On 19 September 1949, sterling was devalued from US$4.03 to US$2.80. However, this did not change the amount of ERP dollars that were available to the UK though it did increase the amount of sterling in the "Special Account" (a counterpart fund to the amount of dollar aid the UK received), which actually had a deflationary effect on the economy and was hoped by the Bank would minimise the inflationary effects associated with devaluation (BE OV46/6, "ERP and Devaluation", 20 September 1949). However, it was also accepted that devaluation would make the terms of trade worse initially though, at the time, the government was unsure how the course of events would unfold as devaluation had created a new and unfamiliar situation (TNA T230/177, "Memorandum from the Foreign Secretary", 18 October 1949; TNA T230/177, "1949/50 Dollar Export Forecast", 22 September 1949).

The Governor of Singapore, Sir Franklin Gimson, informed the Colonial Secretary that the Colonies had been expecting devaluation for some time now; however, there was some annoyance that the value of their Sterling balances had been diminished significantly (BE OV65/3, Telegram no.776 (Secret), 12 October 1949). Furthermore, he relayed that the black market in dollars in Malaya had now been eliminated with the reduced rate, exports to the dollar area had already been stimulated by devaluation and he remained confident that imports from the dollar area to Malaya would soon shrink (ibid.).

This sentiment was echoed in a report following a visit by the Colonial Office's South-East Asia Department to Malaya between June and November of 1949. The report states that, despite the uncertainty over the sterling–dollar rate, the tin industry in Malaya was well organised and productive, as was the rubber industry (TNA CO1045/177, "The Federation of Malaya", 11 November 1949). However, both faced serious problems in the next few years. Both industries could only survive if they expanded. The tin industry needed to discover new fields and prospecting was essential, while the rubber industry needed to expand and consolidate its current estates and replant them with higher-yielding rubber trees, as the only means of successfully competing with synthetic rubber (ibid.; BE OV46/6, "General Memorandum for OEEC: United Kingdom Position in 1950–1951", December 1949). However, the Communist insurgency and the lack of available capital were hampering efforts to develop both of Malaya's vital dollar-earning industries. The insurgency would continue to escalate and the British government still required severe import restrictions to keep the dollar deficit as low as possible.

A telegram from the Commonwealth Relations Office to the Finance Ministers of the Independent Sterling Area, sent in late October, warned that inflationary pressures could wipe out the gains provided by devaluation. Indeed, this warning preceded a statement by the Minister for Commonwealth Relations, Philip Noel-Baker, that the UK would not be meeting the Sterling Area dollar import targets for 1949 and to attempt to do so would have meant "the complete reversal of the whole process of economic recovery and cancellation of contracts on a large scale.... The export drive and the re-equipment of British industry would have come to a standstill" (TNA T236/3995, "Outward (Secret) Telegram no.372 from Commonwealth Relations Office", 22 October 1949).[11] The import target, set at US$1200m (intended to be 75% of the 1948 dollar expenditure), was overshot by US$190m, which Noel-Baker justified by arguing that the overspend took account "of the urgent need to provide the materials upon which our dollar-earning and dollar saving export industries depend" (ibid.).

Noel-Baker concluded the telegram by insisting that the 1949/50 figures would be much improved since more money would be received from the ERP; however, he also acknowledges that ERP dollar aid would be much diminished in 1950/51, which would therefore require renewed dollar economies and the rebuilding of the reserves (ibid.).[12] In a memo for the Organisation for European Economic Cooperation (OEEC), the Bank echoed this point: even with the devaluation of sterling providing a major incentive to purchase British exports, the reduction of dollar imports would still be essential in closing the dollar gap (BE OV46/6, "General Memorandum for OEEC: United Kingdom Position in 1950–1951", December 1949). Indeed, the memo states that exports to the dollar area will need to cover at least 90% of dollar area imports in order to even approach equilibrium and this represented "a completely different trade pattern between the United Kingdom and North America from anything which has existed for the last 35 years" (ibid.). While the level of US imports increased over this period, the overall global supply of dollars fell for the third consecutive year (see Table 3.1).

Essential to the development of this new trading pattern over the next few years was the Sterling Area, which the Bank saw as crucial to British, European and global economic vitality due to the range of Sterling Area goods (particularly colonial goods) being large dollar earners, or dollar savers (BE OV46/6, "General Memorandum for OEEC: United Kingdom Position in 1950–1951", December 1949). This required substantial dollar import reductions in the Sterling Area since the rebuilding of Sterling Area reserves was of the utmost importance to safeguarding

Table 3.1   World supply and use of dollars, 1946–1950 ($ million)

	Annual totals				
Year	1946	1947	1948	1949	1950
Imports	5,168	6,071	7,822	7,066	9,315
Public financial resources: grants and other unilateral transfers (net)	2,279	1,812	4,157	5,321	4,120
Total supplied	13,153	15,471	16,845	16,682	18,209
Total other sources	1,968	5,274	1,159	77	3,628
Total used by other countries	15,121	20,745	18,004	16,759	14,581

Source: TNA T230/177, "World Supply of Dollars", 25 June 1952.

trade. As such, the Bank outlined four policy points to achieve this goal:

- Increase the supply of manufactures and primary goods to dollar markets and other markets that are dependent on supplies from the dollar area.
- Increase the supply of dollar-earning services (e.g. tourism).
- Alter the pattern of production to achieve the above.
- Promote conditions designed to help investment of the surplus countries.

(Ibid.)

All the above points, apart from the second, apply to Malaya. While dollar saving would account for reducing around a third of the dollar gap, the rest would be achieved by stimulating exports through development. For Malaya, this meant the development of the rubber and tin industries. Since the Sterling Area, in total, was in deficit with the dollar area, this increased the importance of colonies like Malaya even more than had been the case over the previous 40 years, when the Sterling Area had provided a surplus to balance Britain's own deficit with the dollar area (ibid.). As such, Britain had an even greater need and responsibility to develop its colonies, which required "above all a high level of investment in the Colonies and this, over a period of years, can be achieved only by a net financial investment from overseas (principally from the United Kingdom) supported by a high level of imports of capital goods and manufactured consumption goods" (ibid.).

The Bank characterised the relationship between Britain and the colonies as "essentially one of mutual advantage", since the colonies relied on the UK for development through finance, manufactured and consumer goods, as well as personnel; while the UK depended on the colonies for raw materials and, in the case of Malaya, the hard currency provided by the sale of its raw materials to the dollar area (ibid.). Malaya then was doubly important to the British economy as it aided in the recovery of Britain's lost reserves and provided raw materials for manufacture – both of which were essential to returning Britain to economic viability (ibid.).[13] However, colonial development was intended to improve those very factors since development was seen as instrumental in developing a surplus with the dollar area.

The Bank then outlined to the OEEC a five-step plan for moving towards resolving the trade disequilibrium:

- general domestic policies: deflationary action, devaluation, increasing productivity, freeing up trade as widely as possible;
- expansion of dollar earnings from trade and services while maintaining imports as much as possible;
- elimination of the dollar deficit on other transactions: capital transactions, Sterling Area payments, payments of gold and dollars to third countries, and the development of existing surpluses – requiring increased exports to the Sterling Area and the rest of the world in order to earn and save dollars;
- recovery of reserves to an absolute minimum of US$2,000m by the end of the ERP;
- strengthening the external financial position as much as possible.

(Ibid.)

These policies rested, however, on ERP dollar aid remaining as was forecast until its predicted end date, and there was little leeway built into these policy priorities.

If these external conditions are not fulfilled, it will be impossible to carry out effectively the policies indicated above, and the United Kingdom position – and indeed that of the whole sterling area and of Western Europe – will be correspondingly weaker, and the United Kingdom will be less able to play her full part in bringing about a "one-World" multilateral trade and financial system.

(Ibid.)

However, the ERP was not resolving the fundamental problem of the global trade imbalance and the UK was still vulnerable to economic upsets due to its low reserves, which, by the end of 1949, stood at £603m, with £131m of dollar reserves available (BE OV46/6, letter to Sir Edward Bridges, 19 December 1949). This was much weaker than the figure indicates, due to the devaluation of sterling. So while the reserves grew towards the end of the year, they only reached a similar level to that of the previous year before they began to fall in April 1949, though the December reserves showed a much improved dollar position. In fact, the dollar reserve position was higher than it had been since November 1946 but both gold and dollar reserves would continue to rise until July 1950, with gold reserves increasing until July 1951 (Bank 1970:162).

The reserves flattered the UK's overall position. The ERP was still supporting Britain's reserve position but not solving the underlying problem. As such, the Bank informed the Permanent Secretary to the Treasury, Sir Edward Bridges, that they were not at all optimistic about Britain's outlook after the end of the ERP (BE OV46/6, letter to Sir Edward Bridges, 19 December 1949). Indeed, the Bank informed Sir Edward that they expected a return to an acute world dollar shortage after ERP finished due to the "deepseated maladjustments in world trade" that still existed and had not yet been resolved (ibid.). This sentiment was echoed in a letter to the UK delegation to the OEEC, emphasising that the only way out of the dollar shortage was through investment in UK and colonial production (BE OV46/6, "International Investment", 6 June 1950). Contrasted with the situation before the Second World War, when Britain's reserves were much greater and it could lose many millions of dollars without precipitating a crisis, the situation was still starkly pessimistic. Indeed, as a Bank memo pointed out:

> A nation which is the centre of a multilateral trading and financial system which conducts transactions with the dollar area alone of $7 billion a year, and which besides that provides the currency in which a large part of the world's international trade is carried on, and which is therefore subjected to every ripple in the world economy, cannot manage with reserves of less than $2 billion. It needs much more to move effectively towards "One-World" objectives.
>
> (BE OV46/6, "General Memorandum for OEEC: United
> Kingdom Position in 1950–1951", December 1949)

Conclusion

This chapter has shown the importance of British reserves to governing strategy, and their notable weakness, a consequence of US productive capacity and Britain's own and continued economic malaise. The most important element of British policy supporting these reserves was the Sterling Area's dollar pool and its most valuable contributor was Malaya. British state managers required both the UK and the Sterling Area to limit imports from the dollar area, and boost exports to the dollar area. The Dollar Drain, and the reserve position, dominated the thoughts of British state managers in this period and this is particularly apparent in three acute moments: the Convertibility Crisis, the ERP and the devaluation of sterling.

The Convertibility Clause was catastrophic for the British dollar problem. The demand for dollars was unable to be met by Britain's line of credit from the US and Canada, or Britain's own dollar earnings, and so convertibility was suspended. While state managers sought to maintain the Sterling Area in this period, this was not because they were under the illusion that the Sterling Area could provide all of the goods necessary for post-war reconstruction, or that the Sterling Area would remain the pre-eminent conduit for international trade in perpetuity, but rather because British state managers believed that this was the best available means to maintaining international trade and Britain's reserve position under crisis conditions at that time.

In order to stimulate world trade further, the US sought to inject an even greater quantity of dollars into the world economy through the ERP. This vast stimulus, again, sought to fuel world trade, the consumption of American goods and the restructuring and reconstruction of Europe's damaged economies. However, with costs rising in Britain faster than elsewhere in the world, Britain was forced to devalue sterling in the hope that this would stimulate exports to the dollar area; however, this was not forthcoming, and crisis conditions remained.

This chapter contains two important ideas of relevance to British imperialism: the mechanisms of the Sterling Area and the value of Malaya to this trading area. Malaya remained a very important source of dollars to the Sterling Area, which pooled all of its foreign reserves in the UK and under the control of the British government. This was achieved through the sale of Malaya's two main natural resources, rubber and tin, to the US. During this period, the British government imposed stringent measures on the members of the Sterling Area. These measures principally took the form of extremely strict import policies and a similarly strict import licensing policy, making it very difficult for any Sterling Area member to import goods from the dollar area for anything other than the most necessary purchases. Furthermore, due to the pooling of all dollars and the significant rationing of these dollars, the British government made sure to keep a very tight lid on all dollar spending. While the British government claimed that dollars were always available to Sterling Area members, and that no member ever "went without", this was the case because of the extremely strict import policies which were set by the Colonial Office.

The purpose of these policies was to limit the drain of dollars from the Sterling Area and to maintain the Sterling Area as a cogent trading bloc, and the largest in the world. Indeed, if the flow of dollars continued unabated from the Sterling Area, the members would inevitably have sought to extricate themselves from the agreement and either "go it alone" or reach an agreement tying their currencies to another. Neither would have been, as British state managers saw, in the interests of Britain or the resurgence of world trade, and thus capital. However, this period also sees attempts by British state managers to secure aid for Malaya and the colonies in order to ensure their economic growth and development, which was not only seen as an essential part of the strategy of boosting the dollar surplus countries of the Sterling Area but was, by its very nature, beneficial to them also.

The chapter seeks to conclude that this dollar drain reveals an economy in crisis, which is best understood as a global overproduction crisis manifest on the one hand as a trade imbalance between Western and Eastern hemispheres, and on the other hand as a shortage of dollars in the global economy. Indeed, officials at the Bank, and Sir Sidney Caine at the Treasury, both characterise the fundamental problem as one of overproduction in the dollar area, particularly the US. The British government sought to aid the reinvigoration of international trade after the Second World War through the manipulation of the markets of the Sterling Area, using import controls and the strict rationing of pooled dollars.

What remains particularly telling is that, during the period 1945–1950, compared with subsequent years, the content of the Bank's archives on Malaya remains unusually empty. However, particularly full in this period are the documents on Sterling Area policy as a whole. One can only conclude therefore that, during this period, the series of bilateral relationships that made up the Sterling Area and Empire were subsumed beneath the overarching institutional framework of the Area, due to the particularly acute nature of the crisis and the measures required to overcome it.

This is consonant with the established literature on the subject (Hinds 2001; Krozewski 2001). However, where this argument diverges from others is in its conception of the Sterling Area. Where other approaches see the Sterling Area and the Empire as a formal institution and analyse it as such, subsuming the individual relationships of the Sterling Area into an imagined idea of the institution of the Sterling Area, the British state sought to force these bilateral relationship to conform to a very strict set of criteria due to the crisis besetting the global economy.[14] Malaya performed a very specific function in its relationship with Britain due to this historically developed relationship with both Britain and the global economy, particularly its dollar-earning capacity derived from its rubber and tin exports to the US. As such, Britain actually required the members of the Area to act in specific ways.

However, the use of these bilateral relationships for a single purpose reveals the particular nature of British imperial strategy in this period. Indeed, as mentioned by numerous state officials, the acute crises that beset the British and global economy were severe and likely to cause the collapse of sterling and bring the British economy into chaos. The only means of avoiding this outcome was by turning these bilateral relationships to a single purpose: dollar saving and accumulation.

The following chapter will look at the period 1950–1955 in British–Malayan relations. It will focus on the continuation of the dollar deficit, further attempts to develop the Malayan economy and the intensification of the Malayan emergency.

4
The Dollar Deficit Continues (1950–1955)

This chapter covers the period from 1950 to 1955 in Britain's relationship with Malaya. This chapter, as with the preceding chapter, charts continuity in this relationship both within this period, and from the last.

As one might expect with an imperial relationship, Britain controlled Malaya's external economic policy as well as its internal economic structure. Britain maintained its control over Malaya's resources, particularly its rubber and tin production that achieve their greatest value in their trade with the US and the accumulation of dollars, which Britain controlled through its management of the Sterling Area's dollar pool. Britain remained keen to develop Malaya economically and stabilise it politically and socially, looking to its eventual independence, for its ultimate insertion into the global economy outside of Britain's direct domination.

The chapter argues Malaya's continuing importance to Britain. Malaya's exports to the dollar area continue to support Britain's reserve position in this period, which becomes especially important as Britain's reserves reach dangerously low levels. Malaya remains, as the Sterling Area's principal dollar pool contributor, a crucial support not only for the Sterling Area but also for the international viability of sterling itself. This is borne out throughout the archival evidence from the period in which ministers, and government and Bank officials, emphasise the importance of Malaya, as well as the continued prosecution of the Emergency and efforts to secure significant loans and grants for the development of Malaya's economy. These efforts show continuity with previous attempts by the British state to develop the Malayan economy, and the reasons behind it.

This chapter concludes by highlighting, despite the perceived changes in Britain's relationship with Malaya, a consistent basis behind this relationship. In Chapter 3, Britain's imperial relationship with Malaya is clearly understood in the classical terms of imperialism as it enforced trade policies and stringent dollar spending limits throughout the Empire. However, this chapter will argue that despite a change in policy, where the British government was no longer imposing such extreme strictures on the Malayan economy, the relationship remains the same. Indeed, the archival material examined in this chapter reveals that no significant shift occurs whatsoever in this relationship. This runs counter to established accounts of British imperial economic relations, particularly Hinds (2001) and Krozewski (2001), and this is a view held widely in British imperial and international history literature, as well as in Malaya-specific literature, such as Kaplan (1990) and White (1996).

This discrepancy in view arises from two sources, in the first instance an understanding of empire as a strategy undertaken by a state in the interests of capital-in-general and manifest as a relationship between states. This is an alternative to a view of imperialism as an institution, a period of history or a type of state. This allows bilateral relationships "within" an empire to be understood in their own terms as historically developed and unique relations that cannot be understood in aggregation with the whole complex of other relationships within that empire. In the second, this argument derives from an analysis of the specific archival documents relating to Britain's relationship with Malaya, which reveal no evidence for discontinuity.

The dollar deficit

Following American pressures, and in addition to cuts in domestic spending, on 19 September 1949 sterling was devalued from $4.03 to $2.80 (Kolko 1972:458). The result was claimed by the British government to have solved the immediate currency shortage: by April 1950, dollar reserves had risen above the "minimum safe level" for the first time since March 1948 (Burnham 1990:134) and were at their highest post-war point. Gold reserves continued to rise for some time (until 1952); however, dollar reserves continued to rise only until July of 1950, reaching a peak of £296m but then began to fall, and would not reach similar levels again until 1958 (Bank 1970:163). This also led to concern at the Bank about the next allocation of European Recovery Program (ERP) aid: as aid was allocated on the basis of reserve figures (the poorer the reserve situation, the higher the allocation), the relative heartiness of the reserves might actually have led to a docking of the UK's allocation but ultimately led to the suspension of ERP (BE OV46/6, "Gold and dollar holdings", 3 May 1950; BE OV46/6, Letter from Rowan to Hitchman, 1 July 1950; BE OV46/7 1 November 1950, "MAC – Suspension of ERP"; BE OV46/7, "United States Aid to the United Kingdom", 8 November 1950). The Chancellor announced in late 1950 that ERP would be suspended from the beginning of 1951, despite the fact that the UK's recovery had been incomplete and the reserves, although having grown considerably, were still inadequate (BE OV46/7, "Suspension of ERP", 15 December 1950).

This reserve position, while ostensibly improving, was still unstable and this was evident from the balance of payments situation in the Sterling Area, particularly the independent Sterling Area (RSA) with regard to their gold and dollar deficits. Australia, New Zealand, India and Pakistan all held large deficits in their balances of payments with the dollar area; Ceylon showed a small surplus and Southern Rhodesia only held a surplus by virtue of gold sales (TNA T236/3995, "Boothroyd to Clarke", 13 January 1950).

The unease over the Sterling Area's unstable position was also raised in an Australian Cabinet meeting in early February and the problem of the dollar deficit was discussed in depth (TNA T236/3995, "Telegram no.87", UK High Commissioner Australia to Commonwealth Relations Office, 7 February 1950). This concern was borne out by figures for the combined gold and dollar deficits of the Sterling Area, which were $1305m in 1949 while the estimated figure for 1950 was $996m. As such the Sterling Area was still suffering from a severe dollar shortage, with the terms of trade still heavily weighing against it (ibid.). This was necessarily a burden on the UK reserves as all Sterling Area reserves were held centrally within the UK's reserves as part of the Exchange Equalisation Account (EEA).

Malayan development

While the Sterling Area was in a parlous situation regarding its ongoing balance of payments problem and the global dollar supply was still very limited, Malaya was facing a rise in the intensity of the Emergency. This prompted the prime minister to create the "Malaya Committee" to provide oversight and discussion on the handling of the Emergency and the development of Malaya. The Committee included the ministers for Defence, the Colonies, Commonwealth Relations and War, the Minister of State and the chiefs of the Armed Forces. The terms for the creation of the Committee mandated it to "preserve peace and order [for] the Federation of Malaya".[1] (TNA PREM8/1126, "Terms for Creating Malaya Committee", 19 March 1950).

The key to winning the Emergency was by winning the support of the local population, particularly the Chinese, as Thomas Lloyd, the Permanent Under-Secretary of State at the Colonial Office, wrote to John Paskin, the Assistant Under-Secretary there, a few days after the creation of the Malaya Committee, following a discussion with Sir John Hay, the Managing Director of Guthries, a major plantation company specialising in rubber and palm oil. However, this was only possible through success against terrorists and the development of the country's economy, he argued. As such, the immediate plans concerning the Emergency were to reiterate commitment to the campaign publicly, liaise more with industrial interests and make propaganda more effective (TNA CO537/5996, "Letter from T Lloyd to Paskin", 28 March 1950).

Henry Bourdillon, the head of the Colonial Office's Finance Department, following a trip to Malaya in early 1949, reported that,

> The Federation is now forced by adverse circumstances to make provision for development. This is truer of tin and rubber than it is of any other Malayan activity, and in the prosperity of tin and rubber HMG have a particularly direct and vital interest. In the case of rubber the great requirement is new planting of high yielding strains, without which the competitive capacity of the Malayan product must rapidly deteriorate. A campaign for improved grading is also urgently necessary in order to nullify the one great advantage which synthetic rubber at present has over the natural product.
>
> (TNA T220/87, "Report on a Visit to Malaya", 6 April 1949)

Bauer (1973) and White (1996) disagree with Rudner (1972; 1973; 1976) in their characterisation of Britain's role in Malaya's development after the war. While Rudner argues that Britain adopted a "hands off" approach to the development of Malaya's rubber industry, both Bauer and White argue that drastic changes occur in development policy with Britain, at certain points, being highly involved in the development of Malayan rubber, with a changing set of policy priorities, which ultimately proved unsuccessful (White 1996:213). As with the Rudner view, Hinds (2001) and Krozewski (2001) also maintain that aid was always piecemeal, limited and undertaken with little commitment by the British state.

This is not borne out by a specific analysis of Malayan development, such as those undertaken by Bauer and White. White (1996:213) also argues that there is continuity stemming from the British desire to maintain dollar earnings from Malaya for the Sterling Area through its involvement in Malayan development. While it is true that Britain saw Malaya as valuable for its dollar earnings, it is a simplistic characterisation of Britain's intent in contributing to the development of Malaya's economy. Indeed, the British state managers sought to prepare Malaya for independence, recognising that development was necessary to stabilise and support Malaya but, of course, the key British interest stemming from development was Malaya's dollar contribution to the Sterling Area dollar pool.

In a Colonial Office report on Malayan development in August 1950, it was made clear that the intention of development was to build a Malayan nation.[2] This was recognised as a gradual task though (which was also commonly accepted), and neither the British nor Malayan government was seeking a rush towards independence at that time (TNA CO967/84, "Notes on Development in Malaya", August 1950). Of Malaya's 51,000 square miles, 80% of the country was jungle, 14% was rubber plantations and 2.4% was rice, while 2.1% was given over to coconut and oil palm. As such, it was a primarily agricultural economy though its tin industry was based on valuable mineral deposits. The report characterised Malaya as well suited for world trade but not for the production of food crops due to its soil and climate; as such, Malaya's development was limited to certain directions (ibid.).

The British government was eager to involve industrial interests in any meetings concerning plans for Malayan development, with a view to increasing cooperation between government and business. As such, John Higham, Assistant Secretary at the Colonial Office, wrote to Sir Henry Gurney, the High Commissioner in Malaya, suggesting that meetings be arranged between the Malayan Rubber Growers Association and the Chamber of Mines with Sir Alec Newboult, the Chief Secretary of the Federated Malay States, and the Colonial Secretary, Jim Griffiths (TNA CO537/5996, John Higham to Sir Henry Gurney, 4 April 1950).

By 1950, the reconstruction of Malaya after the experiences during the war had been largely completed; however, this meant that the "next objective [was] planned development, both social and economic" (TNA CO967/84, "Notes on Development in Malaya", August 1950). The Malayan government had a seven-point scheme for the development of the colony. The plan sought to:

- broaden the base of the economy, as Malaya was too reliant on rubber and tin, which were prone to severe seasonal and price fluctuations;
- emphasise economic activity in which Malaya had a comparative advantage;

- increase food production, particularly rice;
- promote even development;
- pursue development aimed at increasing the total wealth of the country;
- develop the skills of the Malayan workforce;
- and finally, "to aim at making the maximum contribution that its resources permit to the attainment of a balance in the external payments of the sterling area".

The Development Plan also highlighted the desire of the Malayan Federation to help smallholders, who were responsible for 40% of Malayan rubber production, by increasing the yield of their crops through substituting higher-yielding types of rubber. This was intended not only as a means of competing against the high quality and competitive pricing of synthetic rubber but also as a means of reducing support for the communist insurgents in the country (ibid.).

Particular emphasis was placed upon this expected consequence of (and justification for) the Development Plan during a meeting on 2 August 1950 between the Colonial Office and the European Cooperation Administration (ECA) to generate funds for Malayan development. Jim Griffiths called the meeting to discuss the possibility of relaxing the rules governing ECA funds for overseas development, particularly with reference to South East Asia and with Malaya in mind specifically (TNA CO967/84, "Note on meeting with ECA", 2 August 1950).

In the meeting, Griffiths was emphatic about how helpful the ECA funds had been domestically but wanted to make ECA funds do even more work, and be even more helpful. He was particularly keen to highlight to the Americans that Malaya was extremely important to the containment of communism, which resonated very well with the purpose of the ECA. As such, he argued that the counter-insurgency in Malaya was vital for South East Asia, and the worldwide battle against communism:

> The battle against communism in South East Asia could not be won without complete success in Malaya and this battle would be won not only in the jungle, but also in the fields, farms and factories of the country.
>
> (Ibid.)

The Emergency had already been a costly campaign and, when it ceased, its cost could be even more fractious upon Malaya's divided population, he warned, with substantial racial tensions existing between 2.5 million

Malays and 2 million Chinese in Malaya being exacerbated by an economic divide (TNA CO967/84, "Notes on Development in Malaya",
August 1950; CO967/84, "Note on meeting with ECA", 2 August 1950).

The ECA was told that a Commonwealth plan was already being put
together at the time for development of South East Asia (which would
eventually become the Colombo Plan), combining all the resources of
those involved in the Area. However, there was a gap in funding that
could potentially be plugged by funds from the ECA, which, he made
clear

> by stressing again the importance of winning the battle in Malaya
> in the context of the combined resolve of the free countries to con-
> tain communism in the Far East. He felt that it was now possible to
> say that we were beginning to get on top in Malaya. Military suc-
> cess must be secured by economic development in that country and
> throughout our territories in South East Asia.
>
> (Ibid.)

W. John Kenney, the Chief Administrator of the ECA in London, was
reticent about this suggestion, saying that even the ECA's funds were
not unlimited and, furthermore, the ECA would require the Colonial
Office to draw up an integrated programme for development that could
be assessed. However, he did concede that the ECA was inflexible in
where it could actually allocate funds, though that was not something that he could resolve. Kenney, however, reminded Griffiths that
there were counterpart funds unused at the Bank of England, solely for
development purposes that could be put to good use (ibid.).

After the meeting, the ECA and the Colonial Office agreed that the
ECA needed to be supplied with more details about Malayan development, and that both the US and Britain had decisions to make regarding
the use of the funds available to them. However, little seemed to come
from these talks in turning Marshall Aid towards Malayan development
as, shortly after, with the outbreak of war in Korea, ECA funds were
directed towards rearmament programmes (ibid.).

The outbreak of the Korean War was actually good news for Malaya
as rubber and tin prices shot up in 1950, with rubber prices averaging
three times 1949 prices and tin prices jumping by 25% (Lim 1967:317).
Not only did this boost Malaya's contribution to the Sterling Area's dollar pool, it also helped Malaya itself, both economically and in terms of
confidence for future development, as this allowed the Malayan government the opportunity to earn significant tax revenues on the export of

rubber and tin. However, as Sir Hilton Poynton, the Private Secretary to Jim Griffiths, made clear following a trip to Malaya in August 1950, there was little economic collaboration among plantation owners, or among mine owners, in Malaya and so there remained gross inefficiencies in production (TNA CO967/84, "Visit to Malaya by Sir AH Poynton", 4 August 1950).[3]

The hike in global commodity prices came as a welcome relief for Malaya in terms of development, as funds from other sources were hard to come by. With the alteration of Marshall Aid funding, and Britain now spending on rearmament, the Colonial Development Corporation (CDC) was asking for massive returns on any investment because it was run almost as if it were a private company. The CDC dismissed one investment scheme, as that could not guarantee a return of 20% on its initial investment.[4] Indeed, White (1996:227) also points out that CDC loans and schemes were always seen as a last resort. While the CDC was involved in some projects in the Federation, it was never relied upon as a major source of investment due to the high returns they demanded, and that cheaper sources of money were easier to come by through other means.

Poynton was concerned, however, about a problem in Malaya that inhibited the potential for development of rubber and tin: exchange control. He related that while

> exchange control and supply problems were not a burning question in the Federation, except in Penang on the subject of exchange control, where it was argued that they were losing a great deal of trade both in tin and rubber through the inability to spend dollars on buying any tin ore and rubber from Siam.
>
> (TNA CO967/84, "Visit to Malaya by Sir AH Poynton", 4 August 1950)

The need for exchange control and economies in foreign exchange was thus inhibiting the ability of Malaya to develop its economy, which was inimical to the prosecution of the Emergency and Malaya's dollar-earning capacity.

The early stages of Malayan development in the 1950s then see considerable UK involvement through seeking to direct Marshall Aid towards South East Asia and its colonies. With the advent of the Korean War, however, this source of funds was curtailed but was counter-balanced by substantially increased revenues from the booming commodity prices caused by wartime stockpiling. Through the Malayan

Development Plan we see the reasons for Britain's wish to develop Malaya's economy, most notably the resolution of the Emergency and the maintenance of dollar earnings. Whether other priorities can be considered subordinate to these is debatable but not provable, though it is made clear in Colonial Office documents that the intention was to develop Malaya towards eventual political and economic independence. However, what is clear from this is that Britain still remained committed to the development of the Malayan economy and still identified clear benefits from this relationship.

The impact of the Korean War

Towards the end of 1950, the UK had begun to consider alternative reserve strategies due to the boom in commodity prices. Considering the relatively healthy position of the reserves at this time, the UK had options available. The UK had begun to consider going above the US$1200m import ceiling agreed at the Commonwealth Finance Ministers' meeting earlier in the year in order to increase the dollar allocation for certain imports into the UK.[5] (TNA T230/177, "RL Hall to Sir Herbert Brittain", 9 August 1950). It was considered vital to maintain dollar food and raw material imports even if it took the UK above the dollar ceiling due to the threat of war. Indeed, there was even consideration towards converting reserves in gold and dollars into stockpiled goods. If commodity prices rose, there was thus a benefit to holding reserves in goods rather than gold and, if prices fell, there would be benefits in other directions to offset the loss on goods (e.g. the UK would have ready access to large quantities of strategic goods) (ibid.).

Using this reserve strategy, however, required using dollar pool earnings to purchase dollar goods. It was not possible go much above the ceiling without explaining to Commonwealth finance ministers and, therefore, the UK sought their agreement. The solution to attaining the consent of the Commonwealth in allowing the UK to import such large quantities of dollar goods was for the Chancellor to explain it as a defence measure: changing the form of the reserves rather than the ceiling of UK's dollar import programme (ibid.).

Rearmament began with a significant increase in spending on defence goods. The UK agreed with the US that it would manufacture £800m of finished defence material and the equipment for its production. At a meeting to discuss the impact of rearmament on the domestic and export markets, it was agreed that the rearmament load would be concentrated in underemployed areas and in factories where capacity had not yet been met. While some of this spending was attained through increases in productivity and efficiency, the vast majority was achieved through diversions from home and export markets. The diversions from the domestic market meant a reduction in the UK's total production capacity, diminishing Britain's ability to export, while diversions from export markets worsened Britain's balance of payments (TNA T236/2398, "Defence Materials", 22 August 1950).

Labour was a highly limited national resource and it was clear that there would be substantial difficulties arising from the labour shortage, especially with estimates suggesting that the defence programme would require an increase in labour by around 250,000 workers at its peak in three years' time (TNA T236/2398, "Defence Programme", 22 August 1950). It was considered a top priority to engage labour in places "where getting labour [would] do least harm to other national interests", particularly dollar exports (TNA T236/2398, "Labour for Ministry of Supply Orders", 22 August 1950). It so happened that some of the burden of the defence programme would land on declining industries, such as shipbuilding, which would not affect dollar-earning production; however, it was also necessary to increase labour in specialised industries, such as aircraft assembly firms and Royal Ordnance factories, which would affect dollar-earning capacity (TNA T236/2398, "Defence Programme", 22 August 1950).

To minimise the effect on exports, it was proposed that defence supplies and dollar exports would rank equally and have priority over the supply of other goods.[6] It was necessary for priority to be maintained on North American markets if UK exports were to be maintained. It was feared that the UK would then be unable to compete with US domestic deliveries and would confirm the then widely held suspicion that British suppliers were an unreliable source of goods, thus losing the market "for good" (TNA T236/2398, "Defence Materials", 22 August 1950). Of particular importance was equipment for the production of defence materials, which had to be bought abroad so that domestic production was not burdened with their manufacture also.

> machine tools are at the root of industrial production: a falling off in home supplies will, therefore, have a quicker effect on the UK's productive capacity than almost any other shortfall in supplies of engineering goods.
>
> (Ibid.)

This was intended to minimise the disruption to home and export markets for UK-made machine tools and also required the using up of machine tools from Ministry of Supply reserves.

Exports to the Sterling Area were to be maintained and ranked in importance immediately only after defence supplies and dollar exports. The Treasury identified three reasons for this high priority: first, because some exports to the Sterling Area were dollar-saving in that they prevented Sterling Area countries from needing to source those goods from the dollar area; second, some exports were essential for Commonwealth defence programmes; and third, the Treasury identified the Sterling Area and Commonwealth as the UK's best and most reliable long-term market. Furthermore, there was an obligation to the Sterling Area as the UK had recently persuaded Commonwealth Finance Ministers to cut dollar imports by 25% and, therefore, the UK had a duty to supply the deficiency (TNA T236/2398, "Defence Materials", 22 August 1950). The ultimate aim of industrial policy with regard to rearmament was to fulfil the defence obligations of the government by making maximum use of labour resources without damaging economic recovery (TNA T236/2398, "Defence Programme", 22 August 1950).

Meanwhile, figures on the central reserves seemed very optimistic due to the using up of stockpiles of imported goods (particularly raw materials) in the fourth quarter, and considerable price rises also. Overall reserves now stood at £1,147m, a post-war high, though dollar reserves had fallen to £165m. However, high commodity prices were a double-edged sword as it became difficult to import certain goods, which affected the UK's volume of production and its ability to export (TNA T230/177, "RL Hall to Goldman, UK Overall Balance", 3 November 1950). The reserve figures did not show the whole picture though. Increased production that had not been used for consumption at home was held responsible for this, along with wage stability: the increased prices of imported goods were being borne by the consumer, thus freeing equivalent resources for export. However, there was a gap in the reserve figures even then, which was due to invisible income (ibid.).

The Treasury was then concerned about three factors: would there be a sufficient supply of raw materials? Could domestic unrest be contained if the cost of living continued to increase? And how could the case be best presented under the Nitze plan (ibid.)?[7] The immediate response was to suggest a free import policy. There was plenty of demand and a willingness to buy, but supplies were extremely limited. A free import policy would also mean it would be preferable to purchase dollar goods if they were cheaper than non-dollar goods[8] (ibid.). This was mainly an issue of public presentation: it was considered "a bad bargaining position" when import prices were rising, and so too the cost of living, while the balance of payments was improving and the central reserves increasing.

In January 1951, an official memo was written for the Bank to discuss the history of reserve policy and the current purpose of the central reserves. It maintained that the purpose of the UK's reserves was for "use in an emergency to hold a position pending the effect of corrective measures" (BE C43/31, "Central Reserves", 18 January 1951). The recent increases in the standings of the reserves were attributed to a combination of Marshall Aid, devaluation, the drive for exports and the continuation of domestic rationing, though this did also mean a rise in sterling liabilities (ibid.). However, events over the previous two years had shown that, even with exchange control, currency did not flow immediately into the reserves when a depreciation was anticipated. If sterling seemed weak, "the external assets of the Exchange Equalisation Account fall more quickly than the basic trading position would justify; when the exchange is strong, assets rise fast" (ibid.).

The memo ends by making a point about the policy governing the management of exchange control and the changes in external assets of the EEA. It also highlights, yet again, how important the reserve position was to British government policy, and therefore how important were net dollar contributors, like Malaya.

> We must import or die. In order to live, therefore, we must export goods, services and so on, to pay for imports. We want sterling to be used as a reserve currency by other countries as well as a trading currency. A stable rate of exchange (in relation to gold) is considered essential to maintain confidence in sterling as a reserve currency, and so we are denied the use of exchange rate control as a weapon of defence or offence in our external transactions. Domestically we try to preserve a fairly rigid low interest rate structure – in the interests of Government borrowing. Thus we deny ourselves the use of the weapon of a moveable interest rate. We must therefore have large immediately available external assets and be prepared to see wide fluctuation in the amount of those assets because everything else being fixed all the strains and pressures are concentrated on the Exchange Equalisation Account.
>
> (Ibid.)

The standing of the EEA at that point was £1,150m and, while a number of factors had contributed to the increased value of the reserves account, its status as the "safety net" of the British economy meant that it would be perennially prone to crisis and, as such, the current strong position of the reserves was only temporary. Furthermore, as long as this strategy continued, Malaya would remain important to the British economy.

British commitment to Malaya

In a letter from the Governor of Singapore to the Colonial Secretary, the Governor relayed how exchange controls in the whole of Malaya still remained very unpopular (BE OV65/4, "Currency Supplies", 31 January 1951). However, these were still entirely necessary for the health of the Sterling Area's balance of payments and the EEA.

Robert Hall, the Director of the Economic Section of the Cabinet Office, noted in a letter to Otto Clarke, at Overseas Finance, in March 1951, the trick of running down stockpiles of goods and showing an improved balance of payments was working, nobody had yet drawn much attention to this strategy, and Hall felt vindicated by how events had worked out as primary good prices were no longer as expensive as they had been earlier in 1950. This then meant that a change in emphasis could occur, with stockpiles being built back up again (TNA T230/177, "RL Hall to RWB Clarke, Fall in Stocks", 29 March 1951).

Sir Herbert Brittain, also at the Overseas Finance section, in correspondence with Hall, felt that the UK must continue to build up its dollar reserves so that the UK's "policies and dispositions [were] no more hampered by financial needs than [was] absolutely necessary" (ibid.). However, Hall believed that the raw materials situation needed to be taken much more seriously.

> I think that we ought to hold fairly substantial supplies of imported commodities as a permanent object of policy, irrespective of what we think is going to happen about prices in the short run. But beyond this, I feel strongly that we ought to give much more attention to the whole question of our long-run supply position. We are still dominated in our thinking by experience of the 30s, and are not paying nearly enough attention to the implications of a world in which full employment and the development of backward areas have become important considerations of policy.
>
> (Ibid.)

While there may be an ambiguity over which "backward areas" Hall was referring to in the above statement, it certainly applied to the development of Malaya. Independence for Malaya was considered, if not imminent, then certainly not far off. The final point made by Hall is very telling. The development of states like Malaya and its contribution to the support of the British economy was very important and would remain so as long as Britain was committed to the post-war domestic economic consensus. In a joint letter from the major banks of Malaya and Singapore[9] to the Under-Secretary for the Colonies, Sir Thomas Ingram-Lloyd, they expressed a concern over the institution of a new Currency Ordinance. They were worried that the new legislation would have altered exchange limits from a fixed rate to a rate specified by the Currency Commission of Malaya, which might have created uncertainty in the Malayan economy and made the Malayan dollar unstable, which they felt would be especially worrying considering the UK's intention of granting independence to Malaya in the near future (BE OV65/4, "Malaya Currency Ordinance 1951", 19 July 1951). However, in a letter to the Bank of England the following day, William Cockburn, Chief General Manager of the Chartered Bank in London, moderated this concern, since the Ordinance actually required the Colonial Secretary to approve any decisions made by the Malayan Currency Commission (BE OV65/4, "Malaya Currency Ordinance 1951", 20 July 1951).

In a subsequent letter in August, which was copied to the Bank of England, William Cockburn wrote to the manager of the Kuala Lumpur branch to notify him that the Colonial Office and the Malayan government were seeking a loan for the latter and wanted to ask whether the Chartered Bank and the Mercantile Bank would underwrite the flotation (BE OV65/4, "Malayan Loans", 7 August 1951). However, Cockburn was very cool about the possibility of underwriting the public loan because, although very confident about the likely defeat of China and North Korea in the Korean War, the Chartered Bank was still very concerned about Communist influence in the rest of Asia and the continuing Emergency in Malaya. Furthermore, the political instability in Malaya, along with increased levies on rubber and the new currency legislation, had unsettled the money markets, meaning that the long-term loan market in Malaya was very uncertain and, thus, an impediment to borrowing for development (ibid.).

While the Malayan government wanted to borrow from the public rather than the banks to avoid providing inflationary pressure on the economy, the purpose of the loan was to increase prospects for employment in Malaya, which would have led to inflationary pressures. The Colonial Office suggested that the loan would go toward long-term projects and this loan was being used so as not to be a burden on the current revenues of the Malayan government. Cockburn seemed confused by this point, however, since Malayan government revenues were booming from tax receipts on rubber and tin. Indeed, in a *Financial Times* article on 7 August 1951, Sir Henry Gurney, the High Commissioner in the Federation, stated that the Malayan government had a surplus of M$123m (US$14.5m) for 1951 (ibid.).

In an unattributed Bank memo about Cockburn's letter, they condemned the Chartered Bank's attitude as overly harsh. The purpose of the loan was simultaneously developmental and to resolve the political situation.

> One of the most urgent needs for the Federation today is to combat banditry by removing as far as possible the reasons which cause the disgruntled to turn Communist or bandit. This can only be done by resettlement of the "squatters" and large-scale development works such as drainage, irrigation, water-power, housing, etc. The latter have been agreed to be essential measures by Malaya, the UK and America. These things must be done somehow and therefore because they are not "productive" any expenditure on them must in the short run be inflationary.
>
> (BE OV65/4, "Malaya", 10 August 1951)

While this would aggravate an inflation problem caused by high primary commodity prices and the large part of export proceeds going directly to the rubber smallholders, it was considered both necessary and a good way of setting free the money held by smallholders:

> To tap the surplus funds in the hands of these people the Government hopes that premium bonds, lottery bonds, provident funds and a Savings Bank drive will prove attractive.
>
> (Ibid.)

This was certainly preferable to the alternative of seeking loan funds from the London money market, which was difficult politically, with Malaya having to seek Colonial Office approval for such borrowing, and likely to be much more expensive. Furthermore, given that the Malayan Sterling balance had been steadily rising for some time now, the Colonial Office and the Bank would have preferred for Malaya to spend this cash before seeking a loan. However Douglas Godsall, the Financial Secretary of the Federation, felt that Malaya's capricious economy needed those sterling balances as a safety net:

> The Malayan Sterling balances are steadily rising and HMG would like the Federation to use these balances for their development

programme without coming on to the London market. Godsall on the other hand wishes to build up these balances to a sizeable level to constitute a safe budget reserve against the possibility of a collapse in revenue... he emphasised how fortuitous the present boom had been and how, over a series of years Federation revenue comes in fits and starts and how necessary it was to budget for a period of years. He was not really comforted by HMG's assurance that if he used up all his fat then in the last resort HMG would stand behind them.

(Ibid.)

Given Godsall's stance on this issue, the Bank felt that, while it was true that borrowing from the Eastern Banks would be inflationary, this inflationary expenditure was absolutely necessary. The bulk of the loan would be spent locally in Malaya, and it was now considered better than the alternative of using the London balances for expenditure, as there was no point in risking Malaya's safety net in this instance (ibid.).

The true purpose behind the loan, which had not been yet revealed to the Eastern Banks, was that the Federation government needed M$250m for involvement in the Colombo Plan and intended to put a M$100m development plan before the Colombo Plan Council by the end of the year (BE OV65/4, "Eastern Exchange Banks' Participation in Local Loans", 15 August 1951).[10] However, the Federation government wished to pay off the balance of the 1949 loan in order to pass the M$100m loan required to finance the first part of the Colombo Plan, as there would be criticism that Malaya had not yet paid back its previous loan while already asking for more (BE OV65/4, Telegram no.763 (Secret), 19 August 1951). As such, the loan was to be used for clearing the balance of a 1949 loan, stimulating further investment in Malaya, and there was insufficient credit in the Federation to obtain the whole amount – with M$32m going a long way to easing Treasury concerns when Malaya sought the rest from the London market (ibid.).

Godsall had already approached Chartered Bank for a loan of M$32m to be amortised over 20 years, but the bank had been reticent about the loan. Given the intransigence of the Eastern Banks in London towards lending Malaya development funds, Henry Gurney, the Federation's High Commissioner, remonstrated with the Deputy Governor of the Bank of England. He wanted to know how the British government then intended to find development money for Malaya if London banks were unwilling to lend (BE OV65/4, "Eastern Exchange Banks' Participation in Local Loans", 15 August 1951). As noted earlier, Chartered Bank had found it very unusual that Malaya was enjoying such a substantial budget surplus but was not using those funds for development. Indeed, the surplus balances were exceptional, at around M$300m. However, as with the Malayan Sterling balances, the Malayan Finance Committee strongly held the view that Malaya was very prone to boom and bust, due to its economic reliance on the export of raw materials, and so a large pot was necessary in order to weather recessions (BE OV65/4, Telegram no.763 (Secret), 19 August 1951).

While Malaya's Provident Fund would have made up the difference in the worst-case scenario, it was considered much better to match loans on terms that Banks would have accepted as an issue of confidence. The idea was then put forward to induce the Chartered Bank to accept the M$32m figure up to 1960 with a sum of M$3m (ibid.). By this time, however, the Malayan government received support from the Colonial Office saying that if the Eastern Banks did not consent to the loan then the Malayan government should "consider appropriate action against the Banks", which was unspecified (BE OV65/4, Note by the Deputy Governor, 5 September 1951). This action seemed to unsettle the Bank and the Treasury, who immediately called for a meeting between themselves and the Colonial Office, with the Deputy Governor asking specifically for Sir Herbert Brittain's involvement as he considered the issue too important to be dealt with at lower levels (ibid.). However, before the meeting could be arranged, the Treasury contacted the Deputy Governor at the Bank to inform him that the M$3m inducement was put to the Chartered Bank, and Cockburn had said the Board would be content with that arrangement (BE OV65/4, "Malaya: Chartered Bank's participation in local loan", 5 September 1951).

Efforts to resolve the Emergency in Malaya were now well under way, with the implementation of the Briggs Plan having begun in May 1950 and static protection of rubber estates and tin mines beginning in 1951.[11] The Briggs Plan required the forced resettlement of rural Chinese "squatters" (around 500,000 people, about 10% of the whole population), who made up the bulk of the insurgency's support, into guarded villages where communist supporters could be separated from the insurgents, who operated mainly from the jungles of Malaya, and the non-aligned Chinese protected from extortion (TNA PREM11/182, "The Situation in Malaya", 20 November 1951). A report to the Colonial Office on the progress of the counter-insurgency campaign highlighted how important it was to get the Chinese population on side, acknowledging that the war was as much one of morale as it was of actual fighting, because such police would be extremely important (TNA CO537/7285, "Progress Report", 15 October 1951).

While the counter-insurgency campaign was on track for success, it was certainly a burdensome campaign with considerable casualties being reported every month – casualties not just in the military but also rubber planters, as the insurgents targeted Malaya's economic wealth (TNA CO1022/25, "Response to a Parliamentary Question", 6 November 1951; PREM11/182, "The Situation in Malaya", 20 November 1951).

Following the UK General Election on 26 October and the return of a new Conservative government, the new Colonial Secretary, Oliver Lyttleton, only four days after taking office, announced that he would be undertaking a visit to Malaya and Singapore on 26 November 1951 for three weeks, visiting Hong Kong also. The purpose of his visit was broadly to understand at first hand the problems of Malaya and the Emergency, so that the British government would be aware of how best to deal with them (TNA PREM11/122, Telegram no.457, 2 November 1951). However, Lyttleton made clear to the Cabinet before he left that his visit would have more specific goals. First, he intended to reassure both rubber planters and tin miners of the British determination and ability to support them by all means, and to bring the anti-communist campaign to a successful conclusion. Second, he wished to identify the best means of securing the involvement of the Chinese, especially those Chinese currently "on the fence". Finally, he intended to resolve some institutional concerns: settling disputes between police and army; how best to organise and train the police; and who should succeed both Sir Henry Gurney as the High Commissioner of Malaya and Malcolm MacDonald as the Commissioner General of South East Asia (TNA PREM11/182, "The Situation in Malaya", 20 November 1951).

Lyttleton's announcement came shortly before the prime minister asked for information on the situation in Malaya, Britain's contribution to the Emergency and Malaya's value to the Sterling Area and Britain (TNA CO537/7285, "Minutes of Chiefs of Staff committee", 7 November 1951). The initial response to Churchill's request was that, while the Briggs Plan had been successful, "the Communist hold on Malaya is as strong, if not stronger, today than it ever has been" (ibid.). The report for the prime minister emphasised that the major problem was winning the support and loyalty of the Chinese population, on whom the insurgents relied for supplies and support. The conclusions of the report echoed that of the recent progress report for the Colonial Secretary, highlighting that the priority was to build up the police, to include the Chinese also to reassure the Chinese populations themselves and to protect them from internal pressure and external attack (that would force their cooperation with communist insurgents) (TNA PREM11/182, "Conclusions of the British Defence Co-ordination Committee (Far East)", 15 November 1951). The military implications of the Emergency by the end of 1951 were that the Emergency was still very intense and that there could be no reduction in troops for 1952, and that further materiel, particularly armoured vehicles, was required for the successful prosecution of the counter-insurgency campaign (TNA CO537/7285, "Military Implications of the Emergency", 19 November 1951).

The overall report on the situation in Malaya was provided by the Colonial Secretary for the Cabinet and painted a generally pessimistic picture for the colony. The Briggs Plan had been largely implemented by late 1951 and most of the 500,000 "squatters" resettled, along with a number of rubber estates' labourers. However, the next problem was not just protecting these new settlements from direct attack and infiltration but to provide them with the "fullest opportunities to become reasonably prosperous and contented communities, convinced of being much better off as the result of resettlement and willing, therefore, to give increasing and positive help to government". The worry was that, unless this was done, the Briggs Plan had simply presented to the insurgents "an easy target for attack, infiltration and propaganda" (TNA PREM11/182, "The Situation in Malaya", 20 November 1951).

Of similar importance was getting the Chinese willingly involved in the fight against the insurgency. The Malay population had been exasperated at the intransigence of the Chinese in helping with the counter-insurgency and there had already been significant communal tension. Chinese help was considered

> essential not only to bring the campaign to a more rapid conclusion but also to avoid serious communal disorders which would place a further and grievous strain on the British forces. Moreover if the emergency were to end without the active co-operation of the Chinese, the hope of building a single Malayan people might never be realised.

Indeed, this specific resolution of the Emergency was absolutely necessary for building a stable Malayan state (ibid.). This was made abundantly clear in Lyttleton's statement to the Malayan people:

> The British believe they have a mission and they will not lay it aside until they are convinced that intestine strife has been killed and buried and that a true fusion of all communities can lead to true and stable self-government. The road will certainly be long and it runs

through jungle and ravine. But we will protect it, we will stay, we will never quit until the mission is fulfilled... I believe too that even when self government has been attained, the British will have a place and part to play in Malaya.

(TNA PREM11/122, EG Cass to Barry G Smallman, 8 December 1951)[12]

Lyttleton's final sentiment, while undoubtedly rhetorical, is largely accurate. Certainly, Malaya remained important to the British state after 1950, and continued to be so. Malaya's US earnings in 1950 had been US$350m, out of total Sterling Area earnings of US$1,285m but, by late 1951, rubber production had fallen significantly and some estates had even fallen into disuse because of terrorist activity. Particularly problematic was the replanting and maintenance of rubber estates, which was "virtually at a standstill, and prospecting for tin [had] barely resumed after the re-occupation of the country when it had to be suspended because of the lack of law and order". The report went even further to say that if tin prospecting did not resume soon and new prospects found, then its production could not be maintained, let alone increased (ibid.). Lyttleton also noted that there had "recently been an intensification of Communist attempts to break the economy of the country by large scale and brutal intimidation of labour", with the insurgents well aware of the nature of Malaya's importance to Britain. Knowing this, Lyttleton acknowledged that it seemed hard to predict when a reduction of military forces might be permitted but it was certainly not the case now, especially considering the British Defence Co-ordination Committee recommendation that no reduction in the total number of military units could be made before Spring 1953 at the very earliest (TNA PREM11/182, "Conclusions of the British Defence Co-ordination Committee (Far East)", 15 November 1951; PREM11/182, "The Situation in Malaya", 20 November 1951).

The value of successfully prosecuting the Emergency was well accepted even outside of the Cabinet. In a letter to the prime minister, who had requested his advice, Field Marshall Montgomery, while very disparaging of the handling of the campaign and the personnel involved, informed Churchill that there was no doubt about "the urgency of restoring law and order, and good government, in Malaya. It [was] vital from every point of view: economic, military, political, and from the viewpoint of the contest between East and West." Indeed, Montgomery considered the Emergency in Malaya as "the most vital task today in the Empire" and that there was a real danger that the

Emergency could quickly grow out of hand, which could have the most severe consequences for both Malaya and Britain (TNA PREM11/121, "Success in Malaya", 2 January 1952; Letter from "Montgomery of Alamein" to Prime Minister, 4 January 1952).[13]

The dollar deficit intensifies

Newton argues that, while Marshall Aid had not been as effective as had been hoped, the advent of the Korean War had remedied the dollar deficit.

> By the start of 1950, with two years left to run, the Marshall Plan had not succeeded in closing Europe's dollar gap; one third of Europe's imports from America, which now totalled $16 billion, had still been financed by aid. On the termination of this assistance the problems of 1947 threatened to reappear ... but it was the Korean War, which in practice changed priorities in Washington. In 1950 and after, as a consequence of the Korean War and the subsequent global expansion of the American military machine, dollars were pumped into the underdeveloped nations of the Far East. The United States' enthusiastic performance as world policeman finally closed the dollar gap and stimulated international economic growth.
>
> (Newton 1985:179)

However, this is certainly not the case with regard to Britain. Indeed the British dollar deficit was the equivalent of £15.4m in the week ending 17 November 1951, though two further "one-off" payments (US$36m to the European Payments Union (EPU) and US$13m to the British Celanese account) boosted the deficit to £33m. However, the weekly dollar deficit was now around £15m (TNA T230/177, "Gold and Dollar Deficit", 24 November 1951). In fact, the total central reserves had been falling since July 1951 and in November stood at £967m, from a post-war high in June of £1381m. Meanwhile the dollar reserves had been falling precipitously since April 1951, with the November figure for dollar reserves standing at £36m (Bank 1970).

This trend had been anticipated for some time, with the terms of trade deteriorating since October 1950, and by the end of 1951 both visible and invisible exports had fallen short of imports by £521m (Burnham 2003:11). The fall in the terms of trade was due to the increased price of imports combined with increases in the volume of imports into the UK and Sterling Area; indeed, import prices had more than doubled between

1949 and 1951, with the UK's imports increasing by £1,100m in 1951 of which over 60% was due to price rises (ibid.).

By the beginning of 1952, William Strath, the Deputy Chief Planning Officer at the Treasury, recommended to the Chancellor that he use the Commonwealth Finance Minister's meeting on 8 January to "stress that without emergency action there was a real danger of the collapse of sterling" (quoted in ibid.:38). Indeed, Strath further emphasises that the Sterling Area itself "cannot exist in the long-term on an inconvertible basis. If we don't take action, we shall be forced into convertibility in conditions in which we cannot hold the value of sterling" (ibid.). The Bank had already been considering intervening in the New York money market in order to support the value of sterling before the end of 1951, with £5m being suggested as the sum required to shore up sterling's value for the time being (BE C43/31, "Intervention in the New York Sterling Futures Market", 19 October 1951).

The UK's gold and dollar reserves had been dwindling rapidly due to its own and the Sterling Area's deficit with the EPU, which now required a 60% settlement in gold (BE OV46/8, "Future of EPU", 14 January 1952). Sir Donald MacGillivray, then Deputy High Commissioner in the Federation of Malaya, suggested to the Bank of England that the UK and the Sterling Area impose trade restrictions on the EPU. While there was scope for doing this, as the trade with the EPU was not as important as other sources of goods, this measure would simply have shored up the leak rather than reversed it (BE OV46/8, Letter from MacGillivray to Portsmore, 9 January 1952).

The case before the EPU Council for de-liberalising imports became the necessity of maintaining the strength of sterling, which required a strong balance of payments position – this could only be achieved in the short term by limiting imports. Furthermore, since action had to be swift, domestic monetary measures (while better in the long run) were not appropriate and too slow to take effect (ibid.). The EPU had been helpful in reducing the transaction costs in trade but it could not continue without a huge increase in its gold and dollar reserves. An injection of gold and dollars was unlikely to come from the US as American aid was intended to decrease in 1952–1953; as such, if the EPU were to continue, it would be necessary to restructure the basis of intra-European gold payments since its constituent members could no longer afford to contribute to the EPU's gold reserves (BE OV46/8, "Future of EPU", 14 January 1952).

The effects of this crisis were felt very swiftly in Malaya and Singapore, with the Department of Economic Affairs writing to the Chartered Bank to request cooperation from all the Malayan Exchange Bank in meeting the crisis that was affecting the whole Sterling Area.

> You will not, I am sure, need us to explain the very grave conse-
> quences to the prosperity and welfare of Malaya which will follow if
> this crisis is not successfully overcome and if renewed strength and
> stability is not given to sterling.
>
> (BE OV65/4, Letter to Sutherland from
> Gilmour and Spencer, 19 March 1952)

Indeed, Oscar Spencer and Andrew Gilmour, the Malayan and Singaporean Economic Secretaries, respectively, were specific in their request for what assistance the Malayan Exchange Banks could bring to this current crisis.

> What is necessary is that renewed economy should be exercised in
> the expenditure of foreign currencies of all kinds. The purpose of this
> letter is therefore to request all Exchange Banks to scrutinise with par-
> ticular care all applications for credit facilities involving expenditure
> of such currency... This will apply principally to credits for imports,
> and here we emphasise that it is not desired to restrict imports of
> any goods which are clearly essential for consumption by the mass
> of the population or for the development or maintenance of the
> rubber, tin or other industries of the country, or for the entrepot
> trade.
>
> (Ibid.)

Furthermore, they wished to minimise any possibility of resurgence in trade speculation, arbitrage, overtrading or the expansion of credit with regard to these activities unless it was absolutely essential. George Sutherland, manager of the Singapore branch of the Chartered Bank, confirmed that Chartered would do this, as would the other exchange banks, adding that applications for credit using foreign currencies was always subjected to the closest scrutiny (ibid.).

At the end of March 1952, with total reserves now at only £607m, Otto Clarke, Under-Secretary of the Overseas Finance Division at the Treasury, voiced his conclusions about the state of Britain's current crisis.

> We reach the conclusion that the "dollar shortage" is now fundamen-
> tally the inadequacy of British competitive power... It is our own
> weakness, rather than the vagaries of US policy which creates our

crisis. The Americans can help, and usually they don't. But that does not avoid our basic responsibility.

> (TNA T236/3242, "US Dollar Shortage and
> UK Exports", 26 March 1952)

In a memo by the Chancellor, "Rab" Butler, on economic policy, he stated that it would take four years from 1952, setting aside £200m per year, to get the reserves back to the level of July 1951.[14] Indeed, the UK could not rely on financial assistance from the US to help with getting the economy back on track as Marshall Aid was now set to end, and what little remained would be focused on defence spending.

> The experience of recent months has shown that United States aid will not only be greatly diminished in amount, but also closely confined to support of the Defence Programme. Moreover it is also clear that continued reliance on aid is in itself undesirable; it not only weakens our moral position vis-à-vis the United States in international affairs generally, but, by disguising to a greater or lesser extent our true economic position, tends to create the dangerous impression that it may be possible to avoid some of the more painful adjustments that are necessary.
>
> (BE G1/123, "Economic Policy – Memorandum by
> the Chancellor of the Exchequer", 17 May 1952)

This was, of course, not to say that the UK could do without any assistance from the US, Butler wrote, but that aid would only hold value if the UK were to put itself on the road to recovery by its own efforts (ibid.). The draft of the Operation ROBOT announcement, though never given, echoed this sentiment in answering the question of why the UK needed a floating rate of exchange.

> The UK is the banker of the Sterling Area. We hold the gold and dollar reserves upon which the whole sterling system depends. It is an important system, for it finances half the total trade of the world. Its strength and continuity are necessary not only for us but for the whole world. If the reserves are too small or subject to too great strains, then the strength and continuity of the system are endangered. Yet our existing external financial system in fact puts the maximum strain where it can least be borne and where it can cause the greatest damage... Our reserves are not capable of taking the same strain as before the war. We must, therefore, find a system

which does not concentrate all the strain on the reserves. This can be secured by a fluctuating rate – that is by a system under which the £ finds its own level in relation to the $ and other currencies.

> (BE G1/123, "Draft of ROBOT announcement", 25 June 1952)

The ROBOT plan liberated the UK's reserves to become "true" reserves rather than to support the balance of payments deficit. Rather than using them as a quotidian prop to support sterling, the terms of trade and British economic policy, they would only be used when absolutely necessary. In essence, the implementation of this plan would have seen a radical shift in international economic policy (Burnham and Bulpitt 1999; Burnham 2003) Indeed, as the draft announcement made starkly clear:

> Since the war the sterling area has been subject to periodic crises – 1947–1949–1951. Each has been very severe. There must be something wrong with such a system. A major factor is that we have taken on too much and failed to pay our way. Another major factor is that our system results in periodic and violent adjustment.

> (Ibid.)

The impact of ROBOT on the Sterling Area, however, would have been limited. Exchange controls would still have applied in the Area, with stable exchange rates maintained between sterling and the currencies of the Sterling Area, and there would not have been any direct alteration of sterling balances. However, it would have required agreement that the sterling balances not be drawn down below a certain point in order to support the value of sterling (ibid.).

A text written for the Treasury on the global dollar supply, describing the state of the UK's dollar deficit and the reserve situation, declared: "reserves are at such a low level that they urgently require replenishment" (TNA T230/177, "World Supply of Dollars", 25 June 1952). The dollar situation was characterised as fundamentally based on the fact that the US had significantly increased its exports, while its imports had not increased proportionally. Simultaneously, capital had moved to the US but the dollar had not depreciated in proportion to gold in relation to the overall rise in prices. Gold production had been unable to finance this since gold production had fallen in absolute terms: $1,000m before the war and $750m after the war in the non-dollar world. As such, the US trade surplus had been financed after the war by large-scale loans and grants to foreign countries (ibid.).

On the supply side, the US had become more self-sufficient and so this led to the reduction of the supply of dollars paid out for imports and other private transactions. Indeed, dollars paid out by the US since the end of the war had been around 6.5% of US GNP, which was actually below the 6.8% figure between 1925 and 1929. Therefore, even bearing in mind the grants and loans provided by the US since the end of the war (which only reached their peak at 2.5% of US GNP), which are included in the 6.5% figure, the supply of dollars had not even reached the level of the 1920s (ibid.). Indeed, if the US had made purchases on the same scale as in 1925–1929 instead of loans and grants, the world dollar supply would have been much larger. This had been caused by lower levels of private investment and imports in relation to GNP and it was only the Korean War boom that took the figures above those of the 1930s (ibid.).

The IMF and International Bank had, comparatively, provided very few dollar funds after the war. The gold and dollar assets of other countries were highly erratic too, and followed the pattern of Britain's own assets: liquidation in crisis, accumulation during booms. It was assumed that two sources of dollars would decline significantly: dollars from liquidation of assets, and grants/loans from the US. Indeed, the proposed level of US aid for 1952/1953 was $2bn and beyond that year there was considerable uncertainty. With the UK maintaining a dollar deficit of US$250m in 1954, and the RSA (along with South African gold sales) just breaking even, the colonial dollar surplus (and particularly Malaya, which had contributed US$120m, the single largest net contribution to the Area's dollar pool) was as important as ever (TNA CO1030/100, "Exchange Control Problems in Malaya", 16 September 1955). Indeed, even with the low price of rubber in this period, Malaya was still a consistent high dollar earner (Table 4.1).

The Treasury sought to predict the supply of dollars in 1956 to give a very general idea of the situation facing the British economy in the

Table 4.1 Net current balance for Malaya, 1952–1956 (£ million)

	1952	1953	1954	1955	1956
Dollar Area	71	43	37	68	51
Other non-Sterling Area	6	−2	−6	−1	1
Sterling Area	−58	−58	−37	−24	−42
Total all areas	19	−17	−6	43	16

Source: BE OV65/5, "Federation of Malaya: Sterling Assets, Trade and Balance of Payments", 24 January 1957.

latter half of the 1950s, and what action could be taken. The forecasting of supply was closely linked to predicting the level of demand and supply in the US, and thus GNP. At 1951 prices, the Treasury predicted this would be about $40bn by 1956 but this was an optimistic figure supposing continued growth at 4.5% (TNA T230/177, "World Supply of Dollars", 25 June 1952).

Since the war, prices of US imports had increased but volume had not recovered, with the ratio of volume to GNP steady between 1.9% and 2.1% during the period 1946–1949. The Korean boom raised this ratio to 2.3% and 2.2% in 1950 and 1951, respectively, but this did not constitute a trend due to the extraordinary circumstances and the small sample. Indeed, it reflected the "increase in purchases, particularly of raw materials, for stockpiling and the increase in imports of industrial materials and semi-manufactures … which were temporarily in short supply but for which the normal source [was US] home production" (ibid.). US imports were mainly industrial materials and foodstuffs that were not produced in the US – for example, natural rubber.[15] This was exacerbated by the Second World War, making the US even more self-sufficient and moving the import:GNP ratio to even lower levels.

Since the demand for imports is a "derived demand", the volume of imports was closely related to GNP. This was borne out by figures which showed that devaluation and large price fluctuations had little effect on the US import:GNP ratio. The rise in imports due to the Korean boom consisted of the traditional imports, as well as some manufactures. There was some stockpiling but the chief reason was simply a temporary issue: US domestic production could not keep up with a very rapidly rising demand. For some products home supply had been exhausted but, against this, rearmament and the fear of war encouraged even greater self-sufficiency through the development of synthetic and alternative products from the home market (ibid.). Synthetic rubber was an example of this, with the development of the synthetic rubber industry during the Second World War largely concentrated in the US with a production capacity of over one million tons per year (White 1996:64). This provided serious competition to Malayan natural rubber, and was a perennial concern for the Malayan government and rubber growers.

There was little optimism that the import:GNP ratio might change unless the level of demand remained at the Korean boom level and this would only be helpful if US domestic production could not keep pace with demand, which was highly unlikely and, therefore, the Treasury forecast an import:GNP ratio of 2.2% for 1956. The text also indicates how helpful it would be to have the International Bank and Export Bank

supplying dollars to developing countries. Indeed, there was some optimism that UK pressure could be brought to make this a reality, and was
in fact the best chance of increasing the global supply of dollars:

> Grants and loans to under-developed countries are almost certainly
> the most hopeful way of increasing the world dollar supply. The risk
> of social unrest and political revolt in the backward countries already
> provides strong political pressure in their favour... But the world dol-
> lar position will not be greatly improved if this merely leads to an
> erratic flow of dollars allotted by Congress every time the political
> position in an area becomes critical... It is most important for eco-
> nomic reasons – and for political reasons too – that the flow of dollars
> for development should expand at a stable rate.
>
> (Ibid.)

However, the document makes a further caveat that to rely on dollars
from the developing areas of the global economy would be foolish.

The document predicted that, taking the dollar supply as an index
with 1947 being 100, 1950 being 119 and 1951 standing at 122, the
global dollar supply in 1956 would be 114. Therefore, even with an
optimistic evaluation of current trends, the world dollar supply would
actually shrink. Furthermore,

> since incomes in the rest of the world must be expected to rise in
> the intervening period, and since at the same time rearmament may
> continue to divert resources away from dollar saving and from export
> expansion in third markets, the task of restraining demand for United
> States goods to this level is likely to present a substantial problem,
> particularly if the geographic distribution of dollars is taken into
> account.
>
> (Ibid.)

Europe's share of US imports had fallen from 50% before the First World
War, to 30% in the inter-war period and to 15% since the end of the
Second World War. America's, in the same time, had risen from 34% to
58% in the same period. However, US exports had not changed radically.

Europe's dollar problems can be seen as the consequence of Europe's
inability, partly as a result of the obstruction of East-West trade and
the failure to find substitutes for United States products elsewhere,

to reduce its dependence on United States' supplies as rapidly as the United States has reduced its dependence on European produce.

(Ibid.)

There was little reason to think that this trend would reverse, as "Europe appears to stand little chance of increasing its exports of manufactures to the United States very substantially" (ibid.). If anything, there was likely to be a further fall in Europe's dollar supply but this would be offset by further dollar aid to developing countries.

This led to further optimism that developing areas would then receive significant dollar aid, thus boosting the world supply of dollars.

> With this pattern of dollar supplies it seems certain that the principal way in which the United Kingdom and other European countries will have to balance their dollar accounts is by a reduction in the dependence on United States products through the substitution of supplies from other areas. The alternative is to earn dollar surpluses in third countries.
>
> (Ibid.)

This meant Canada and Latin America; however, the UK and Europe had traditionally had deficits with these countries since the war. The document concluded by stating that the problem of the dollar deficit was so fundamental to the British and European economies that the best option available was import substitution.

> We must rely for a major part of the solution of the dollar problem on the substitution of alternative supplies for imports from the United States. Moreover, unless it can be corrected by commodity agreements or other means, the great instability of the dollar supply...makes it the more desirable that we should become less dependent on the United States for our most essential imports, particularly since their prices are fixed by price support policies and do not move in sympathy with United States import prices.
>
> (Ibid.)

The development of Sterling Area countries, particularly developing colonies like Malaya, was essential to maintaining British economic policy given the continued and persistent problem of the limited global dollar supply. Malaya itself was still supplying over a third of all the

Sterling Area's dollars (Hack 2000:303). A letter from the Colonial Office to Douglas Godsall in Malaya showed that the UK was very concerned about development in Malaya, even showing concern about how the policies of UK banks had an impact upon credit availability in Malaya. Since the banks in Malaya were only branch banks, with central offices in London, this meant that the local banks did not act according to the preferences of the Malayan government or, in some instances, the conditions of the Malayan economy (BE OV65/4, Letter from Hulland to Godsall, 19 July 1952).

Following the base rate rise in the UK on 12 March 1952 from 2.5% to 4%, Godsall asked the Colonial Office whether Malaya should follow the UK's deflationary policy too, as the local banks were taking advantage of the difference between British and Malayan loan markets. If the local rates were low, the balances were remitted to London to obtain the higher rate there; but if they were too high then the measure of restriction might be overdone and development impeded. For both the Colonial Office and the Malayan governments, it was hard to determine the appropriate course of action (ibid.).

In a follow-up letter from the Bank on the subject, at Hulland's request, the Bank of England made clear the position on sympathy rate changes for Malaya. The measures undertaken in the UK to restrict credit were, it explained,

> primarily designed to meet conditions in the United Kingdom and although there is an essential financial connection between this country and the Colonial Territories, the measures were not necessarily intended to apply automatically to all the Colonies. Credit conditions vary wildly in the Colonies and credit control, either restriction or expansion, is not an end in itself; we are naturally anxious to satisfy ourselves that any form of credit control which might be pursed in the Colonies is designed in the best interests of the Colonies in the light of their current economic circumstances.
> (BE OV65/4, Note on Letter from Hulland to
> W Godsall, 1 August 1952)

The Bank then suggested to Hulland that he ask Godsall exactly what economic conditions were like in Malaya currently. This was done with the particular purpose of discovering exactly how important banking credit was to development in Malaya, as well as to provide the Bank with up-to-date information on credit availability in Malaya also (ibid.).

Malayan downturn

Malaya's economy was undergoing a severe downturn and the cost of the Emergency was now becoming burdensome. The Emergency had cost Malaya around £30m in 1953 (around 30% of state expenditure and about 50% of the federal budget) and was estimated to cost around £23m in 1954, and by 1955 was expected to account for 30% of state revenues and 40% of the federal budget (TNA CO1022/2, "The Emergency", 29 December 1953; BE OV65/4, "Economic impact of defence expenditure", 25 October 1955). Estimates of Malaya's budget deficit for 1953 were around M$97m, but these proved extremely optimistic (TNA CO1022/2, "Malayan Budget", 1 September 1953). While Malaya broke even in 1952 at M$725m, there was still a budget surplus of M$330m from previous years, in addition to a loan of M$100m. Budget expenditure had been M$850m for 1953, reducing the surplus to only M$220m, of which only half was actually expendable. These financial difficulties were especially worrying as social and economic development was considered essential to the resolution of the Emergency; furthermore, the financial troubles had already resulted in pressure to resume selling rubber to China, which had been halted in 1951 following the communist victory in the civil war (ibid.). However, it was reiterated in the Foreign Office report, and in a public statement to the Malayan press later that year, that the British government would come to Malaya's aid if it encountered serious financial difficulties (ibid.; TNA CO1022/2, "Statement to the Malayan Press", 11 August 1953).

Britain had already provided Malaya with a grant of £6m to support its deficit, along with loans from Brunei and Singapore of £4.5m and £3.5m, respectively. However, with revenues from rubber levies unlikely to exceed £10m, Malaya was facing a serious balance of payments problem, which might require cuts in social and economic programmes that were essential for maintaining the successes achieved in the Emergency (TNA CO1022/2, "The Emergency", 29 December 1953). As such, given the prospect of dealing with the Emergency for the foreseeable future, Malaya faced a "severe economic depression" and was tasked with a major development programme that could not be postponed. Therefore, there were two options: either finding cheaper methods of resolving the insurgency or seeking economic aid from outside Malaya to cover the budget deficit over the next few years (ibid.). Both of these options were to be implemented.

In early January 1954, an International Bank for Reconstruction and Development (IBRD) mission to Malaya was being arranged in London to arrange a development package for Malaya. Preliminary discussions centred on generating lists of contacts and important people within the Malayan rubber and tin industries for the IBRD delegation to meet during their visit (TNA CO1045/177, "International Bank Mission to Malaya", 11 January 1954). At a meeting at the Bank of England later on that month, Bank officials met with IBRD officials to discuss the problems of Malayan development and "the need for a profitable economy at current prices of rubber and tin which was important both from the Malayan point of view and the UK point of view". Also discussed was the development of Malaya's financial market, including the establishment of a Malayan Central Bank, which it was agreed would be best to plan now rather than being hastily drawn up just before or after independence occurred (BE OV65/4, "IBRD Mission to Malaya", 20 January 1954; TNA CO1030/627, "Federation of Malaya", 27 February 1958). This prompted the Bank of England to take a much closer interest in Malaya's financial system and to begin planning for the eventual establishment of the Central Bank in Malaya, with the IBRD's recommendation to set one up having been assured but not yet announced (BE OV65/4, "Malayan Banking Statistics", 15 September 1954).

It was well known that Malaya depended for its economic well being on rubber, particularly the export of rubber, more than any other commodity, even tin. Indeed, from 1950 to 1954, rubber accounted for 65% of the value of the Federation's exports. In 1952 Malayan GDP had fallen from the 1951 level of $5,550m to $4,693m, and continued to fall in 1953 to $4,271m and $4,208m in 1954, finally rising in 1955 to $4,931m (Lim 1967, p.317). The years 1951–1955 had seen extreme fluctuations in the price of rubber and the correlation between price changes and the economy as a whole was remarkably close.[16] With the majority of rural Malays and Chinese working at a subsistence level on small rubber plantations, a large portion of the Malayan population was affected by the future of rubber prices. Unless government investment increases their consuming power, they will continue to be susceptible to "politicians who promise them something better" (BE OV65/6, "Federation of Malaya: The Economy", 23 June 1959).

Natural rubber cultivation is a lengthy process and so natural rubber prices tended to be much higher compared with synthetic rubber (a rubber tree has an economic life of 30–35 years and the first seven are unproductive). This had been exacerbated in Malaya due to the painfully slow replanting process that had been made difficult as a result of the deprivations of the Second World War, and almost impossible due to the Emergency. Despite this, natural rubber could actually be

produced more cheaply than synthetic. However, that was not currently
the case, and with many estates approaching a major replanting period
in late 1955, the price of natural rubber remained high, which stimulated further investment in synthetic rubber research and production in
an attempt to reduce those costs (TNA PREM11/873, "Dispatch to Prime
Minister from High Commissioner, Federation of Malaya", 2 August
1955).

European estates were notoriously reticent to spend money to change
practices and the smallholders were infamously improvident, with little sense of saving up for a rainy day. As such, government – both the
Malayan and British – involvement was essential and was required to
revitalise the whole Malayan rubber industry. This meant financial support in replanting, as well as reducing taxes on exports, in order to
reduce the costs of the development of Malayan rubber. It was felt by
the High Commissioner of Malaya, Sir Donald MacGillivray, in a letter to
Churchill, that this would eventually reap dividends through increased
yields and increased production (ibid.). This plea by MacGillivray was
entirely successful, with the UK offering to support the replanting
process in Malaya with financial assistance (ibid.).

On 8 September 1955, the Malayan Federation announced an
amnesty for all communist insurgents, with the Chief Minister of
Malaya, Abdul Rahman, saying that he was willing to meet Chin Feng,
the leader of the Malayan Communist Party (MCP). Singapore echoed
this announcement with a similar amnesty for insurgents. However, due
to the conditions of the amnesty, all insurgents who surrendered were
to be interred indefinitely, so there was actually no increase in surren-
ders. Chin Feng stated publicly that he rejected the amnesty and would
only meet and negotiate as an equal (TNA FO371/116941, Telegram
from McGillivray to Colonial Secretary, 18 November 1955), though
there had already been a preliminary meeting between the Malayan
government and the MCP to discuss the format of future meetings
(TNA FO371/116941, "Top Secret Memo", 10 November 1955).

The British government were wary of the amnesty but refused to
accept any concession made by the Chief Minister on the release of the
"core" group of insurgents who might still have undertaken subversive
activity in the Federation and Singapore, nor would the British government accept any formal recognition of the MCP (TNA CAB128/29,
Conclusion 37(55), 25 October 1955; TNA FO371/116941, Telegram
from MacGillivray to Colonial Secretary, 18 November 1955). Indeed,
the UK was actually fearful that the Malayan government was seeking
early independence and had come to believe that independence was

conditional upon the resolution of the Emergency, and this was the true reason behind the amnesty and the beginning of negotiations with the MCP. However, it was emphasised to the Chief Minister that this was not the case and that independence and self-government for Malaya were not in any way contingent on the conclusion of the Emergency (TNA FO371/116941, "Emergency in Malaya", 22 November 1955).

Certainly, this seems an unusual matter for the British state to be so concerned about if we consider the view held by Hinds (2001) and Krozewski (2001) that 1953 sees the beginning of the end of the British Empire. The 1953 date is linked to a period of trade liberalisation within the Sterling Area. However, an episode in late 1955 shows how willing the British state was to accommodate the desires of Malayan rubber producers (TNA FCO141/7479, Officer Administering the Government Federation of Malaya to Colonial Secretary, 16 October 1956). This episode sees the British state retaining the import duty on synthetic rubber following a request by the Malayan Rubber Growers Association (ibid.). This is not to undermine White's (2004; 2010) rejection of the gentlemanly capitalist approach. On the contrary, the Colonial Office held a very dim view of the Rubber Growers Association, as a stubborn and conservative organisation (TNA FCO141/7479, Colonial Office to MacGillivray, 16 November 1955). Moreover, even bearing trade liberalisation in mind, what we discern from the archives is not a caesura but the status quo. Malaya remains valuable to Britain and the Sterling Area throughout this period for the same reasons it had before: principally, its dollar earnings. This even led Abdul Rahman to thank the Colonial Office for their continued commitment and support for Malaya, its economy and dollar-earning capacity (TNA FCO141/7499, Statement from the Tunku, 7 January 1957).

Conclusion

The chapter has shown that the continued reliance on British reserves to support British domestic and international economic policy meant that the dollar deficit was a problem of the highest order for British state managers. Indeed, the situation was still very serious and the cause of the problem had not been resolved; the global supply of dollars was limited by the terms of trade between the US and the rest of world, which is clearly understood by state managers as an issue of competitiveness between US producers and the rest of the world. This has been substantiated by reference to the dwindling of UK Central Reserves, the concern shown by the Treasury and the Bank over the global supply of dollars after the end of Marshall Aid, and the continued dollar deficit of the Sterling Area. This meant that Malaya remained extremely important to Britain, as it was still the highest net dollar earner in the Sterling Area. Britain's dominance of Malaya was used to the advantage of British economic and monetary policy by aiding in the maintenance of the UK's reserve position. The purpose of which, ultimately, was to resolve the crisis affecting the global economy fundamentally, by allowing for the reconstruction of the British economy, which would permit greater exports to the dollar area and, ultimately, a shift in the balance of trade and a return to an "equilibrium" in the global trading system.

The impact of the Korean War altered the nature of American aid, focusing it upon European rearmament, and boosted the price of raw materials. This highlighted to Britain that they had very limited autonomy to resolve this problem, as well as how much pressure was being placed on the reserves. The Korean War also provided a huge boon to the Malayan economy, improving its revenues substantially, due to the increased price of raw materials. However, this was short lived and the prices of raw materials collapsed, leading to curtailed GDP and export revenues in Malaya. Britain, therefore, had to look towards the development of other countries to supply dollars. Indeed, Britain's relationship with Malaya is most keenly revealed in its attitude to Malayan development. Britain was deeply committed to Malaya and its development: seeking loans for Malaya, providing grants and financial support itself and trying to arrange for ECA funds for Malaya before the Korean War.

It seems difficult to support the idea that Britain's support of Malayan development was confined solely to the importance attributed to its dollar-earning potential. Certainly, this was a major factor in Britain's commitment to Malayan development but not the only one. Indeed, state officials repeatedly associate the development of Malaya with nation-building, the resolution of the Malayan Emergency, the security of the Far East and, of course, to ensure that it provided its maximum potential for contributing to the Sterling Area dollar pool. Also frequently associated with development was Malaya's preparation for eventual independence from Britain, which itself contained a number of sub-goals: trying to alter Malaya's boom-and-bust economy due to its reliance on rubber and tin production, increasing food production and reducing ethnic and economic divisions.

This relationship, then, is better understood not through claims of a zero-sum exploitation of Malaya by Britain but, rather, through trying to understand the historically developed relationship between these two states, and their respective relationships with the global economy.

Certainly, Britain would benefit materially from Malaya's economic development but this manifested itself in a number of ways, not simply in Malaya's dollar contribution, and this is repeatedly stated throughout the documents presented in this chapter. Britain maintains strict control over Malaya's economic policy, using its dollar earnings to support sterling's position as an international currency. However, we see that Britain seeks to create in Malaya, through its development programme, a state that is well suited to the global capitalist economy and will remain valuable to Britain for the foreseeable future, by trying to resolve issues of boom and bust, as well as ensuring the competitiveness of its rubber industry against synthetic alternatives through replantation drives, and by trying to create a state that is both politically and economically stable.

One point that remains clear from this period, however, is the continuity in the relationship between Britain and Malaya. We see this in the persistent problem of the global dollar shortage, the desire to develop Malaya's economy and a complete lack of any suggestion that there is a cleavage in Bank or National Archives. While absence of evidence is not evidence of absence, one would expect, if the Hinds (2001) and Krozewski (2001) and theses were correct, that we would see a noticeable shift in the official mindset towards Malaya during this period. Indeed, they argue that the move towards trade liberalisation in 1953 marked a clear discontinuity in Britain's relationship with the Sterling Area more broadly. However, when looking closely at official documents of the specific relationship between Britain and Malaya within the Sterling Area, we find no evidence of a discontinuity. In fact, we see a reiteration of the major importance of Malaya to British economic policy. This then supports the view that there is greater analytical value to be derived from understanding imperialism not as a type of state, or an institution, but as a state strategy manifest as a relationship between states, which can only be fully understood through close analysis of that relationship.

Chapter 5 will provide an analysis of the period 1955–1960, featuring financial and constitutional discussions over Malaya's independence in 1957 and Malaya's introduction into the Sterling Area as a full and independent member.

5
Malayan Independence and the Sterling Area (1955–1960)

This chapter charts Britain's negotiations with Malaya concerning its eventual independence, including Malaya's relationship with the Sterling Area, its exchange controls, membership of the International Monetary Fund (IMF) and plans for the future development of Malaya.

This chapter looks at Malaya's growing sense of independence from Britain in this period, even before formal independence is declared. This is particularly apparent through Malaya's use of its Sterling Area membership, and its value to the Area, as a bargaining chip in political negotiations with Britain, with Singapore considering not renewing its exchange controls. This chapter also sees two similar episodes, with Malaya negotiating its own level of expenditure in foreign exchange, rather than having it imposed by Britain and the negotiation of an independent dollar reserve. Each of these incidents brings into question Malaya's relationship with the Sterling Area, and so too to Britain. Malaya is aware of its importance to the UK and the Sterling Area and repeatedly uses its value as a net contributor of dollars as a bargaining chip to achieve certain political goals, whether political credibility in Malaya, early independence or improved terms during constitutional negotiations.

The establishing of the Malayan Central Bank also sees a landmark in Malaya's independence, giving Malaya the ability to manage its own monetary policy. This precedes the desire to accumulate its own dollar reserve, which again brings Malaya's relationship with the Sterling Area into question. This period also sees the de-escalation of the Malayan Emergency, with little violence occurring after 1955 and periods of total inactivity by insurgents during this period. The Emergency was declared over in 1960, though had been effectively over for five years prior to that.

A prominent debate in imperial economic relations literature cen-tres on the relative importance of *de facto* convertibility of 1955, and the *de jure* convertibility of 1958. Where Schenk (1994, 1996) argues that the 1955 date was the more significant, Hinds (2001) and Krozewski (2001) argue that 1958 saw the final end of coherent eco-nomic relations between Britain and its empire. Their approaches are broad, looking, in Schenk's case, at the history of the Sterling Area as an institution for managing sterling, and in Krozewski and Hinds' cases, at the broader economic relations between Britain and its empire. These have been summed up by the authors themselves as distinc-tions between "economic" and "political" approaches to the subject: where Krozewski and Hinds see themselves as trying to understand British foreign relations, Schenk is trying to understand British eco-nomic performance (Krozewski 1997:850). White (210:175) also makes the point that the Sterling Area offers a clear element of continuity in terms of Malayan international economic history; however, what White does not note is *how* this was important in terms of the relationship with Britain, in other words as an imperial relationship. While this is certainly preferable to the Krozewski–Hinds thesis, it stills fails to com-prehend the significance of that continuity in terms of British governing strategy.

This chapter covers the chronology of *de facto* and *de jure* convertibility. Contrary to the general consensus in the literature on British imperial economic relations, this chapter maintains that Malaya's relationship with Britain remains fundamentally unchanged. While Malaya begins to act more independently, and indeed receives formal independence, from Britain, Malaya simply acts more indepen-dently *within the relationship that already exists*, using the nature of the relationship to its own advantage and not actually challenging its basic structure. This accords with the conclusions of Chapter 1.

The chapter focuses on a political crisis over exchange control in Singapore; the Financial and Constitutional Talks over Malayan inde-pendence; a Malayan request to Britain for an independent dollar reserve; and the search by the newly independent Malayan state for development funds. Each of these moments sees repeated emphasis placed by British officials on the continued value and importance of Malaya to the Sterling Area and the efforts by British state managers to maintain the nature of the relationship between Britain and Malaya. Furthermore, what both Krozewski and Hinds both see as discontinu-ity in 1958 does not feature in the archival documentation between Britain and Malaya. On the contrary, rather than seeing the complete breakdown of imperial economic relations in 1958, we see repeated efforts by British state managers to sustain the relationship with Malaya.

Malaya's own understanding of its value to the Sterling Area, and hence to British economic and monetary policy, reveals the nuance of the imperial relationship. While the institutional arrangement provided by the Sterling Area permits Britain to centrally pool convertible currency reserves and for sterling to be used as a reserve and trading currency by a wide variety of states, it is this arrangement that simultaneously permits the domination by Britain of Malaya to its own ends but also for Malaya not only to recognise its own value and leverage benefits from that but for Britain, in recognising that value, to seek to maximise it, resulting in development, economic growth and increased political independence. The imperial relationship then cannot be understood as a one-way domination of one state by another but a relationship characterised by the domination of one state by another, featuring the possibility for constraints and opportunities on both sides.

Exchange Control Ordinances

Towards the end of 1955, the Federation of Malaya was drawn into a dispute mainly between Singapore and Britain; however, given the nature of the constitutional arrangement between the governments of Malaya, whatever one government chose to do had enormous repercussions on the others. Indeed, the Bank considered both their economies and external trade only fully comprehensible as a single whole (BE OV65/5, "Federation of Malaya: Sterling Assets, Trade and Balance of Payments", 24 January 1957). As such, when the chief minister of Singapore, Saul Marshall, decided to use the collective dollar earnings of Malaya as a bargaining chip in future constitutional settlements, the Federation became drawn into that argument. Indeed, the relationship between the Federation, Singapore, Sarawak and Borneo was such that the British government at first treated the situation as if the entirety of Malaya were making these demands. Furthermore, the nature of the bargaining chip used by Marshall was such that it was keenly felt throughout the entirety of Malaya, and a particularly sensitive issue for Britain too.

Marshall's action, *prima facie*, does not seem to be too brazen. Marshall merely stated his intent only to renew Singapore's Exchange Control Ordinances for six months, which was a much shorter period than was normal.[1] The Governor of Singapore, in correspondence with the Colonial Office, believed that Marshall intended to use the issue of exchange control renewal as a bargaining chip in the upcoming Constitutional

Talks in London; it was believed, by Marshall, that Singapore was so vital to the Sterling Area that London would not dare call his bluff. However, when informed by the Governor that Singapore was only instrumentally valuable as the entrepôt market for the Federation's actual dollar earnings, Marshall was quite surprised. Indeed, the Governor believed that Marshall had a view to securing the dollar earnings of Malaya as well as using them as a tool to his political advantage (TNA CO1030/100, "Extract from letter from Governor of Singapore to Colonial Office", 5 November 1955).

Alan Lennox-Boyd, the Colonial Secretary, in a telegram sent in late November 1955, relayed the implications of removing exchange controls in Singapore to Sir Donald MacGillivray, the High Commissioner of the Federation.

> Quite apart however from the local effects there would be inevitable repercussions outside the Federation and Singapore, since Her Majesty's Government would be obliged, however reluctantly, to take steps to protect their own interests and those of the sterling area. It will surely be apparent to your Ministers that, so long as exchange control remains necessary for the sterling area, it would be impracticable for one territory within the area to abandon controls without undermining the effectiveness of the controls in the area as a whole. Her Majesty's Government would therefore be obliged to take steps to prevent Singapore, with its highly developed financial mechanism, becoming a wide breach in the defence of the sterling area.
>
> (TNA CO1030/100, Telegram no.164, 23 November 1955)

He also emphasised to MacGillivray the great threat this action posed to the economies of both Singapore and the Federation even if Britain did not take protective measures to insulate itself and the Sterling Area from Malaya's lack of exchange control. Lennox-Boyd believed that, if Marshall went through with his threat to remove exchange controls, the Malayan economy would be prone to speculation on the Malayan dollar and be unable to prevent capital flight from its territories (ibid.). This also highlights the continuing importance of the Sterling Area to Britain, and Britain's desire to protect the Sterling Area's exchange controls.

The Bank of England felt that, taken in isolation, Singapore's threat to abandon exchange controls was not particularly worrisome.[2] However, the Bank was extremely concerned about the precedent that this would set in the Sterling Area. Their main worry was that other members of the Area would follow Singapore's example, which would force Britain to either abandon all exchange controls within the Area, for which Britain was entirely unprepared, or else impose exchange controls against members of its own currency area, which seemed absurd and contrary to the reasons for the Sterling Area (BE OV65/4, Sterling Area: Abandonment of Exchange Control in Singapore (SECRET), 29 November 1955). However, the Bank did acknowledge that the abandonment of exchange controls was a necessary consequence of the move towards convertibility and the Collective Approach and was, therefore, ultimately a desired policy outcome (ibid.).

This threat from Marshall prompted the Colonial Office into action to consider how best to put forward the argument to Singapore and the Federation (if it was convinced to support Saul Marshall's plan) to remain in the Sterling Area, highlighting the advantages of staying in the Area and the disadvantages of leaving. Malaya was, after all, still very important to the UK and the Sterling Area, being the highest net dollar earner to the Area at US$120m in 1954. The only other member of the Area approaching Malaya was British West Africa with earnings of around $100m/year; however, British West Africa and Malaya were unique in that Malaya's own net dollar earnings were greater than the rest of the colonies' earnings combined.[3] Coupled with the fact that Britain itself was a net dollar spender of US$250m in 1954 and the Independent Sterling Area (including South African gold sales) only broke even, Malaya still remained extremely important to the maintenance of the Sterling Area, which was still vital to British economic and monetary strategy (TNA CO1030/100, "Exchange Control Problems in Malaya", 16 September 1955).

The argument that was drawn up was based upon a memo created for a Colombo Plan consultative committee meeting earlier in 1955, but was never actually submitted or used at the time. The memo stated concern that the common view in Malaya was that membership of the Sterling Area had become detrimental to Malaya's economy, with Malaya's dollar earnings used solely to meet dollar spending of other members, or to accumulate reserves to benefit the rest of the Area at Malaya's expense. The comparison between the greater freedom in dollar expenditure enjoyed by Hong Kong, the UK or the independent members of the Sterling Area, and Malaya's own exchange controls only provoked further anger at this difference (ibid.).

The economic view was not straightforward either. Malaya could leave the Sterling Area, as its dollar earnings were large enough to change the backing of its currency from sterling to the dollar easily enough and in a short period. Furthermore, with sterling having been devalued already since the war and serious discussion having been given to a floating exchange rate, as well as a great deal of speculation about the rate of sterling, Malaya might well have benefitted from basing its currency on the strongest and most stable currency in the world, the US dollar. Furthermore, any devaluation would be due to Britain's balance of payments problems, and not Malaya's. If devaluation did occur, Britain would benefit most from the boost given to the reserves, since they were held by the UK (TNA CO1030/100, "Malaya and the Sterling Area", 27 September 1955). However, the Colonial Office responded that the issue of devaluation could be rejected on the basis that the UK was "sternly resolved" to maintaining the sterling–dollar rate.[4] Furthermore, if devaluation did occur, the Malayan Currency Commission had the power to decide whether they wished to devalue the Malayan dollar in sympathy, as Pakistan did in 1949 (BE OV65/4, "Malaya Currency Ordinance 1951", 19 July 1951). The Sterling Area required no perpetual fixity in exchange rates of its members' domestic currencies, just that sterling be used in international transactions (TNA CO1030/100, "Malaya and the Sterling Area", 27 September 1955).

Indeed, the Colonial Office was well aware that this sense of injustice could not simply be dismissed as pure propaganda, or ignorance. This idea of colonial exploitation had become deeply embedded in the beliefs of the commercial and industrial sectors in Malaya, and the Colonial Office were worried that the issue of Malaya's membership in the Sterling Area would shift from an economic issue into a political one (ibid.). As such, it could become a widely held public view that the Sterling Area was synonymous with colonial exploitation and domination by a foreign power, which would be extraordinarily difficult to respond to, other than to say that there were independent members of the Sterling Area who enjoyed the benefits brought by the Area (TNA CO1030/100, "Malaya and the Sterling Area", 27 September 1955). This might also have led to the belief that a dollar-based economy was synonymous with independence. The Colonial Office was then eager to develop an argument for the Sterling Area based on the idea of mutual confidence and partnership on an equal basis (ibid.).

The first point to emphasise in this vein of argument is that the Sterling Area was a diverse collection of economies with common interest in maintaining the stability of sterling, through internal economic policies and by limiting expenditure external to the Area. The nature of these measures varied between countries, though there was a sense of complementarity present in the Area.

The different parts of the Sterling Area fall into two main categories –
those that are net dollar earners and those that are net dollar savers.
Borneo and Sarawak, for example, are net dollar savers owing to their
oil production, because the oil they produce might otherwise have
to come from dollar sources. Similarly, the United Kingdom is a net
dollar saver because its exports to the rest of the sterling area take
the place of goods which would otherwise have to some from the
USA. To say that Malaya is a net dollar earner which earns dollars for
the benefit of the United Kingdom rather than for itself is therefore
an over-simplification. Each party benefits the other, and it is quite
impossible to state in precise quantitative terms the benefits which
each confers and receives.

(TNA CO1030/100, "Exchange Control Problems
in Malaya", 16 September 1955)

Since different parts of the Area had different economies, they therefore
required different import policies. This idea of complementarity then
rested on a more fundamental idea that each member of the Sterling
Area performed a certain function for the rest of the Area's members.
Britain's function in the Sterling Area was to manufacture cheaply and
export its goods.

Many of [the UK's] exports will contain a dollar element which is
not charged against the receiving country's accounts. There is, thus,
clearly a case for the United Kingdom to purchase in the cheapest
market the raw materials it requires for its manufactures. This is the
reason why the United Kingdom has placed many of its raw material
requirements from the dollar area on [Open General Licence].

(ibid.)

Malaya, on the other hand, produced mainly raw materials and needed
to buy the cheapest machinery required for production. However, this
machinery was specialised in nature and did not lend itself to an open
licence, which was used to justify the lack of dollar open general licences
in Malaya. Indeed, the Colonial Office argued "Malaya has never . . . been
prevented by dollar restrictions from purchasing cheaper dollar equipment where this is available" (ibid.). It was argued by the Colonial Office
that the issue was more one of difference and complementarity than
exploitation and servitude.

In fact, the record of Her Majesty's Government in recognising
that other territories in the Sterling Area (whether dependent or

independent) have their own particular problems which cannot be met by any stereotyped formula will bear the closest scrutiny. There is scarcely a territory, however small, in which some departure from standard practice is not in operation.

(Ibid.)

This understanding of the Sterling Area and the Empire by British state managers lends further credence to the understanding of imperialism as a relationship between states, and certainly undermines understandings of the Empire as a monolithic institution. The Colonial Office was in fact confident that, as long as the issue did not become clouded with emotion, and in concert with an upcoming liberalisation of Sterling Area dollar imports, it was likely that Malaya could be easily convinced that its dollar earnings were not being used simply to "subsidise the extravagances" of other members of the Sterling Area; however, it was not the same argument as that of Malaya's membership of the Sterling Area (ibid.).

The best argument presented for Malaya's retention of Sterling Area membership was actually an issue of reserves. Sterling Area membership meant that Malaya actually required fewer reserves than existing outside of it since it did not need to hold reserves in the currencies of other Area members, as all trade was conducted using sterling. Furthermore, the more countries in a monetary area, the fewer reserves they would need since they would need no foreign currency for the trade between themselves.

Given the Sterling Area's internal trade amounted to £3,354m in 1954 and its external trade was £3,061m, the currency reserves held on behalf of members was therefore around half of what it would be otherwise (ibid.). This was further accentuated by the complementary nature of the Sterling Area's economies – reserves could be even lower than they might be. Seasonal and cyclical variations in economies could be smoothed over, as the terms of trade varied in a complementary manner and, in times of austerity, substitute goods were found within the Area also.

The nature of Malaya's economy, it was argued, meant that it had a natural direction towards the Sterling Area. Generally, this meant that Malaya purchased a large quantity of goods from Sterling Area countries, particularly the UK, and sold a great deal of goods outside the Area (TNA CO1030/100, "Malaya and the Sterling Area", 27 September 1955). Indeed, this historically developed and unique relationship between Malaya, Britain and the global economy highlights all the more the importance of understanding the specific nature of these relationships rather than as aggregated under the title of an empire; furthermore, this is the official understanding of British imperial relations by British state managers.

> Malaya's trade pattern of course emerged long before exchange control was thought of and it developed along its particular lines simply because this was its natural bent. Membership of the sterling area thus implies a certain natural outcome of Malaya's trading needs and has resulted in sterling area banks, insurance companies and shipping companies developing to meet those needs. Similarly sterling area finance has largely contributed to Malaya's development.
>
> (TNA CO1030/100, "Exchange Control
Problems in Malaya", 16 September 1955)

Thus, if Malaya left the Sterling Area, these benefits from her "natural development" would be forsaken: sterling would become a foreign currency and Malaya would have to develop her own reserves of both sterling and other foreign currencies to overcome trade fluctuations. Furthermore, imports from Malaya and investment in Malaya would therefore be foreign currency commitments and treated accordingly. This would then make the whole system of trade and its ancillary features much more difficult, particularly for Malaya.

> The effects on Malaya's economy would not be easily calculable. But it is clear that, if Malaya's own balance of payments with the rest of the world (including the sterling area) were adverse, she would have to restrict imports from all sources. This would be likely to happen at a time when the sterling area itself was moving towards convertibility and non-discrimination in trade.
>
> (Ibid.)

Indeed, Malaya's current dollar surplus meant that she must have a current sterling deficit. Where Malaya's sterling deficit was not caused by dollar import restrictions requiring Malaya to buy sterling goods, Malaya would have to sell dollars to the UK to get hold of sterling (TNA CO1030/100, "Malaya and the Sterling Area", 27 September 1955). Similarly, where import restrictions required Malaya to purchase sterling goods, this could also exacerbate her deficit with the Area though it was nowhere near the whole deficit (ibid.). Certainly, in this regard, Malaya was definitely paying a price for membership of the Sterling

Area, though the Colonial Office was adamant that this price was worth paying for the benefits it purchased.

> But is it not worth it, for the freedom which she thereby obtains in sterling area markets for her exports and re-exports, for the uncontrolled import of capital she gets, for her access to the London Market for the investment of her reserves, and for all the intangible advantages that flow from the free use of the currency and the trading machinery through which between 1/3 and 1/2 of the world's trade is conducted?
>
> (Ibid.)

These benefits would have been impossible for Malaya to participate in if it had left the Sterling Area. Furthermore, the Colonial Office emphasised the reciprocal nature of the Sterling Area quite clearly, acknowledging that Britain did benefit from Malaya's membership but that did exclude the fact that Malaya benefitted from membership also.

> We do not deny that her membership of the sterling area is of advantage to us: but this is perfectly consistent with it being of advantage to her too. Moreover as we progress towards the non-discriminatory and convertible world which is our major objective the membership-fee of controls should progressively be lightened.
>
> (Ibid.)

One further argument maintained that switching to the dollar might have made Malaya seem more appealing to dollar investment, and given the US further reason to protect the natural rubber industry from synthetic rubber competition (TNA CO1030/100, "Exchange Control Problems in Malaya", 16 September 1955). However, the dollar area was no guarantee of investment from the US, or of protection from synthetic rubber. In fact, Sterling Area membership was seen as an attraction for US investment, judging by former deals between independent countries and colonies, and Canada received no benefit from protectionism by close association with the dollar area, the Colonial Office noted. Not only were the benefits of membership of the dollar area generally exaggerated, but severing links with the Sterling Area would be a severe blow to Malaya's economy and would have had far-reaching effects (TNA CO1030/100, "Malaya and the Sterling Area", 27 September 1955).

The argument that Malaya would do better in the dollar area is based on a mass of misconceptions. Yes, Malaya has a large trade with the dollar area but her largest trade is with the Sterling Area. If Malaya had to join one (which she would as her currency is not used in international trade) then the Sterling Area would be the obvious choice ... So long as the great bulk of Malaya's trade is with non-dollar countries – whether sterling or non-sterling – it seems inconceivable that she would gain anything on balance by severing her links with the only important non-dollar currency used in international trade.

(Ibid.)

With the argument prepared, or at least dusted off, the Malayan Joint Ministers Conference in Singapore, on 7 November 1955, saw Marshall announce that Exchange Control Ordinance would indeed only be renewed for another six months. Donald MacGillivray relayed Marshall's realpolitik reasoning to Alan Lennox-Boyd. To Marshall, the basis behind his strategy was entirely political. At the upcoming Constitutional Talks in 1956, he intended to press Lennox-Boyd for early independence for Singapore in 1957.[5] However, Marshall expected this to be dismissed out of hand and that was why he wished to make an issue of Exchange Control Ordinance.

The only weapon to hand was the Malayan dollar surplus and so he proposed to use that by deliberately and openly threatening to deny its use to the Sterling Commonwealth by the abandonment of exchange control if he did not get what he wanted on the political front.

(TNA CO1030/100, Telegram no.687, 7 November 1955)

MacGillivray told Marshall that this course of action was very dangerous to Malaya economically and that even a fully independent Malaya would need some kind of exchange control. He further emphasised to Marshall that the British would call his bluff and serious damage could be done to the Malayan economy in the meantime. Marshall responded by saying that it would be impossible for the UK to call his bluff, even if they wished to, as the independent Sterling Area would intervene and force Britain to accept the terms. According to MacGillivray, Marshall said, "he wanted to put a loaded pistol on the table, knowing that the Secretary of State and Sterling Commonwealth could never let him use it" (ibid.).[6] Marshall reckoned that either the British would be forced to accept or the Colonial Secretary would order the Governor of Singapore to extend the Exchange Control Ordinance by fiat, and dismiss Marshall. The first would be a success and the second would reveal a dictatorial side to British rule and strengthen Marshall politically among the Singaporean public.[7] However, Marshall acknowledged to MacGillivray that this bargaining strategy was useless without the support of the Federation, as the Federation was the source of the vast majority of Malaya's dollar earnings (ibid.; TNA CO1030/100, "Exchange Control", 9 November 1955). Both Marshall and the British then sought the Federation's support.

Marshall had already sought the support of Abdul Rahman, the Chief Minister of the Federation, at the Joint Ministers Conference and, indeed, there was support in the Federation due to the widespread belief among the estate owners (of which a great number were in the Federation government) that Malaya would do well out of leaving the Sterling Area (TNA CO1030/100, "Exchange Control Problems in Malaya", 16 September 1955). However, his plan required the support of the entire Alliance Party in the Federation and this was not forthcoming (TNA CO1030/100, Telegram no.143, 9 November 1955).

At the Joint Ministers Conference, Marshall put forward a series of arguments in favour of his proposal for using Exchange Control Ordinance as a bargaining chip in Constitutional Discussions with London:

- Malaya as a whole lost more by exchange control than it gained.
- The Central Bank proposed by the International Bank for Reconstruction and Development (IBRD) mission would give Malaya further financial independence and, following formal independence, this might help in finding a future away from the Sterling Area.
- The ruling parties in both Singapore and the Federation were committed to independence in 1957.
- A six-month extension would see Ordinance expire in June 1956, by which time Britain would have to respond to demands for accelerated self-government.
- Taking a hard line with the British government would politically strengthen the Malayan chief ministers and governments.
- Singapore could not act alone. The Federation and Singapore's interests were conjoined and Abdul Rahman's support was vital.
  (TNA CO1030/100, "Exchange Control", 9 November 1955)

These arguments put forward by Marshall were completely rejected by Singapore's own Minister for Economic Affairs; however, Marshall was uninterested in the technical considerations of his arguments – he was solely concerned with the political success of his gamble.[8] Furthermore, arguments from economic considerations actually improved Marshall's sense of confidence, as Sir Robert Black reported to Lennox-Boyd:

> The more we attempt to argue on financial and economic grounds that it is essential for Malaya to stay in the Sterling Area, the more convinced, of course, the Chief Minister may become that he has a powerful weapon and therefore he will be the more determined to use it politically.
>
> (TNA CO1030/100, "Exchange Control", 9 November 1955; FCO141/7437, Telegram from Governor of Singapore to Colonial Secretary, 9 November 1955)

Indeed, Sir Hilton Poynton, Private Secretary at the Colonial Office, underlined this point, as well as the importance of the whole situation, to Leslie Rowan, the head of the Overseas Finance division at the Treasury.

> I think you will agree that refusal by Singapore and the Federation to continue exchange control amounts in effect to the withdrawal (or expulsion) of Malaya from the Sterling Area. However alarming this may be to the UK and the [rest of the Sterling Area] I think it would be tactically unwise to let Marshall think we were alarmed on this ground since it would enhance the value of this manoeuvre in his eyes as a form of political blackmail. Moreover if the price asked is early full self-government there would be nothing to stop Marshall and his friends doing whatever they want when they have got full self-government.
>
> (TNA CO1030/100, AH Poynton to Sir Leslie Rowan (SECRET), 16 November 1955)

The next step lay with Abdul Rahman. It was considered very unlikely by the Colonial Office that he would agree to Singapore's suggestion, though the Colonial Office was aware of the possibility. Sir Robert Black advised the Colonial Office that, if worse came to worst, he could reject the six-month extension or force a further extension after the six months; however, he warned that both courses of action would lead to a constitutional crisis, and would be used by Marshall to further his own agenda (TNA CO1030/100, "Exchange Control", 9 November 1955).

This then led the Colonial Office to discuss the issue with the Bank. The Colonial Office believed that there were only two possibilities in calling Marshall's bluff. First, they could refuse to let the Ordinance lapse. Marshall would then resign and the issue would become one of public opinion; however, while the argument that seeing Ordinance lapse would be detrimental to Malaya's economy was clear, making a good case of it in a public setting would be difficult and unlikely to be successful (TNA CO1030/100, AM MacKintosh to DMB Butt, copy to Loynes, 11 November 1955).

Second, and the only reasonable alternative, was to stop Marshall gaining any support from the Federation. This could only rest on the fact that Britain would consent to accepting the lapsing of Exchange Control Ordinance, and that the consequences to Malaya's economy would be catastrophic. The advice sought by the Colonial Office from the Bank was clarification as to whether the British government could afford to call Marshall's bluff, or whether Britain was required to stop it as the trustee of the Sterling Area. The Colonial Office also asked for a document detailing the merits of the Sterling Area and the demerits of leaving to join another currency bloc (TNA CO1030/100, AH Poynton to Sir Leslie Rowan (SECRET), 16 November 1955).

> What seems to us to be needed is a paper written in simple language for the layman, divided perhaps into two parts: the first would set out the very meagre advantages which would accrue to Malaya if she were to ally herself with the US dollar; the second would show the immediate and formidable disadvantage which would follow on severance from the sterling area. This could ... be pitched fairly strong and include the blocking of the £300m Malayan Sterling Balances.
>
> (Ibid.)

Marshall was aware that he could not use Exchange Control as a bargaining tool unless his ministers supported it, and, crucially, the Federation government supported it. Poynton then suggested to Rowan that the High Commissioner in the Federation and the Governor of Singapore should be pressed to convince the ministers in both governments to reject Marshall's proposal (TNA CO1030/100, AH Poynton to Sir Leslie Rowan (SECRET), 16 November 1955). However, if they were unable to persuade Marshall to give up his idea before he left Singapore for London, then it would be made an issue in London at the Constitutional Talks. The line agreed between Poynton and Rowan was that the Colonial Secretary would discuss it but only as an economic matter. However, if Marshall persisted in the issue at discussion, then Lennox-Boyd would have to tell Marshall that if he insists on pursuing this course it will be necessary for the Governor to use his reserved power to put the necessary legislation through, and that in doing so he will publish a clear statement of the economic reasons for his action and thereby make it apparent that Marshall had been set upon a course which could not be other than gravely damaging to the interests of Singapore.

(Ibid.)

This worst-case scenario would then require the Governor of Singapore, the High Commissioner of the Federation and the British government to make a strong case to the Malayan public for the justifications of their actions.

Lennox-Boyd remained hopeful that MacGillivray would see success in his efforts to persuade ministers not to pursue threats to abandon Exchange Control in Singapore, or the Federation. Lennox-Boyd telegrammed MacGillivray that he should remind ministers in Singapore and the Federation that economic setbacks would mean political setbacks (referring to independence); he also emphasised to him that the exchange controls of the Federation and Singapore were "of vital significance to the economic life of the [sterling] Area" (TNA CO1030/100, Telegram no.164, 23 November 1955). However, he also asked MacGillivray to emphasise that linking the two subjects for political or constitutional progress could lead to catastrophe economically and politically (ibid.). Indeed, Lennox-Boyd told MacGillivray that even the minimum measures to protect Britain and the Sterling Area from a potential Malayan free-exchange area would have enormous consequences for Malaya. Outlining these measures, he told MacGillivray that controls would have to be set up between the Sterling Area and Malaya, as well as a restriction on Malayan development capital and the severe hindrance of the traditional banking relationship enjoyed by Area members (ibid.; BE OV65/4, Sterling Area: Abandonment of Exchange Control in Singapore (SECRET), 29 November 1955). In essence, it would have effects that were almost synonymous with Malaya's withdrawal from the Sterling Area; however, Britain was adamant that this outcome would not occur.

Above all, Lennox-Boyd was hopeful that Federation ministers were deterred from Marshall's proposed course of action by the economic arguments made, and that they would therefore not support Marshall's proposal. MacGillivray wrote back to Lennox-Boyd two days later to tell him that he had met with Abdul Rahman. Rahman had told him that the Federation was extremely unlikely to support Marshall's proposal, though Marshall was coming to discuss the issue with him on 26 November (TNA CO1030/100, Telegram no.745, "Exchange Control", 25 November 1955; FCO141/7437, Telegram from High Commissioner, Federation, to Colonial Office, 25 November 1955).

MacGillivray also relayed that the members of the Singapore Executive Council had informed him they did not intend to recommend that Exchange Control be extended for only six months just to exert political pressure, as there were no good economic reasons for doing so (ibid.; FCO141/7437, From Governor of Singapore to Secretary of State for the Colonies, 29 November 1955).[9] Four days later, Exchange Control Ordinances were renewed by one year, rather than six months. Governor Black told Lennox-Boyd that Marshall justified his climbdown by saying that "his bargaining position [was] sufficiently strong not to have to make use of the exchange control weapon. In the circumstances he had no option but to abandon the idea" (ibid.; CO1030/100, Telegram no.156, 29 November 1955).

Despite the eventual climbdown from Marshall's initial position, both Malayan and British interests are brought to the fore in this short crisis in British–Malayan relations. Britain maintains that Malaya's membership of the Sterling Area is still vital both to its own economic interests and Malaya's. Marshall's position, while still political grandstanding to achieve greater political independence, reveals that it was in Malaya's interest to remain in the Sterling Area; to do otherwise would be, if not catastrophic for the Malayan economy, then certainly very difficult to extricate itself from the Sterling Area and reinsert itself into another currency area. This then highlights the nature of this imperial relationship: both Britain and Malaya benefitted from the current arrangement, as they had since 1945. The arguments generated by the British government to support continued Malayan membership of the Sterling Area, and the retention of exchange controls, reveal the continued value of Malaya to the British (and vice versa) but the arguments do gloss over the fundamental basis of the Sterling Area: it is, in essence, and fundamentally, an institution to support Britain's economic policy and position. However, this episode also reveals the dynamic nature of the relationship and proves that the relationship cannot be reduced to that basic quality of the Sterling Area. Indeed, Marshall's gamble reveals how Malaya's value to the Sterling Area can be presented as an opportunity for the benefit of Malayan (or Singaporean) policy.

Constitutional Talks

With the resolution of Exchange Control Ordinance renewal settled going into the Constitutional Talks in London in early 1956, the Talks looked set to be dominated by the issue of imports of synthetic rubber to Britain. The Colonial Office had been approached by the Federation's Minister for Economic Affairs, who wanted to know why Britain was using the dollar pool to purchase synthetic rubber rather than simply purchasing Malayan natural rubber (TNA CO1030/58, "Import of Synthetic Rubber into the United Kingdom", 2 December 1955). There was some anger in Malaya that, for all Britain's declarations of support concerning development, Britain was unwilling to support the Malayan rubber industry with its custom. The British government had approved an import programme for 70,000 tons of synthetic rubber in 1956 from the US, which corresponded to a drop in orders for Malayan natural rubber by 70,000 tons for that year.

The Treasury responded to the request by pointing out that the UK abided by rules common to the entire Sterling Area – dollar expenditure was acceptable as long as it was for essential purchases. Synthetic rubber imports were considered essential purchases as the efficiency and competitiveness of the UK rubber manufacturing industry relied on them. The Treasury maintained that the import programme in 1956 was not excessive and therefore was a justifiable use of dollars. The Treasury also refused to review the programme (ibid.).

The Colonial Office sent a letter to Donald MacGillivray a few days after the initial Treasury response to reiterate the reasons for the synthetic rubber imports, and the stubbornness about maintaining them. In the letter, Lennox-Boyd emphasised that this policy was entirely consonant with Sterling Area rules but aimed ultimately at the convertibility of sterling. This aim could not be accomplished until the Sterling Area's balance of payments had been strengthened and the only means of achieving that was to improve the efficiency, productivity and competitiveness of the British economy. The argument then proposed by the Colonial Office and the Treasury was that the import of synthetic rubber was justifiable in terms of Britain and the Sterling Area's general economic policy (TNA CO1030/58, Colonial Office to High Commissioner, Federation of Malaya, 13 December 1955).

Average natural rubber prices in 1955 had reached a post-Korean War high of around 34 p/lb, which had stimulated the competitiveness of synthetic rubber production (Lim 1967:317). The use of synthetic rubber was also preferred for a great deal of rubber manufacturing end uses, and Lennox-Boyd argued that the import of synthetic rubber in this instance would greatly reduce the need to import any more in the future. Furthermore, since European rubber manufacturing industries had not had access to Britain's rubber markets, their industries were considerably more efficient and competitive than Britain's own (TNA CO1030/58, Colonial Office to High Commissioner, Federation of Malaya, 13 December 1955).

While Lennox-Boyd was very eager to emphasise that Malaya's rubber and tin industries were essential to the dollar earnings of the Sterling Area, their protection could not come at the price of British and the Sterling Area's development as a whole. Indeed, the Colonial Office made it clear that import controls on essential dollar imports were contrary to the Sterling Area's economic policy, and also asserted that General Agreement on Tariffs and Trade (GATT) obligations required that Britain should not employ quantitative import restrictions for protective purposes, despite using exactly the opposite argument in the mid-1940s to justify quantitative import restrictions (ibid.). The Colonial Office's final point was to say that imports of Malayan rubber into Britain were at such a low level that swapping synthetic imports for Malayan imports would have little effect indeed. Natural rubber was principally consumed in the US market, where natural and synthetic rubber were in free competition (ibid.).[10]

The arguments put forward by both the Colonial Office and the Treasury to the Federation, and subsequently reiterated by the High Commissioner in Malaya, settled the matter on the specific issue of synthetic rubber imports. However, the concern over the issue was merely a manifestation of a more fundamental problem running throughout the Britain–Malaya relationship: the use of dollars earned by Malaya. This became the theme of the Financial Working Group in the Constitutional Talks held in London between January and February 1956.

In a Bank memo, a copy of the brief for the Malayan Minister for Economic Affairs was discussed by John Fisher (the Deputy Chief Cashier), Sir George Bolton and Lucius Thompson-McCausland in detail. Financial issues and exchange policy were to be discussed in relation to Malaya's imports from the dollar area and its dollar spending, as well as its future financial ties with Britain and the Sterling Area. The Minister's brief contained three demands and one offer:

- Full membership of the Sterling Area, so that Malaya will be consulted on matters of common policy and will be invited to attend finance ministers' meetings.
- Britain was to accept that Malaya's capital requirements were to be met in the London market, to the tune of £20m over the next five years.

- Malaya was to have freedom to import from dollar sources, and to have free access to its own dollar surplus in order to develop its economy to expand trade with neighbouring countries.
- In return for the above, Malaya would pledge full collaboration and cooperation on all matters affecting sterling and convertibility.

(BE OV65/4, "Malaya", 17 January 1956)

The first demand was not discussed because it was wholly acceptable. For the second demand, the Treasury reported it could not assure the Malayan delegation that this was possible, though there were precedents for that to occur.[11] The third demand was considered the most important and an immediate issue for the Talks, and saw the Bank provide an insight into divisions on Sterling Area policy within the state management.

> If Malayan ministers press for freedom on dollar imports and if this is largely conceded (whether for political reasons or otherwise) it will make an irreparable breach in the wall of dollar restrictions around the Colonies which the Treasury seek to maintain – and which we are anxious to lower.
>
> (Ibid.)

Once again, the Bank's major concern was that it would set a dangerous precedent for the Sterling Area. If this were permitted, it would be difficult to deny similar concessions to other countries (e.g. the colonies of the former British West Africa) and therefore, according to the memo, the Colonial Office too would have to abandon its current efforts to keep all colonies on the same exchange policy (ibid.). The Bank then was much more committed to the Collective Approach than the Colonial Office or the Treasury, who were still committed to the maintenance of exchange controls around the Sterling Area. However, by this point, the Collective Approach had been widely accepted by British state managers and the Sterling Area and, therefore, the Bank, as Burnham (2003:184) argues, was much more eager to act swiftly to achieve Convertibility than the Treasury (and also the Colonial Office).[12]

One possibility of getting around Malaya's demand for free dollar imports was to use Hong Kong as a "back door" through which Malaya could buy all the dollar goods it needed. Hong Kong's special status was brought up by the Malayan delegation, since the former had much greater dollar freedom than any country in the Sterling Area (BE OV65/4, Letter from Emanuel to Simons (SECRET), 23 January

1956). However, this was because Hong Kong was an entrepôt area for China, Korea, Macao and Taiwan and sold large quantities of goods to these territories and in return received large quantities of dollars, which Hong Kong was permitted to use freely (BE OV65/4, "Hong Kong Free Market", 26 January 1956). Hong Kong's dollar earnings actually provided a net contribution to the Sterling Area, while sterling accounts in the colony were restricted and the Hong Kong government enforced this by strictly limiting the sale and purchase of sterling. Furthermore, the Malayan dollar was linked to sterling through statute but the Hong Kong dollar was a *de facto* link, with no strict basis in law. Unlike Malaya, Hong Kong was not legally obliged to back its currency with sterling or to issue against sterling at a fixed rate. As such, Hong Kong was seen as a very special case (BE OV65/4, "The Federation of Malaya – Constitutional Conference", 30 January 1956).

A free market like Hong Kong's is contrary to the fundamental principles of the Sterling Area and to HMG's obligations to the IMF. The arrangements in Hong Kong are in effect a compromise between its two roles as an outlet for China and neighbouring countries and as a Sterling Area territory; they can only be justified because of the exceptional circumstances, which are of over-riding importance to the economic existence of the territory concerned.

(BE OV65/4, "Hong Kong Free Market", 26 January 1956)

It was then put to the Malayan delegation that there was no justifiable comparison between the Malayan and Hong Kong economies, which they were satisfied with (BE OV65/4, "The Federation of Malaya – Constitutional Conference", 30 January 1956). John Fisher made one further point, that the most basic and convincing argument against a Malayan free market was Malayan development. Malaya required stability in order to develop and, as such, fluctuating exchange rates would run contrary to this since they would require a barrier between Malaya and the Sterling Area instead of the current statutory arrangement (ibid.; BE OV65/4, "Singapore: Free US Dollar Market", 4 February 1956).

Given the failure of the comparison between Malaya and Hong Kong, a member of the Malayan delegation approached the Chief General Manager of Chartered Bank, Howard Morford, to tell him that the Malayan delegation was now considering setting up Singapore as a free market in US dollars, as in Hong Kong. Morford asked P.L. Hogg at the Bank to see whether there were good arguments that could be mustered by either the Bank or the Treasury to dissuade the Malayans from this course of action (BE OV65/4, Letter from Morford to PL Hogg, 31 January 1956).

The purpose behind this determination to achieve free use of dollars was, of course, for Malaya to expand its primary and secondary industries, and a free market was seen by the Malayan delegation as attracting overseas capital to invest in the Malayan economy. However, the Bank was adamant that there was no guarantee of this and that a free market could actually encourage instability and uncertainty (BE OV65/4, "Singapore: Free US Dollar Market", 4 February 1956). Further, if it were just Singapore becoming a free market then exactly the same arguments applied as if Malaya as a whole wished to have a free market: exchange barriers would be required, it would strain the link between currencies and it was entirely dissonant with Malaya's professed intention of staying in the Sterling Area and committing to the obligations inherent to that (ibid.).

By the end of the Constitutional Talks in mid-February 1956, a provisional agreement had been reached about the lead-up to the Federation's independence. The Talks had led to an agreement that an elected Malayan finance minister would take over all responsibility for internal and external finance from the (London-appointed) Financial Secretary with immediate effect. Malaya would remain in the Sterling Area after independence, which was scheduled for August 1957, and Malaya would send delegates to all future meetings of finance ministers. Control over the Federation's dollar spending would move from Whitehall to the Federation government, who would then be tasked with applying Sterling Area policy to Malaya as a whole (BE OV65/4, "The Federation of Malaya – Constitutional Conference", 13 February 1956). Assurances were given to Malaya that "sympathetic consideration" would be given to Federation borrowing in London for development purposes (ibid.). Furthermore, Britain pledged to give fair treatment to overseas capital investment in the Federation and agreed to aid in meeting the costs of the Emergency after independence (ibid.). The final report on the constitutional conference characterised the agreement made between Malayan and British delegations on the Sterling Area:

> We had a full and frank discussion of the Federation's position in the Sterling Area. The Malayan Delegation indicated that it was the view of their Government that membership of the Sterling Area was to the common advantage of the Federation and the other members and that it was their intention to remain in it after attaining

full self-government. There was general recognition by the United Kingdom representatives of the importance of the Federation's contribution to the strength of the Sterling Area through the direct earnings of dollars from rubber and tin.

> (TNA CAB129/79, "Federation of
> Malaya", 21 February 1956)

A letter from Herbert Brittain, second secretary at the Treasury, to Thomas Lloyd, Permanent Under-Secretary of State at the Colonial Office, a week after the Constitutional Talks emphasised how important the colonies were to the British economy and how crucial it was still to maintain strict limits on dollar expenditure.

> We cannot regard Colonial economies as "entirely external" to that of the United Kingdom. Such description would, indeed, have little meaning. For years now it has been necessary to emphasise the inter-connectedness of internal and external problems, and...vigorous internal measures are necessary to relieve the balance of payments...The fact remains, however, that external spending, even in the sterling area, has a more direct and a larger effect upon our reserves and the status of sterling than expenditure at home, and has for that reason to be examined with special care.
>
> (TNA CO1025/56, Brittain to Lloyd, 20 February 1956)

Colonial Sterling Balances had recently risen, and this was helpful to Sterling's position and also therefore to Britain (TNA CO1025/56, Letter from Lloyd to Brittain, 3 February 1956). However, Brittain emphasised clearly to Lloyd that the Colonies could not be permitted to run down their sterling balances by spending freely as this would still place too great a strain on the reserves, they would dwindle to nothing in the process and the colonies would suffer as much from that as Britain (ibid.). Britain's dollar reserves in February 1956 were still very low at £77m, with gold reserves at their lowest level since June 1953 at £703m (Bank 1970:162).

Immediately following the Constitutional Talks, a new Minister of Finance, as per the agreement with Britain, was appointed in the Federation. Colonel Henry Lee was ethnically Chinese and had been bestowed the honorary rank of Colonel by Chiang Kai-Shek. His political activities were decidedly anti-communist and he was a very wealthy man, holding considerable business interests in both the Federation in Singapore in rubber estates and tin mines (BE OV65/4, "The Federation of Malaya – Minister of Finance", 29 February 1956). Lee, like British officials, did not want to see Singapore become a free dollar market. Lee became the key figure in all of Britain's financial discussions with Malaya until 1959, and during this time the same issues dominated Britain's relationship with Malaya, even after independence (ibid.).

Financial discussions

In early June 1956, Malayan ministers met with representatives from the Eastern Banks to discuss the setting up of an investment corporation to stimulate industrial development in the Federation to the tune of M$10m. While the Banks wanted a majority government share in the corporation, the Federation government sought to have the corporation based on majority private investment (BE OV65/5, "Malaya: Industrial Development Corporation", 8 June 1956). The Federation was also using the terms of the creation of a central bank as a bargaining chip for the setting up of the investment corporation and, in a letter to the Bank of England, the Mercantile Bank felt that the setting up of the corporation revealed a desire to cut ties with Singapore (ibid.).

While the Colonial Office admitted they were not aware of the creation of the Industrial Development Corporation, they informed the Bank that this was usual for colonies heading towards independence and there were precedents for it. However, they acknowledged that, ordinarily, the Colonial Development and Food Corporation (CDFC) would provide funds for the corporation but the Malayan government had not approached the CDFC for funds (ibid.). Colonel Lee also contacted the British government at this point to ask for financial aid for Malayan development; however, the Colonial Office was reticent to approve any funds unless the details of a specific development plan were provided, but these had not yet been drawn up by the Federation (TNA CO1030/903, Letter from J. Hennings to Mr Johnston, 18 June 1956).

Certainly, the Federation was very eager to gain access to large amounts of ready cash to spend on development in the run-up to independence (BE OV65/6, "Malaya", 20 August 1958). Indeed, by the end of June, Donald MacGillivray telegrammed Alan Lennox-Boyd to inform him that the Federation had asked him about lifting the rubber embargo against China (TNA CO1029/112, High Commissioner, Malaya to Colonial Secretary, 30 June 1956). The High Commissioner had informed Colonel Lee that the British government would require an end-use certificate due to security concerns about its application; however, this would probably be meaningless and therefore he suggested using a quantitative restriction instead and proposed an initial limit of 2,000 tons of rubber (ibid.).[13] The embargo on rubber exports to China was ultimately relaxed. It was too difficult to get end-use agreements from the Chinese government, but Malayan exports assured Sir Robert Black that their rubber exports were used only for civilian purposes. These shipments constituted the first rubber exports to China from Malaya since 1951 (TNA CO1029/112, "Telegram no.482: China Trade Controls: Rubber", 9 October 1956).

By August, however, Britain was forced to deal with the repercussions of the nationalisation of the Suez Canal, an action described in the Bank as imperilling "the survival of the UK and the Commonwealth, and represents a very great danger to Sterling" (BE G1/124, "Sterling and the Suez Canal Situation", 1 August 1956). A letter to the Governor of the Bank highlighted that the use of economic warfare against Egypt would be detrimental to Britain, especially to the reserves (ibid.). This was not catastrophic at the time, as the reserves had reached a comparative high-point with dollar reserves at £137m and gold reserves at £722m (Bank, p.162). However, the Suez crisis, due to both economic warfare and the effect on sterling, diminished the reserves significantly. By the end of August dollar reserves had fallen to £88m and by the end of November had fallen again to £47m, with gold reserves at £655m (ibid.).

By even mid-November, George Bolton, in discussion with Leslie Rowan, agreed that Britain could not continue to take losses as they had been and still hope to maintain the rate of sterling, which was essential since if that rate could not be maintained, "there [was] a grave risk of the Sterling Area coming to an end" (BE G1/124, "Discussion with Leslie Rowan", 13 November 1956). They agreed that an appeal to the US to help maintain parity was necessary since "it is a major interest of the US to maintain Sterling and to prevent the collapse of the Sterling Area" (ibid.); however, this was not forthcoming and the reserve situation only abated with Britain's unconditional withdrawal from the Suez Canal Zone, with dollar reserves rallying up to £166m by the end of the year (BE C43/31, "Exchange Market Tactics", 3 December 1956; BE Statistical Abstract no.1 1970, Table 27:162).[14]

Against this backdrop, Financial Talks between Britain and the Federation were being prepared, starting on 17 December 1956. The Federation had begun to worry about revenues after independence, as the IBRD's report on Malaya's economic development suggested that rubber prices would fall between 1957 and 1960 (IBRD 1955:48; TNA CO1030/903, Galsworthy to Monson, 3 December 1956). The

Federation then sought further financial assistance from the British government but the Colonial Office was reticent to accede to, what they termed, Malaya's "exorbitant demands", considering them extremely unreasonable (TNA CO1030/903, Galsworthy to Monson, 3 December 1956).

In communication with the Colonial Secretary, the Commissioner-General of South East Asia, Sir Robert Scott, reiterated the High Commissioner's plea that the Colonial Office accept Malaya's request for generous aid. He emphasised that the financial situation in Britain would certainly be better suited to the economic arguments for doing so but these arguments supported broader political ones (TNA CO1030/903, Letter from Commissioner-General, SE Asia to Colonial Secretary, 6 December 1956). While there were substantial British investments in Malaya, running to hundreds of millions of pounds, plus the invisible earnings accruing from shipping, banking and insurance, this was not the best argument for being generous with Malayan development aid.[15]

> The main economic argument for financial aid is, quite simply, dollars. On the prosperity of Malaya and on the stability of its economy depends one of the biggest single sources of American dollars at the disposal of the Sterling bloc, if not indeed the biggest individual source. Malaya earns some hundreds of millions of dollars a year, a quarter or more of the total dollars accruing to the whole sterling area. Surely the greater the strain on sterling, the greater the need to conserve such a vital source of dollars. If that can be done by sterling expenditure, it is cheap at almost any price.
>
> (Ibid.)

Essential to Malaya's source of dollars was the rubber industry, and Abdul Rahman contacted the Colonial Secretary the day after Sir Robert Scott's letter to assure him that rubber replantation was the highest priority in the Federation's development plan (TNA CO1030/904, Tunku Rahman to Colonial Secretary, 7 December 1956).

The Colonial Office were initially very concerned that the financial discussions would be focused on Malaya's relationship with the Sterling Area, and prepared another document detailing the value Malaya gained from remaining in the Sterling Area (BE OV65/5, "Questions affecting the Federation of Malaya in relation to Sterling Area Policies", 12 December 1956). However, in conversation with the Bank, the Colonial Office was informed that Malaya's position in the Sterling Area were unlikely to come up again since the issue had been extensively covered in the Constitutional Talks at the beginning of 1956; instead, the discussions were most likely to focus on finance for Malaya's defence and development programmes (BE OV65/5, "Malaya and the Sterling Area", 28 December 1956).

Given Britain's weakened state following the Suez crisis, the Financial Talks were difficult. The Malayan delegation demanded that Britain meet half the cost of the Emergency,[16] and help to meet the costs of Malaya's development plan. The Federation then asked for a £100m grant to bridge the gap between Malaya's capacity and requirements (TNA CO1030/903, "Note for Prime Minister", 8 January 1957). The British delegation responded starkly by saying that the British government did not and could not give direct financial aid to independent members of the Commonwealth for development since it was considered "a normal economic activity in which any independent Government must stand on its own feet", and there was a stated suspicion among the British delegation that, if the costs were spread out, the Federation could meet them (ibid.). The Malayan delegation, which included Abdul Rahman and Colonel Lee, were extremely disappointed with this response from the British.

However, as had been agreed in the Constitutional Talks in early 1956, Britain would provide financial aid to meet the costs of the Malayan Emergency. This was not only seen as a contribution to the Emergency but also to the Federation's development plan as it freed up significant resources, with the development of Malaya "recognized to be in itself an important contribution to the fight against communism" (TNA CO1030/903, Telegram no.59, 10 January 1957). Britain agreed to provide an annual grant of £3m for the following three years and, at the end of those three years, the British government agreed to review the Federation's financial position and then decide on whether to activate a fund of £11m for further assistance, to be spread over the next two years (ibid.).[17] In addition, Britain offered to use previously promised funds of £6.5m to the Federation to further expand its armed forces, as well as supplying equipment up to the value of £5.5m (ibid.; TNA CO1030/627, "Federation of Malaya", 27 February 1958). These amounts would be in conjunction with a grant to the Federation for development from the unspent balance of the Federation's Colonial Development and Welfare allocations at the date of independence, a sum of around £4.5m (TNA CO1030/903, Telegram no.59, 10 January 1957). In all, this amounted to grants of nearly £37m until 1961, about which both Abdul Rahman and Colonel Lee were very pleased (ibid.).[18]

With Malayan capital expenditure very high at around M$260m, Malaya needed as much money as it could get. However, despite a recommendation in the IBRD report (1955:212) that Malaya could seek local development loans worth around M$10m per year through the Malayan Post Office Savings Bank (POSB), the Bank of England was extremely reticent to support this notion (BE OV65/5, "Federation of Malaya Post Office Savings Bank", 30 May 1957). There would be a great risk of capital loss to the POSB, since there was no limit on the amount of government stock the POSB could purchase, the POSB's portfolio would be extremely limited and "in an economy as dependent as the Federation on the vicissitudes of the world markets for tin and natural rubber, the interests of depositors must surely be carefully watched and not sacrificed for development expedience" (ibid.). So while British officials were eager for Malaya to have as much cash as possible to spend on development, this was not the key priority – Malayan development was instrumental in terms of dollar earnings, but also and importantly, the stability of the economy and the Malayan political establishment.

Despite the relative distance now from Suez, the effects were still being felt in the British economy, including the prolongation of oil supply difficulties; however, both Leslie Rowan and Denis Rickett were sanguine, in a letter to Cameron Cobbold, about the position of sterling due to the resolution of domestic political instability through Prime Minister Eden's resignation at the beginning of 1957, and the boost likely to be given to sterling through the seasonal effect on Sterling Area commodities (BE C43/31, "Exchange Policy", 11 January 1957).

With independence only four months away, Malaya began the process of applying for membership of the IMF, the International Finance Corporation (IFC) and the IBRD. The Colonial Secretary forwarded to the High Commissioner in Malaya the details of the process of application. Since the Federation and Singapore shared a single currency, the IMF expected both countries to act in a unified manner and this required a single central bank for both territories, which had previously been recommended by the IBRD (IBRD 1955:652; BE OV65/5, "Telegram no.1065, Application by the Federation of Malaya for Membership of the IMF and the IBRD", 6 May 1957).

By the beginning of August, less than a month before independence, the committee on Malaya's membership to the IMF recommended terms for its admittance. Malaya was required to pay an IMF quota of US$45m, with a subscription fee of 3.5% of that payable in gold or convertible currencies (US$1.575m). However, since Malaya had no independent holdings of gold or dollars because it was a member of the Sterling Area, it was required to hand over its current dollar and gold earnings to the IMF until the 3.5% subscription was met (BE OV65/5, Octavio Paranagua to Colonel Lee, 2 August 1957). Once the subscription had been paid, Malaya would join the IMF and the rest of the quota would be paid in Malayan dollars at a previously agreed value. Malaya would then have access to the IMF's resources in any currency it wished up to the amount of its initial gold payment (US$1.575m), though the IMF would charge 1% for this service (ibid.).

With Malaya accepted as a member, and the details clear on how Malaya should proceed as a member of the IMF, the IBRD and the IFC, Abdul Rahman sent a letter to the High Commissioner in Malaya requesting that Britain pay the lion's share of Malaya's subscriptions to these organisations (BE OV65/5, "Application by Malaya to IMF, IBRD, IFC", 19 November 1957). Since Malaya's reserves were held in the general pool of the Sterling Area, Abdul Rahman requested Britain

> to make on behalf of the Federation the gold and dollar payments set out above to the Fund, Bank and Corporation respectively. The payments, together with any consequential charges incurred, should, it is suggested, be debited to the Federation Government Account with the Crown Agents for Overseas Governments and Administrations.
>
> (Ibid.)

As such he requested that Britain pay US$875,000 for the IMF, US$500,000 for the IBRD (in gold to the Bank of England) and US$277,000 in US dollars to the Federal Reserve Bank (ibid.).[19]

With independence granted to Malaya on 31 August 1957, Malaya assumed a full membership of the Sterling Area and the Commonwealth (TNA CO1030/627, "Federation of Malaya", 27 February 1958). An interview with Lord Kilmuir, the Lord Chancellor, was arranged for the BBC to discuss Malaya's independence from the British Empire and the Treasury was asked to provide some answers to the questions that would be asked. Most of the questions focused on Malaya's membership of the Sterling Area, and the Treasury, Bank and Colonial Office advised the Lord Chancellor to avoid speculative answers and only talk about details if pressed, and then only to emphasise the benefits of the Sterling Area, from information which the Bank, Treasury and Colonial Office had generated numerous times previously in persuading Malaya to remain as part of the Sterling Area after independence (BE OV65/5, Hennings to Charles, 10 September 1957).

The Bank, however, suggested to Lord Kilmuir that if the topic of Malaya's dollar earnings came up, he should emphasise that Malaya's dollar earnings could not be considered in isolation, as "the fact that she chooses to convert them into Sterling and hold her reserves in that currency instead of in dollars enables her to obtain the advantages of Sterling Area membership" (ibid.). This became a particularly pointed issue with Malaya seeking its own dollar reserves, independent from the Sterling Area's general pool, following independence.

Over a month after Malayan independence, Britain's reserve position was still extremely precarious, leading the Chancellor, Peter Thorneycroft, to make the following statement to the Cabinet:

> We have been near to the edge of economic disaster. We are still near the edge. Over the past two months we have lost £185 millions from our gold and dollar reserves. The reserves at the end of September were down to £660 millions, only two-thirds of what they were at the end of 1954, despite the £200 millions which we drew from the International Monetary Fund (I.M.F.) last year and the £37 millions which we gained by not paying last year's interest on the American loan.
>
> (TNA CAB129/89, "The Economic Situation", 14 October 1957)

While the Chancellor cited the means of supporting the UK position as the dollars the UK had already borrowed and deflationary domestic policies, Malayan dollars at this point were as crucial as ever in propping up Britain's precarious reserve position, and discussions over Malaya's position within the Sterling Area still retained particular significance.

Following independence, the Colonial Secretary submitted to Parliament his Annual Report, detailing the events in Malaya up to 31 August 1957. His report revealed that the Emergency had declined in seriousness in 1957 as it had in the four years previously. In fact, in July 1957, it was the first month since July 1948 in which the communist insurgents had not killed anyone, there were also no reported casualties by the security forces in Malaya and there were no major incidents relating to the Emergency (TNA CO1030/627, "Federation of Malaya", 27 February 1958). The prosecution of the Emergency was considered by the Colonial Office to have been extremely successful, with around half of the whole country declared free of insurgent activity. Indeed, by 31 August 1957, the number of active terrorists had dropped from a peak of 8,000 in 1951 to around 1,830, with an estimated 10,000 terrorists killed, captured or surrendered since the Emergency was declared in

1948; and security forces had suffered around 9,000 killed, wounded and missing in the same time (ibid.).

Despite concerns over the Federation's budget, the end of 1956 saw it turn out better than expected, due to the maintenance of rubber prices (though rubber prices did fall marginally from a high in 1955) and tin prices, as well as increased receipts from import duties and expenditure being smaller than expected. An expected deficit of £5.7m became a surplus of £6m, though this certainly did nothing to calm the Federation in regard to either future revenues or the capricious nature of an economy based upon the prices of raw materials (ibid.). As such, Britain had agreed that the Federation could seek to raise loans for development on the London markets after independence. Coupled with the debate over an independent dollar reserve, and the specific terms for the creation of a Malayan Central Bank, the issue of Malaya seeking loans from the London money market became a serious issue in the relationship between Britain and Malaya in the immediate post-independence period.

Independent dollar reserves and frantic borrowing

The debate over Malaya's membership of the Sterling Area continued even after Malayan independence, despite the issue having apparently been resolved in the Constitutional Talks in early 1956 and the Financial Talks in late 1956. Certainly, there did not seem to be any specific reason for the constant generation of arguments to remain in the Sterling Area by officials in the Colonial Office, the Treasury and the Bank. A letter from the Bank to the Treasury, 11 days after Malayan independence, makes a suggestion for one further argument for Malayan Sterling Area membership: access to the London money market.[20]

> For developing countries, this is a valuable facility even though access to the market needs to be regulated because of the general shortage of capital. The Federation are hoping to raise £10mn in the London market in the next four years.
>
> (BE OV65/5, "Malaya", 10 September 1957)

In early 1958, the Malayan prime minister was already enquiring of the Bank of England whether the Federation could borrow the agreed £10m from the London market that year. Abdul Rahman sought the cash to cover the cost of the Emergency not paid for by the UK and to support the cost of development – revenues had continued to drop since both rubber and tin prices had fallen in consecutive years since 1955 (BE OV65/5, "Malaya – London Market Borrowing", 24 January 1958).

The Malayan Treasury's general reserves were £59.75m, with £13.75 in Malayan dollars and the rest in sterling.[21] However, the free reserves were estimated by the Bank to be at around £27.5m, which would be reduced to £5m by the end of 1958 due to the budget deficit, and accounted for only two weeks' worth of spending (ibid.). It was believed Malaya could find around £8.5m from local long-term borrowing to bolster its reserves but, with a budget deficit in 1959 expected to be as high as £16.25m, the Federation required further funds. As such, the Federation was seeking access to the London money market, as promised to them by the British government in 1957, for the sum of £10m.

The Bank and the Treasury were very reticent to let Malaya borrow from the London money market since they believed that Malaya had not sought US aid strongly enough, and that Malaya would find it easier to draw on her sterling balances in the near future. Crawshaw at the Overseas Finance section of the Bank was particularly vehement about Malaya seeking the full £10m in 1958.

> As to being allowed – I would hope they would not while they have such large sterling funds (whether earmarked or not). If they spend all their funds, I do not think they should be given more, since they will have put too much strain on us already. As to ability – independent Malaya would be a newcomer to the London Market and should only borrow a modest figure (say not more than £3mn) on the first approach. £10mn in this year is just not on.
>
> (Ibid.)

In a subsequent letter from the Commonwealth Relations Office to Britain's High Commissioner in the Federation, the High Commissioner was advised to avoid the question of permitting the Federation to approach the London market entirely and echoed Crawshaw's sentiments almost exactly.

> We do not therefore wish to provide Malaya with access to additional Sterling until it is absolutely essential to meet our commitment under the 1957 financial settlement which provided for the possibility that Malaya might raise £10 million in the London market over five years.
>
> (BE OV65/5, "Telegram no.133 (secret), Financial Situation", 29 January 1958)

The reasons cited for this reticence were that British officials felt Malaya was well provided for with its own reserves, it would gain access to its own sterling balances soon, it had already taxed Britain's resources somewhat in recent months and it had made no concrete overtures to the US for aid (ibid.).

The search for money to support Malaya's budget problems was in difficulty at this point.[22] Loans and credit from the US were not forthcoming and, according to the Secretary for the Federation Ministry of Finance, there was "some soreness in Kuala Lumpur at CDFC's failure to secure support in the London market and at the apparent distrust of Malaya, which is revealed" (BE OV65/6, "Malaya", 20 August 1958). In discussions with the Secretary, Leslie Rowan emphasised that simply having access to a market did not guarantee access to credit and that persuading investors was a difficult prospect. However, he suggested that Britain could offer the services of the Export Credit Guarantee Department (ECGD) but had no idea of any specifics (ibid.).[23]

Following the suggestion by the Federation that Malaya could set up its own money market, the Bank became extremely concerned, vociferously opposing the idea and prompted the Bank to have another look at the arguments for Malaya's continued membership of the Sterling Area (BE OV65/5, "Federation of Malaya", 14 April 1958; BE OV65/5, "Amendments to Henley's letter on Malaya – Sterling Area", 18 April 1958).[24] This turned out to be well timed as, two months later, Geoffrey Gould, the Principal Assistant Secretary in the Federation Treasury, approached Henry Jenkyns, a Treasury official, at the Conference of Commonwealth Officials to relay to him Colonel Lee's intention to acquire an independent dollar reserve for Malaya (BE OV65/5, "Malayan Desire to Hold Dollars", 11 June 1958). Gould said that Lee wanted the independent reserve for five reasons: other countries had them; prestige; to enable Malaya to "indulge in a spending spree unobserved"[25]; to make borrowing from the US easier; and as a hedge against a fall in the value of sterling holdings (ibid.; TNA T236/5151, "Telegram no.756, Dollar Reserve", 18 October 1958).

Jenkyns immediately told Gould that the British government certainly did not favour the holding of independent reserves by Area members since one of the reasons for Sterling Area membership was centrally held foreign currency and gold reserves, with members holding sterling as their reserve currency. Furthermore, he told Gould, the central reserves were used as much as possible to pay for dollar goods (ibid.). Gould replied that, due to Malaya's membership of the IMF,

Malaya could only accumulate US$6m before being required to use 50% of any further dollars accumulated to repurchase their own currency, a proposal in which Colonel Lee did not see any sense (however, this turned out to be a misunderstanding about IMF statutes). Jenkyns considered this a minimal sum that would not be practically problematic but still problematic in principle (ibid.).

The initial response within the Bank to Malaya's request was to accept that, given the eventual set-up of the Malayan Central Bank, some level of independent dollar reserve would have to be agreed to eventually just to cover commercial banks' dollar transactions, and especially because the Federation was still such an impressive dollar earner (BE OV65/5, "Federation of Malaya – US Dollar Transactions", 19 June 1958).[26] However, while a working balance of US dollars would be necessary, spending money on it was considered foolish by the Bank bearing in mind the budgetary constraints and balance of payments difficulties the Federation was facing at the time, especially when this was leading them to borrow heavily from abroad. Furthermore, Malaya had already started drawing on its sterling balances, which was putting strain on sterling (ibid.).

However, in response to Crawshaw's sentiment, Leslie Preston, the Principal at Dealing and Accounts Office at the Bank, disagreed that it was inevitable that the Federation would eventually develop some level of independent dollar reserves. He felt that the better option would be to permit certain money dealers in the Sterling Area the authority to cover exchange transactions instead of relying on central banks. This would manifest itself in Malaya as it had done previously, through authorised dealers in Singapore. Indeed, Preston wanted to avoid entirely the possibility of giving Malaya an independent reserve on the principle of the matter (BE OV65/5, "Federation of Malaya – US Dollar Transactions", 24 June 1958).

In a letter back to Jenkyns, Crawshaw emphasised to him that it would be difficult to deny the Federation's request for an independent dollar reserve since it was a sizeable dollar earner by its trade with the dollar area through Singapore. He felt that denying the request would ultimately lead to a number of problems.

> It will be difficult to resist such a request as the Federation is a sizeable US dollar earner as a result of its trade through Singapore. If too many difficulties are made, the Federation may be tempted to increase its own US dollar earnings by requiring exports to Singapore onsold to

the USA to be invoiced in US dollars or by trying to divert its exports to the dollar area away from Singapore.

(BE OV65/5, "Federation of Malaya – an independent
US dollar holding", 11 July 1958)

However, despite the problems arising from rejecting the request, and even if the principle of allowing Malaya to build up its own dollar reserve were conceded, Crawshaw advised Jenkyns that it would be a mistake due to Malaya's current budget difficulties. Furthermore, the argument based on its necessity for central bank transactions did not stand up, as the Bank's powers of issue were to be in abeyance for some time (ibid.). The fact that it was a sum of only US$6m was also misleading, since the Federation would not have been required to make purchases of its own currency out of reserves greater than US$6m, as those obligations were not applied to reserves below the country's IMF quota, which was US$25m. So, the obligation to purchase Malayan dollars would only have arisen if reserves in gold and dollars rose above US$25m (ibid.).

In a statement to the press on 17 October 1958, Colonel Lee made clear the deficiency he felt Malaya had.

Every Commonwealth country in the sterling bloc has a dollar account in the United States. Malaya became an independent country only recently and it has therefore not got an account in the United States.

(TNA T236/5151, "Telegram no.756, Dollar
Reserve", 18 October 1958)

Compounded by the fact that Malaya had to inform the Bank of England in order to spend dollars or gold due to a lack of a dollar account, and that it would be a matter of convenience and not affect Malaya's dollar spending, Colonel Lee felt it was entirely reasonable for Malaya to have independent dollar reserves. He also cited Malaya's huge contribution to the Sterling Area dollar pool, providing around US$300m net each year (ibid.).

The Central Bank of Malaya was established on 24 October 1958 and Colonel Lee gave a speech to mark the event in which he described the purpose for setting up the Central Bank. While the Central Bank's operations would be initially modest with a maximum of M$60m from government deposits and M$20m from commercial banks' deposits, Lee felt that the Central Bank would encourage Malayans in all walks of life to make use of the banks in Malaya and so contribute to the funds available for investment in Malaya (BE OV65/6, "Federation of Malaya", 15 January 1959).

> One of the Federation's greatest needs was to obtain sufficient capital to finance our development and...we could not afford to spend at the rate required unless funds were forthcoming from domestic savings or overseas borrowings. We cannot depend on getting outside financial help whenever we want it and, in any event, there must be some limit to the amount we may prudently borrow overseas, therefore we must do all we can to encourage the savings habit in our people.
>
> (BE OV65/6, "Banking Bill", 1 December 1958)

Colonel Lee then saw the Central Bank, at this time, as a means of expanding the money supply and providing great deal of credit to sustain Malaya's spending, which had been extremely difficult to come by over the past year.

> A realm of opportunity is opening before the Federation's banks as our development plans get under way – opportunities for expanded and more diversified business and greater branch representation as hitherto untapped or under-developed resources all over the country are converted into real wealth.
>
> (Ibid.)

The legislation that established the Central Bank also provided licensing laws for banks to operate in the Federation. The purpose was, ostensibly, to ensure that the Federation had oversight on the viability and integrity of the bank in question; however, the true purpose was to ensure that the Federation government could legally ban the Bank of China from operating in its territory (ibid.).[27]

> The Government has reviewed the role of foreign banks in the Federation as an independent country and has decided, as a matter of policy, that no bank which in its opinion is under the effective control of the Government of another country should be permitted to operate in the Federation. The Government feels strongly that with the financial resources of their governments behind them such banks, if permitted to operate here, could as they expand their

activities, exercise an undue influence on the financial and overseas trading affairs of the Federation and in this way may constitute a threat to the economic and, indeed, the political independence of the country.

Therefore, for a banking licence to be granted, the foreign bank had to have the majority of its capital not owned by a foreign government, and a majority of its board could not be appointed by a government or some agency acting on its behalf (ibid.). While Malaya grew into its formal independence, this did not change the fundamental dynamic of the relationship. The dollar reserve sought by the Federation was limited and did not constitute a break with the mechanisms of the Sterling Area for dollar pooling; furthermore, Malaya still sought substantial development through the Sterling Area and from the UK.

At this point in the chronology of events, one particular moment is seen by both Krozewski (2001) and Hinds (2001) as the final cleavage between Britain and its Empire: the move to *de jure* convertibility in December 1958. Prior to and after this event, we would have seen a change in the relationship between Britain and Malaya. However, on the contrary, what we see is a clear maintenance of this relationship and continuity from the post-war problems to 1960. Immediately prior to this point, not only do we see British concern about the possibility of a Malayan independent reserve, but also repeated emphasis about how important Malaya remains to the Sterling Area and to the British economy. Moreover, after 1959, we see a further intensification of British development aid to Malaya through a number of channels to avoid the everyday problems that arose from fluctuations in the rubber and tin markets.

The search for capital

At the beginning of 1959, both the Bank and the Commonwealth Relations Office drafted reports on the state of the Federation's political and economic development, and prospects for the future. The Bank was highly optimistic about the prospects for Malaya, having done better than the Bank hoped or expected (BE OV65/6, "Federation of Malaya", 15 January 1959). The Bank expressed some concern that the three main political parties were effectively "racial protection societies rather than political parties", and the Government, the Alliance Party, comprised the right-wing elements from each of the parties (ibid.).[28]

The High Commissioner in the Federation, George William Tory, submitted a report on Federation's economy to the Commonwealth Relations Secretary, Alexander Douglas-Home. He argued:

> The day-to-say fortunes of the Federation reflect the day-to-day fortunes of the rubber and tin markets. Even at yearly intervals, changes of fortune can be explained almost entirely in terms of market forces originating outside the Federation itself; one need not look far beyond the figures of output and prices for rubber and for tin.
>
> (BE OV65/6, "Federation of Malaya: The Economy", 23 June 1959)

Certainly, this was apparent in statistics of the Malayan economy, and therefore had a massive effect on Malaya's finances and its development budget. In 1953, Malayan GDP had fallen to M$3,883m from M$4,153 in 1952 and M$5,000m in 1951, where the price of rubber had been 50.84 p/lb in 1951, 28.34p/lb in 1952 and only 19.91p/lb in 1953 (ibid.; Lim 1967:317,323).[29] Malaya's economy had been particularly vulnerable to the violent fluctuations in the price of raw materials during the Korean War, though it was still the case that Malaya's economy was susceptible to these price movements. In 1957, GDP stood at M$4,852m while the price of rubber was at 26.09p/lb, in 1958 GDP was M$4,700 and rubber at 23.5p/lb and 1959 saw GDP grow to M$5,411 and the price of rubber also jump to 30.05p/lb (ibid.).

The yield from the rubber crop represented a quarter of national income. Malayan rubber production was growing steadily by 1959, having stood at 638,000 tons in 1957, 663,000 in 1958 and 698,000 in 1959 (Lim 1967:329). The Federation then expected to produce around 850,000 tons of rubber by 1965 but predicted that national income would actually be lower than in previous years due to competition from synthetic rubber forcing the price of rubber down (BE OV65/6, "Federation of Malaya: The Economy", 23 June 1959); furthermore, there was little optimism for the expansion of other sectors of the economy in the meantime (ibid.). Improving productivity and efficiency was unlikely to contribute a great deal to the economy either, as this required significant development aid.[30] [31] As such, the High Commissioner was pessimistic about the prospects for the Malayan economy over the next few years.

> It seems difficult to resist the theoretical conclusion that the existing standard of living is unlikely to be maintained over the next few years, and that in all probability it will decline. The chances

of an improvement seem extremely remote unless unforeseen extra-neous factors, such as the outbreak of a limited war of the Korean pattern, force up the prices of rubber and tin to inflationary levels, and given the threat from synthetic rubber, any prosperity based on high prices for the natural product must be something of a fool's paradise.

(Ibid.)

The "everyday" effects to this economic problem were likely to have a significant political impact too. Most rural Malays worked at a subsis-tence level on small rubber plantations and so were greatly affected by rubber prices. George Tory warned that, if the government was unable to change this basic problem, subsistence workers in the Federation would continue to be susceptible to "politicians who promise them something better" (ibid.).

Given the difficult situation that the Federation felt itself in by 1959, it came as no surprise that a *Financial Times* article, entitled "Does £ Area Club Mean Much Now?", reopened debates about the merits of staying in the Sterling Area. W.H. Wilcock, Governor of the Malayan Central Bank, wrote to Eric Haslam to inform him that Malayan politicians had once again begun discussing the value of remaining in the Sterling Area, and requested a document be drawn up by the Bank of England to detail the benefits of Sterling Area membership (BE OV65/6, WH Wilcock to Eric P Haslam, 13 June 1959).

Haslam responded by criticising the *Financial Times* article for present-ing the Sterling Area as a "one size fits all" institution when this was not the case (BE OV65/6, Haslam to Wilcock, 9 July 1959). There were no universally applicable advantages to Sterling Area membership, and it was still a very important component of the global economy.

> The Sterling Area is constantly changing in its scope and character, in response to changing circumstances, but it embraces a mechanism which the world – and particularly the members of the Common-wealth – cannot do without if international trade is to expand and flourish.
>
> (BE OV65/6, E. P. Haslam to W.H. Wilcock, 23 June 1959)

The only element of the Area that could be described as truly univer-sal was that it was "a voluntary association of countries who have a strong mutual interest in maintaining sterling as an international cur-rency and are prepared to shape their monetary and foreign exchange policies accordingly" (ibid.). Indeed, what is quite telling is that this was the official British mindset and how imperial relations and the Sterling Area were understood by the Bank: as a mechanism which managed a complex set of bilateral relations that had historically developed and could not be understood, in fact, as a unitary institution. Moreover, we see yet again Bank officials reiterate the continuity in the Britain–Malaya relationship even as late as 1959. With Malaya, this was certainly advantageous, he argued, as its fortunes were so closely tied to the Sterling Area that the establishing of exchange controls between Malaya and the rest of the Area would severely weaken Malaya's economy. The absence of those barriers stimulated commercial and financial transactions, as well as inspired confidence in the Malayan economy (ibid.).[32] While exchange controls were likely to be relaxed in the next few years given the growing sense of independence the Federation had, not only from Britain but also from Singapore, Haslam argued that the Federation would remain in the Sterling Area and trade in sterling, since it was the currency in which most world trade was still conducted – and the vast majority of Malaya's own trade (ibid.).

A meeting on 9 September 1959, between the Chancellor, Heathcoat-Amory, and Colonel Lee took place to discuss Malayan development and the establishing of the independent Malayan dollar reserve.[33] Colonel Lee began by referring to the previous offer by Leslie Rowan to take up ECGD credits to provide some support to the Federation's trade; he had noted its success in India and felt that a similar scheme would help with the Federation's short-term financial difficulties (TNA T236/5151, "Note of a Meeting in the Chancellor's Room", 9 September 1959). Lee went on to make two further points. First, with the negotiations concerning Britain's level of support for Emergency operations coming up, he wished to let the British government know that the Federation was seeking significant assistance from the British. Second, he raised the issue of Malaya's independent dollar reserves and stated the new figure of a reserve of US$25m (ibid.).[34]

The Chancellor responded by saying that, although he was sympathetic to Malaya's desire to hold dollar reserves, it was the practice of the Sterling Area to concentrate their reserves in sterling, with gold and convertible currency reserves pooled centrally in London. This was essential to the Sterling Area system, he maintained, and it was this, as much as anything else, which allowed the UK to keep capital moving freely to and in the Sterling Area (ibid.). As such, if Sterling Area members sought to hold substantial reserves in currencies other than sterling, this would undermine the Sterling Area, and therefore Heathcoat-Amory asked Colonel Lee to "keep the Malayan independent reserve to modest proportions" (ibid.).

Colonel Lee said he was seeking a separation of the Exchange Control and import licensing machinery (and therefore the statistics relating to them) from Singapore; this would allow the Federation freedom from the "financial nexus" tying it to Singapore, which he saw as problematic if there were a change of government in Singapore. This separation would also highlight "that Malaya was a significant earner of dollars for the central sterling area reserves" (ibid.) and therefore justify the Federation's request for an independent dollar reserve.[35] The Chancellor accepted the difficulties facing Malaya but stressed that the size of net dollar contributions was not a factor in the decision to grant a reserve:

> Insofar as a particular Commonwealth country's balance of payments position with the non-sterling world formed a basis for our policy, we would be interested in its position viz a viz the whole non-sterling world and not with the dollar area only.
>
> (Ibid.)

This seemed particularly curious, as the basis for British policy towards Malaya had rested mainly on the fact of Malaya's trade surplus with the dollar area. Therefore it seems reasonable to conclude that the Chancellor's response to Colonel Lee was intended to distract from that particular avenue of argument due to its high likelihood of success.

Lee's agenda was stark in that he was entirely focused on finding as much money as possible for Malayan development, since the Malayan economy was still prone to fluctuations due to its reliance on tin and rubber prices. He not only brought up the issue of borrowing from the London money market this year, which the Chancellor rejected as, he claimed, conditions were currently neither favourable for Commonwealth financing nor in Malaya's interest to seek a loan from London (though the base rate was at 4% then, its lowest rate since early 1955), he also suggested to the Chancellor that a Commonwealth Bank be set up to entice capital investment from outside of the Sterling Area (ibid.).[36] Lee also urged that sterling Convertibility occur as soon as possible, to which the Chancellor replied that it was the aim of the British government to move towards Convertibility but he would not make any commitments unless it was certain they could be carried out (ibid.).

In a subsequent meeting between the Governor of the Malayan Central Bank and officials from the Treasury and Bank of England, the Malayan figure for the size of independent reserves was set at US$25m.[37]

Wilcock, the Governor, implied that this was by far the most conservative figure that had been discussed in the Federation government, and would be accumulated over two years (TNA T236/5151, "Malaya", 24 September 1959). It was made clear to Wilcock that the desire to hold these dollar securities was a "serious difficulty of principle" for the British government. Wilcock assured the Treasury and the Bank that there was no desire to diversify currency backing at this stage. The desire for independent reserves was because:

> The Government was accumulating surplus funds as a result of the high price of rubber and there was some lag in development spending. He had recommended to Ministers that they should not disturb their existing holdings of UK Government stocks, but should build up dollar holdings from their accumulating budgetary reserve.
>
> (Ibid.)

Wilcock also suggested that if the British government were totally intransigent about Malaya's dollar reserve, the Federation would likely concede the issue (ibid.).

The Federation, according to a memo by the Central Bank's Board, still sought to establish a money market and a stock exchange in Malaya as a means of redirecting the Federation's well-organised banking system's short-term investment towards Malaya itself; however, the development of a money market was limited until the Central Bank became a bank of issue and a lender of last resort (BE OV65/6, "The Establishment of a Money Market and Stock Exchange in the Federation of Malaya", 28 October 1959).

In late November, the House of Representatives in the Federation passed legislation permitting the Federation to invest up to M$75m (equivalent to US$25m) in securities guaranteed by foreign governments or international financial institutions. Tan Siew Sin introduced the bill by saying "this would not only allow the Government a more flexible investment policy, but would enable the Government to take any favourable opportunities for sound investment which might arise" (TNA T236/5151, "Malayan Holdings of US Dollars", 27 November 1959).[38] It seemed, to both the Bank and the Treasury, that the Wilcock/Tan Siew Sin plan explained to them in September was being implemented (ibid.). This did cause some concern within both the Treasury and the Bank that Britain was, in a sense, required to be on best behaviour with the Federation now, since if Britain somehow upset the Federation, the latter might decide to press ahead more quickly to the

US$25m figure, or increase it. Though, at the time, the dangers of the Federation rushing to achieve this accumulation of dollar reserves was unlikely since they had much less incentive to speculate against sterling than they had only a couple of years previously due to its much improved position (TNA T236/5151, "Malayan Holdings of US Dollars", 1 December 1959).

In late February, the Deputy Governor informed the Treasury that the Federation had made its first purchase of dollars from the Bank of England, the sum of US$4.5m using sterling funds held for the Federation government, which was executed without question since it was accepted that the Malayan Central Bank had "the right to draw on the reserves by virtue of its position as a Sterling Area Central Bank" (BE OV65/6, "Federation of Malaya: Independent Dollar Reserves", 21 March 1960). Since the Federation's total sterling assets were £287m and the quantity of dollars the Federation was purchasing was very small, the Bank and Treasury were happy that they were spreading out their purchases as promised (TNA T236/5151, "Unknown to Taylor and Mackay", 25 February 1960; TNA T236/5151, "Malayan Dollar Purchases", 1 March 1960).[39] However, the Bank was still concerned that, as there was no specific agreement between the British and Federation governments about the Malayan dollar reserve (only a verbal agreement between the Treasury and the finance minister), the Federation could pass fresh legislation at any time to exceed the M$75m limit though they were happy that it had some basis in law (BE OV65/6, "EBF" to Hogg, 10 March 1960). As such, the Bank hoped for some consultation between governments but there was no reason to assume that was going to be the case.

Tan Siew Sin was due to arrive in Britain as part of an official visit at the end of 1960. In a background note, prepared by the Bank for his visit, the Bank described the situation in the Federation as "buoyant" due to high rubber prices (now at 32.16p/lb) and increasing volumes of tin exports, which meant GDP for 1960 stood at M$5,921m (BE OV65/6, "Federation of Malaya", 12 September 1960; Lim 1967:317, 329). The Federation's official sterling balances stood at £129m, having grown from £100m in 1959 and £65m in 1958, and the Federation had also acquired US$5.5m of its independent dollar reserve by September 1960 (BE OV65/6, "Federation of Malaya", 12 September 1960). The Federation's budget was to see a surplus in 1960 due to the higher rubber prices, which permitted it to pay back a loan to Singapore of £3.5m that was taken out in 1953 to pay for the cost of the Emergency (which had also been declared as at an end on 12 July 1960) (ibid.).

While the development programme of 1956–1960 was curtailed due to financial austerity, external finance had come from the IBRD, the Development Loan Fund (DLF) and the Brunei government. The CDFC lent £0.25m towards a hydroelectric scheme in the Cameron Highlands, the ECGD signed a £2.25m credit for telecommunication equipment and the British government had also provided Commonwealth Development and Welfare (CD&W) allocations and grants towards the Emergency (BE OV65/6, Henley to C.C. Lucas, 25 October 1958; BE OV65/6, "Federation of Malaya", 12 September 1960). The background note makes mention of the offer made by the British government for the Federation to borrow £10m from the London money market; however, it claims that this offer was not picked up on despite repeated requests by Federation ministers for the money, which were consistently rejected by British officials and never actually used (BE OV65/6, "Federation of Malaya", 12 September 1960).

The IBRD and the Federation government were, by that time, drafting a new development plan for 1961–1965, which was expected to have a budget of M$1,500–2,000m – double the budget of the previous plan – and would be found largely internally with the help of the Malayan Central Bank (ibid.). The Central Bank had been gradually assuming its new role in Malaya, though individual banks themselves still responded to the London base rate (e.g. in June 1959, 5–6%, though they did not in January 1960). A new currency agreement between the Federation, Singapore and Borneo Territories was agreed in February 1960, which afforded a number of major changes to Malaya's monetary policy: it removed the supervisory powers of oversight of the Colonial Secretary; provided an increase in Federation representation on the Currency Board; and broadened the permitted field of investment for currency funds to include dollar securities (though the Federation was not using these to purchase its dollar reserve) (ibid.). The background note concludes on the point that the Federation and Singapore had begun negotiations for a customs union, which would ultimately pave the way for unification (as Malaysia) when Singapore declared independence in 1963 though this would ultimately prove to be short-lived (ibid.).

Conclusion

This chapter has looked at four major events in the relationship between Britain and Malaya: the renewal of Exchange Control Ordinances; Constitutional Talks concerning independence; Financial Talks concerning independence; and the Malayan demand for an independent dollar reserve. Each of these events has also featured, to some degree, Malaya's struggle to find large amounts of development capital.

Each event has brought into focus Malaya's relationship with Britain, both before and after formal independence. As such, the chapter concludes that the fundamental relationship between Britain and Malaya does not substantially change following formal independence, as the relationship is still ultimately governed by the logic and nature of the Sterling Area mechanism as a means of managing Malayan economic and monetary policy to benefit Britain. Malaya remains important to the Sterling Area throughout this period, a fact cited by officials in the Bank, Treasury and Colonial Office, due to its large dollar-earning capacity and the continued inability of the Sterling Area and Britain to balance trade with the dollar area, which is revealed by state managers and also through the meagre size of Britain's currency reserves.

Even after independence, when the formal vestiges of empire were removed, Malaya's relationship with Britain is still managed by these same factors and they continue to dominate the relationship. Britain identified in Malaya a prime support for the Sterling Area, which was itself a key component for the maintenance of sterling as an international currency and for Britain's economic vitality. As such then, Malaya continued to play a vital role in Britain's international economic policy. Without Malaya, more stringent import restrictions on dollar area goods and further emergency measures, which would have required a significant change in the quality of life for citizens of Sterling Area countries, would have been necessary and these would have seriously retarded Britain's economic recovery, as well as the recovery of global trade which was vital to Britain's economy.

The various arguments brought up by officials in the Bank, Treasury, Colonial and Commonwealth Relations Offices in this period concerning Malaya's role and membership of the Sterling Area are convincing. They reveal, explicitly, Malaya's continued importance to the Sterling Area, British economic policy and the nature of the relationship between Britain and Malaya. While Britain certainly used Malaya to its own advantage, Malaya too benefitted from this relationship. The historical development of trade within the Sterling Area had seen Malaya hold a deficit with the UK and a surplus with the US (the very basis by which she was so valuable to the UK as a dollar earner), which meant that exiting from the Sterling Area would have been too costly to reasonably consider. This was recognised by Malayan state officials both prior to and after formal independence from Britain and ensured that they would continue to support Sterling Area membership due to the advantages it brought the Malayan economy. Hence, the imperial relationship between Britain and Malaya is characterised by constraints and opportunities. Britain could not mercilessly abuse Malaya since development was essential to its continued value and, indeed, Malaya did continue to be valuable to Britain due to its persistent trade imbalance with the US. Nor could Malaya simply extract itself from the imperial relationship since its economy depended upon the continuity of this relationship.

This period particularly has been seen in terms of discontinuity.[40] However, in close examination of documents in both Bank and National Archives, we see a very strong continuity in the relationship between Britain and Malaya. The same reasons prevail in this period that prevailed prior to, and throughout this period. Moments one would think of as intuitive caesuras – Schenk's *de facto* convertibility, Hinds and Krozewski's *de jure* convertibility and the numerous phases postulated by the scholars of British imperial history and decolonization – simply do not bear fruit in terms of how state managers, both British and Malayan, view the relationship between the two states.

Analysis of British imperialism has been quite limited due to its scope: broad and monolithic, with little account taken of the specific relationships that actually constituted the Empire. There is also a sense of formal Empire that ends with independence – in particular, Krozewski (2001:213) attributes any idea of post-independence continuity to sympathetic elites in the periphery, which is itself empirically problematic when considered in light of the Saul Marshall controversy; however, Malaya remains in the Sterling Area, a mechanism designed to support sterling and the British economy, not simply due to a pro-British elite, but due to the historically developed relationship with Britain. As such, when we look at the historical record, and we critically assess what we mean by the British Empire, informed by an open Marxist understanding of imperialism that situates the strategy in terms of the nature of the capitalist state and social relations, we see that there is not one history of the British Empire but actually a series of particular relationships between Britain and other states that are historically, politically, economically and geographically conditioned.

Concluding Remarks

While the study of imperialism has been dominated by the question of historical periodisation, across a number of disciplines, a central theme of this book has been the importance of critical theoretical and historical enquiry into imperialism itself. The first chapter of this book established a theory of imperialism that avoided key problems in the scholarship on both British imperial economic relations, and on imperialism as a broader phenomenon.

The prevailing ideas of British post-war imperial relations are discontinuity, decolonisation and decline. These ideas stem fundamentally from an understanding of the British Empire as a monolithic institution and this is manifest in the extant literature on the topic, which sees British imperial relations analysed as a whole and in aggregate. Not only has this been shown as conceptually problematic, but the book has also shown that British state managers themselves did not consider it in this way. This is particularly important given that it is British state managers, under historically developed conditions, who determine governing strategy. As such, the relationship between Britain and Malaya can only be meaningfully understood in terms of the broader goals of British state managers within the global economy.

By criticising this way of thinking and analysing British imperial relations from an open Marxist perspective, as a strategy undertaken by states and manifest as a relation between states, we can see an alternative history of British imperial relations with Malaya. Furthermore, this history of the British–Malaya relationship is more intelligible as a steady and continuous relationship, rather than one characterised by discontinuity and disjuncture.

The enduring value of the open Marxist understanding of imperialism derives from its coherent account of the state and crisis situated in the exploitative and contradictory nature of global capitalist social relations. This has specific and particular value through understanding the role Malaya played in Britain's strategy to mitigate the precarious situation facing the global economy after the Second World War. In understanding imperialism as a strategy manifest as a relationship between states, not only are we obliged to study the individual relationships of the Empire but, when we do, we find them unique and divergent from the history of the rest of the Empire: dynamic, characterised by nuance, and embedded in the nature and historical development of capitalist social relations and the capitalist inter-state system.

However, it is quite easy to understand why the general consensus in the literature is discontinuity. Chapter 3 provided an account of the immediate post-war period, when the whole of Britain's imperial dominion was marshalled, with the acute nature of the post-war crisis actually bringing a sense of homogeneity to the British Empire. Archival research for this period reveals a great number of communiqués directed "to all colonies", even in files dedicated specifically to Malaya and Singapore, which themselves are rarely referred to directly during this five-year period. What is particularly curious is that the "to all colonies" communication is rarely found subsequent or prior to this period. However, as with the myth of Cacus, appearances are often deceiving.

Discontinuity is not revealed by a close analysis of the documentation from Bank and National Archives concerning British–Malayan relations. On the contrary, not only do we see a strong continuity, but also the moments at which one might intuit natural caesuras in the relationship do not provide them. Krozewski (2001) and Hinds (2001) both argue that 1953 and 1958 see profound disruption in British imperial economic relations; however, the Archives reveal that this description of Britain's broader relationship with its aggregated empire provides little relevance to its relationship with Malaya specifically. Malaya's importance to, and handling by, Britain after both of these moments remains consonant with and identical to the previously existing relationship. Furthermore, the phases of Empire as argued by Holland (1984; 1985), Kaplan (1990) and Darwin (1988; 2006) and manifest in the work of others, including both Krozewski (2001) and Hinds (2001), also find little purchase when considering the relationship between Britain and Malaya in isolation. White (2010), while identifying the Sterling Area as an element of continuity within Malayan international economic history, fails to understand this relationship in terms of British governing strategy. As such then, while White identifies one aspect of continuity, its significance as an imperial relationship is lost.

The implications that derive from this observation of British–Malayan relations are that the history of the British Empire and the Sterling Area is not that of monolithic institutions but a complicated and nuanced history of the complex set of relations that comprise and manifest as these institutions. As such, we can only truly understand the history of the British Empire by developing an alternative history of it: a history of the relationships between the states of which it was comprised and not the reified institution that it is understood to be.

British imperialism and Malaya

Throughout the period 1945–1960, Britain used its dominion over the Malayan state, both before and after independence, to improve conditions for capital accumulation in Britain itself. In a time of domestic consensus politics, Britain had adopted an economic strategy by which economic strain was placed principally on the UK's foreign currency and gold reserves. Britain's commitment to keeping the base rate of interest low also meant that foreign funds were unlikely to accumulate in the UK and therefore reserves would remain low, British banks would lend elsewhere (where they could), but the money supply in the UK itself (of sterling) would remain relatively flexible. This developed from a commitment to an interventionist domestic economic policy, allowing the government and the market to borrow cheaply, but had a constrictive effect on external economic policy upon which the stresses and strains of domestic policy were concentrated.

The UK held that the Sterling Area was a vital and necessary component of the international trading system and its own economic policy and, therefore, required maintenance. The source of the UK's benefit from this relationship lay in Malaya's trade surplus with the US, which provided it with large amounts of US dollars. Due to the mechanism of the Sterling Area, these dollars were pooled centrally in Britain's own reserves and rationed out to those with the most need. These dollars were not used solely to support Britain's own imports from the US but as a means of maintaining the Sterling Area, itself the principal prop to Britain's economic recovery and growth, and the means through which sterling was maintained as an international currency. It is also worth considering the role of the Sterling Area as an imperialist institution, an imperial management tool for the British state.

Britain, in this manner, acted to resolve a global economic crisis manifest as a dollar shortage through the actions of state managers to solve Britain's own economic problems. The ultimate goal of British state managers was to improve Britain's economic performance. With the relative failure of both the European Recovery Program (ERP) and the Anglo-American Financial Agreement (AAFA), the only sustainable way of achieving this was to increase the global supply of dollars through increasing exports to the US. Malaya's role then, as the largest single supplier of dollars in the Sterling Area, was to provide a stopgap measure to the broader problem, and this permitted greater quantities of US goods into the Sterling Area, which were necessary for reconstruction and the maintenance of the UK reserve position. Even after 1955, the dollar situation was still serious. The balance of trade with the US was still in deficit for Britain, and the reserve position was still weak. As such, Malaya's role within the Sterling Area remained fundamentally the same, as Britain still gained great benefit from its dollar earnings and Malaya still found advantage to remaining in the Sterling Area.

Malaya did not immediately wish to divest itself of the Sterling Area upon independence in 1957, but used its importance to the Sterling Area (and thus Britain) as a means of securing more generous terms both financially and economically. Even when the British state was effectively blackmailed by the Singaporean First Minister to grant independence earlier, the bluff was called as Malaya refused to back this strategy since it would have done great harm to both Malaya and Singapore had Saul Marshall actually carried through his threat. However generous the terms might have been, Malaya was entirely dependent on the Sterling Area for trade and economic development. This dependence was historically developed and was to the advantage of Britain and Malaya, and pointed out repeatedly to the Malayan governments. Malaya was, on independence, bought cheaply at twice the price.

This book has also maintained that Britain did not mercilessly exploit Malaya – that it was not a one-way relationship with the sequestration of Malayan dollars and capital away from the colony to Britain. While Britain dominated Malaya, and used the colony as a means of supporting its own economic and monetary strategy, which was ultimately to the benefit of the UK, this ultimately depended on Malayan social stability, economic vitality and development. Malaya benefited from this relationship through British commitment to suppress the insurgency, along with material and financial support in reconstructing and improving the rubber and tin industries, as well as provisions being made for investment into the Malayan economy. Furthermore, Malaya itself could not simply "opt out" of this relationship, even if it were deemed an exploitative one, as Malaya had historically developed a deficit with the Sterling Area along with its surplus with the dollar area. It had become, in effect, economically integrated into the UK's trading bloc, which provided not only the disadvantages of dollar sequestration and import control by the British government but came hand-in-hand with the advantages of using sterling as an international trading and reserve currency, access to a large international market and an inherent interest by the UK in ensuring that Malaya's economy was both stable and growing. Indeed, the prevailing view of state managers in the Archives is not of British villainy seeking to exploit the Malayan, but is entirely concerned with the daily business of running a state. British imperial strategy was, in effect, to support domestic economic strategy through the manipulation and development of foreign states and markets, of which Malaya was a particularly important example.

As Burnham (2003:185) notes, the origins of the crises of the late1960s and the 1970s lie in Britain's response to the post-war economic crisis, which was itself a result of the state's response to the crisis of the interwar years and Britain's relative economic decline at the end of the 19th Century. The devaluation of 1967 ultimately led Britain to unilaterally withdraw from, and thus cause the total collapse of, the Sterling Area. However, certainly up to 1960, we find the mechanisms of the Sterling Area still in use with regard to the particular relationship Britain held with Malaya, which continued to pool its dollars in the Sterling Area's reserve.

Imperialism and accumulation

As Simon Clarke (1994) has pointed out, the fundamental contradiction upon which capitalism is based is that between the production of use-value and exchange-value, and the supremacy of the latter over the former. The global overproduction crisis that characterises the early to mid-20th century stems directly from this contradiction. From this contradiction, capital seeks ever greater means of increasing productivity from which to capture additional surplus value, leading to competition between capitals. Those capitals that are successful and outcompete their rivals remain in the market, while the circuits of their rivals are destroyed. This process leads to productive capitals producing ever more use-values beyond the consumptive powers of the marketplace, beyond the capacity of society to actually purchase these commodities at a profit. Without an outlet for this commodity form of capital, without their purchase, there exists a glut of commodities – they have been overproduced, hence an overproduction crisis. This is the exact nature of the crisis between Eastern and Western hemispheres during this period –

capital in the US had, much earlier than the Second World War, become the most competitive capital in the world and was substantially out-producing the productive capital in other territories, becoming a prolific and speedy supplier of essential goods domestically and internation-ally. Due to the creation of monetary and trading blocs in the inter-war period, this overproduction crisis presented itself as, *prima facie*, a cur-rency shortage. The creation of trade blocs in the inter-war period was intended to safeguard the capitals of national states from foreign com-petition; however, due to the global nature of capitalism, this merely provided a stopgap measure and, ultimately, the overproduction crisis presented itself yet again albeit in a different form, as a dollar shortage, which persisted into the early 1960s (Burnham 2003:175).

The role of the state in regulating the circuit of capital, both domesti-cally and internationally, is vital to the reproduction of capitalist social relations. The national state acts as a "processing node", essential to the maintenance of global capitalist relations. The action of the national state is essential for the maintenance of international economic vital-ity. It achieves this through avoiding or resolving the periodic crises that beset capitalism and act as "blockages" to the circuit of capital, taking a variety of forms. The state acts to resolve these crises through actions both domestic and international. One such strategy is imperial-ism. Imperialism is not to be understood as some fantastical activity pursued by a specific type of state but a potential activity available to all states, depending on historical contingency. It is this historical contingency that needs to be explored and analysed in order to fully understand imperialism. This thesis has attempted to understand the particular historical relationship between Britain and Malaya during a period of acute political economic strain, in order to understand how imperialism has manifested and been conditioned by the historical, economic and geographical contours of this specific relationship.

The potential for imperialism is, in effect, an aspect of the state that cannot be separated from its nature as a capitalist state. Furthermore, the implementation of an imperialist strategy reveals the nature of the international state system and how it is characterised by global capitalist social relations. The value of an open Marxist approach is that it seeks to offer a totality of social relations: imperialism, crisis and the state-form all spring fundamentally from the same contradiction and the same set of social relations. They are all fundamentally capitalist in nature.

The global movement of capital is highly revealing and illustrates the nature of the problem. The highly productive US was booming, though ultimately in just as much trouble as the rest of the world if the trade imbalance continued. While various remedies were attempted, they did not prove successful in the long term and acted merely as a palliative to the fundamental problem, which actually required the reconstruction of the British economy to the extent that its exports were capable of competing with US goods both internationally and in the dollar area. With US dollars being increasingly concentrated in the dollar area, US trade was effectively dwindling and ultimately would have realised itself in a major world crisis even worse than the one with which British state managers grappled in the post-war period. As it is, the various attempts to improve European and Eastern trade with the US succeeded, with Malaya being one element of that struggle.

The final hope of this book is that imperialism, as a phenomenon of the society in which we all live, should be further studied and understood in that context. This book has, deliberately, focused on one small aspect of one small moment of British imperial relations; however, imperialism itself persists in altered forms that appear simply as globalisation, or the actions of international institutions, or as an international campaign against terrorism. This book started by highlighting the importance of history and theory through invoking the myth of Cacus, and it will end on the same note. It is only by discovering the origins of imperialism, in terms of its historical development and the social conditions from which it springs, that it can be truly understood as a persistent and constant element of global society.

Appendices

Dramatis personae

These details have been gathered from a number of sources, including National Archive and Bank documents, as well as Burnham (2003), Fforde (1992) and White (1996). They are not exhaustive of every character mentioned in the thesis but are intended to provide a reference for the most frequently cited names.

Sir Robert Black
Governor, Singapore (1955–1957)
George Bolton
Executive Director of the Bank of England (1948–1957)
Henry Bourdillon
Assistant Secretary, Colonial Office (1947–1954)
Assistant Under-Secretary, Colonial Office (1954–1959)
Deputy UK Commissioner for Singapore (1959–1961)
Sir Edward Bridges
Cabinet Secretary (1938–1946)
Permanent Secretary to Treasury (1946–1956)
Harold Briggs
Director of Operations, Federation of Malaya (1950–1951)
R.A. 'Rab' Butler
Chancellor of the Exchequer (1951–1955)
Sydney Caine
Deputy Under-Secretary of State, Colonial Office (1947–1948)
Third Secretary to UK Treasury (1948)
Head of UK Treasury and Supply Delegation to Washington (1949–1951)
Thomas Catto
Governor, Bank of England (1944–1949)
Allen Christelow
Under-Secretary, UK Treasury and Supply Delegation to Washington
R.W.B. 'Otto' Clarke
Under-Secretary, Overseas Finance Division (1947–1953)
Cameron Cobbold
Deputy Governor, Bank of England (1945–1949)
Governor, Bank of England (1949–1961)
Sir William Cockburn
Chief General Manager, Chartered Bank of India, Australia and China (1940–1955)
Arthur Creech-Jones
Secretary of State for the Colonies (1946–1950)
Sir Stafford Cripps
Chancellor of the Exchequer (1947–1950)

Hugh Dalton
Chancellor of the Exchequer (1945–1947)
Alexander Douglas-Home
Secretary of State for Commonwealth Relations (1955–1960)
Chin Feng
Secretary-General of Malayan Communist Party (1947–1955)
John Fisher
Deputy Chief Cashier, Bank of England (1950–1959)
Oliver Franks
British Ambassador, US (1948–1952)
Andrew Gilmour
Financial Secretary, Singapore (1946–1949)
Seconded for Special Duties, High Commissioner's Office, Federation of Malaya
   (1949–1951)
Secretary for Economic Affairs, Singapore (1951–1953)
Sir Franklin Gimson
Governor, Singapore (1946–1952)
William Gorell-Barnes
Personal Assistant to Prime Minister (1946–1948)
Assistant Under-Secretary, Colonial Office (1948–1960)
Jim Griffiths
Secretary of State for the Colonies (1950–1951)
Sir Henry Gurney
High Commissioner, Federation of Malaya (1948–1951)
George Hall
Secretary of State for the Colonies (1945–1946)
Robert Hall
Director of the Economic Section, Cabinet Office (1947–1953)
Economic Advisor to UK Treasury (1953–1961)
Sir John Hay
General Manager, Guthries (1930–1963)
UK and Colonial Delegations to International Rubber Conferences (1946–1957)
Derick Heathcoat-Amory
Chancellor of the Exchequer (1958–1960)
Sir Thomas Ingram Lloyd
Permanent Under-Secretary, Colonial Office (1947–1956)
W. John Kenney
Chief of Mission, European Cooperation Administration (1948–1950)
Chief of Operations, European Recovery Program (1950–1952)
Colonel Sir Henry Lee
Minister of Finance, Federation of Malaya (1956–1959)
Alan Lennox-Boyd
Secretary of State for the Colonies (1954–1959)
Oliver Lyttleton
Secretary of State for the Colonies (1951–1954)
Malcolm MacDonald
Governor-General, South East Asia (1946–1948)
Commissioner-General, South East Asia (1948–1955)
High Commissioner, India (1955–1960)

Sir Donald MacGillivray
Deputy High Commissioner, Federation of Malaya (1952–1954)
High Commissioner, Federation of Malaya (1954–1957)
Harold Macmillan
Chancellor of the Exchequer (1955–1957)
Sir Alec Newboult
Officer Administrating Government of Malaya
Philip Noel-Baker
Secretary of State for Commonwealth Relations (1947–1950)
Sir John Paskin
Assistant Under-Secretary, Colonial Office (1948–1954)
Sir Hilton Poynton
Private Secretary to Colonial Secretary (1943–1959)
Permanent Under-Secretary, Colonial Office (1959–1966)
Leslie Thomas George Preston
Assistant Principal, Dealing and Accounts Office, Bank of England (1948–1953)
Deputy Principal, Dealing and Accounts Office, Bank of England (1953–1957)
Principal, Dealing and Accounts Office, Bank of England (1957–1968)
Abdul Rahman
Chief Minister of Malaya, Malaysia (1955–1970)
Leader of Alliance Party (1953–1970)
Bernard Rickatson-Hatt
Press Officer, Bank of England
Leslie Rowan
Second Secretary, UK Treasury (1947–1949)
Second Secretary, Head of the Overseas Finance Division (1951–1958)
Ernest Rowe-Dutton
Third Secretary, UK Treasury (1947)
Oscar Spencer
Economic Secretary, Federation of Malaya (1950–1955)
Minister for Economic Affairs, Federation of Malaya (1955)
Economic Adviser and Head of Economic Secretariat, Federation of Malaya (1956–1960)
Sir Gerald Templer
General Officer, Commanding-in-Chief Eastern Command (1950–1952)
High Commissioner and Director of Operations, Federation of Malaya (1952–1954)
Chief of Imperial General Staff (1955–1958)
Lucius Thompson-McCausland
Advisor to the Governor of the Bank of England (1949–1965)
Peter Thorneycroft
Chancellor of the Exchequer (1957–1958)
G.W. Tory
High Commissioner, Malaya (1959–1960)
Sir Henry Wilson-Smith
Second Secretary, UK Treasury (1948)

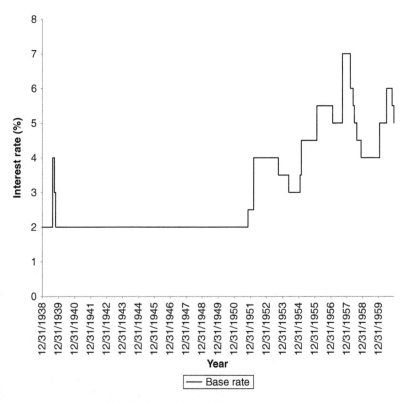

Figure A.1   Bank of England base rate, 1938–1960
Source: Bank of England Statistical Abstract no. 1 (1970).

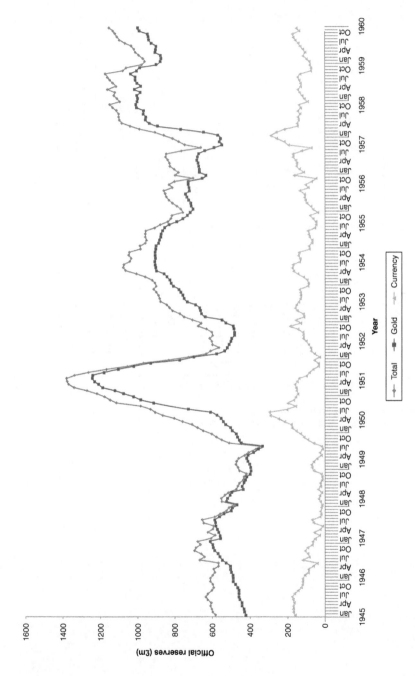

Figure A.2 UK reserves, 1945–1960
Source: Bank of England Statistical Abstract no. 1 (1970).

Figure A.3 Natural and synthetic rubber, 1945–1960
Source: Colin Barlow; The Natural Rubber Industry: Its Development, Technology, and Economy in Malaysia; Oxford University Press, Kuala Lumpur (1978).

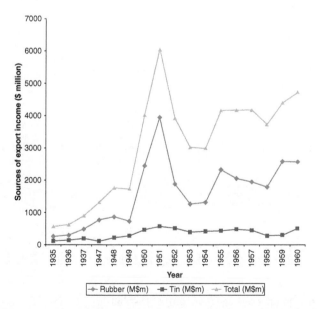

Figure A.4 Pan-Malayan rubber and tin export and total export income, 1935–1960
Source: Lim (1967).

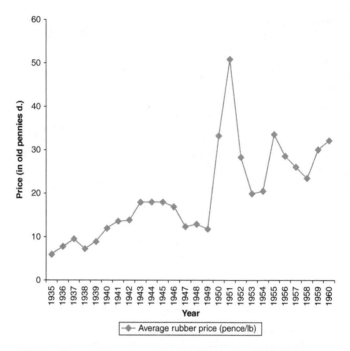

Figure A.5   London yearly average natural rubber price, 1935–1960
Source: Lim (1967).

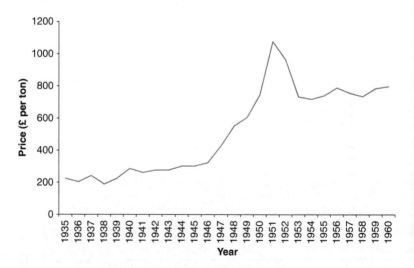

Figure A.6   Tin price average (London), 1935–1960
Source: Lim (1967).

Notes

Introduction

1. See, inter alia, Strange (1971), Tomlinson (1982; 2003), Holland (1984; 1985), Stockwell (1984), Darwin (1988; 2006; 2009), Pollard (1991), Reynolds (1991), Cain and Hopkins (1993), Krozewski (1993; 1996; 1997; 2001), Coates (1994), Schenk (1994; 1996), White (1996; 1997; 2000; 2003), Young and Tomlinson (1997), Young (1998), Hinds (1999; 2001) and Harper (2001).
2. See, for example, McKenzie (1986), Porter (2004), Wilson (2004), Hall (2006) and Makdisi (1998).
3. See, for example, Said (1978; 1993), Barringer and Flynn (1997), Cooper (2005) and Howe (2009).
4. Good examples of this approach include Burnham (1990; 2003), Kettell (2004), Rogers (2012).
5. See *Journal of Imperial and Commonwealth History* 41:4 (2013).
6. For an elaboration on the concept of state managers, see Block (1987).

1 Conceptualising British Imperialism

1. See, inter alia, Wright (1954), Greaves (1955), Bell (1958), Conan (1961), Strange (1971), Newton (1985) and Schenk (1994).
2. One potential counter-example to this claim is Bell (1958), who does focus on four states within the Sterling Area. However, Bell's focus is not on the relationship but the particular institutional mechanisms provided by the Area (ibid.:1958). The states on which he focuses offer examples of these mechanisms. Moreover, these examples are not backed up with archival evidence. The lack of focus on specific bilateral relations is a point also made by both Krozewski (1993) and Schenk (1994; 1996:135).
3. For examples of the exceptions, see Newton (1985), Cain and Hopkins (1993; 2002), Schenk (1996). Particularly noteworthy is Schenk (2010), whose account of the decline of sterling is masterful, especially in regard to understanding its decline in a global context. She points out that even in 1947, 87% of foreign currency reserves were held in sterling and that only by 1955, and following a major devaluation, did global dollar reserves become larger than sterling reserves (ibid.:31).
4. Both Strange (1971:96–103) and Schenk (1993) provide accounts of the establishment of the Malayan Central Bank in 1959. Where Strange argues that Britain was resistant to its establishment due to a desire to have Malaya still economically dependent on Britain, Schenk argues that Malaya was not entirely enthusiastic about the prospect of full monetary independence from the UK, which she argues was due to both the potential political and economic difficulties posed by uniting Malaya with Singapore, and the desire to represent institutional continuity after independence to ensure Malaya

remained an enticing location for foreign investment. While both accounts are very interesting, Strange's account provides no primary sources to support her conclusions, and Schenk's account is historical and ultimately fails to provide a critical explanation behind the logic for Malaya's reticence to enthusiastically pursue monetary independence. For example, there is no reflection upon the fact that both Malaya and Britain see continuity within the Sterling Area as a means for economic stability – it is merely presented as the reason for Malayan reluctance to pursue monetary independence. Furthermore, this book, while certainly concerned with economic and monetary issues, does not intend to focus at great depth on the establishment of the Malayan Central Bank, its origins in the International Bank mission to Malaya in 1954, or the specific nature of the negotiations in its setup.

5. This is a view echoed by Krozewski (1993).
6. See, for example, Krozewski (1993:260) and Schenk (1994:6).
7. Krozewski (1996b:15) also argues in an earlier work that British economic and monetary links with its empire converged immediately after the war up until 1951, due to repeated crises and strains in this period. Subsequent to this, with Britain attempting to integrate into the liberal world order, links with empire began to diverge until 1958, when Britain's relationship with its empire was effectively severed.
8. Schenk (1996:871) points out that the general consensus among state managers was that the sterling balances were not particularly important to government policy, especially by the end of the 1950s, as the benefits (their existence was a manifestation of sterling's use as an international reserve and transactions currency) and disadvantages (Britain could not redeem these liabilities all at once due to their size and function) they provided could not be easily reconciled. Indeed, when analysing the archival documentation, the sterling balances do not feature with much frequency or importance in terms of Britain's relationship with Malaya.
9. Kettell (2001:20) further develops this point in the unpublished version of his thesis by identifying more specifically the problems inherent to such approaches towards exchange rate policymaking:

> In addition to their individual and specific difficulties, the approaches to exchange rate policy-making outlined above are also open to challenges on broader methodological grounds. In particular, these approaches can be criticised for their failure to address the more fundamental and logically prior question of why society itself takes the form that it does. Whilst attributing causal importance to the relation between public and private actors, the political and economic characteristics of individual countries, and the role of interest groups, traditional approaches make no attempt to understand why these social phenomena themselves should exist, but instead treat them in a taken-for-granted, ahistorical, positivist manner. The key difficulty this poses for an understanding of exchange rate policy-making is that there is no means of tracing any internal connection between the aims and motivations of policy-makers and the characteristics of the wider society in which they operate. The relation between political behaviour and socio-economic factors has thus to be derived in an exogenous and speculative fashion, leading to systematised

accounts that are more descriptive than analytical, and which ignore the fundamental constraints that are imposed upon exchange rate policy-making by the structural composition of society itself.

10. This has become a generally well-accepted theory in the literature as a way of describing the manner in which British business operated in the colonies (see Cain and Hopkins (1993; 2002) and Dumett (1999) for further discussion on the concept), and dominates accounts of relationships between business and state in the literature on Malayan business. See, inter alia, Jen (1955), Puthucheary (1960) and Jomo (1988).

11. See, for example, Amin and Caldwell (1977). A later response to Amin and Caldwell was provided by A. J. Stockwell (1998), who argued strongly against the use of the concept of neocolonialism to explain British policy before and after independence (though Stockwell is mainly concerned with post-independence policy) in Malaysia. Stockwell (ibid.:152) argues that British officials were not as obsessed about British investments, or Malayan dollar earnings, as is generally understood but were mainly concerned with regional security and a "grand design" to unite Singapore and the Federation. This is not an entirely convincing argument mainly due to methodological considerations: Stockwell relies entirely on prime ministerial and Cabinet documents to make his case, and his work does not use any Treasury or bank documents to support his argument. As such, there is no account of Malaya's role in and value to the Sterling Area, or convincing argument (or proof provided) for ignoring the economic factors in Britain's relationship with Malaya. This criticism is also made by Schenk (2008).

12. White (2000; 2003) provides further analysis of British involvement in Malaysia after independence, from 1957 to 1970. White's analysis is a little under-theorised and, despite referring to Darwin's (1988) thesis on British decolonisation, does not engage with the literature on the Sterling Area despite its crucial role in providing the basis for Britain's international economic policy. This is also true of Pathak (1988), whose analysis of British foreign policy towards Malaysia from 1957 to 1967 is also atheoretical by his own admission, arguing that to use theory is "tantamount to the quest for utopia" and instead relies on what he calls "historical method" (ibid.:271. Pathak relies very little on archival analysis, using only a handful of documents but depending mainly on interviews and secondary sources. His ultimate conclusion (ibid.:273) is that Britain turns from an "empire" into an "ordinary state", thereby creating a typology of states but does nothing to substantiate how an abstract "state" can change form from an "imperial state" to an "ordinary state". This concept of the "ordinary state" is also not critically reflected upon.

13. White (1997) also provides an analysis of development policy within Malaya from 1945 to 1957, and this focuses upon debates within the literature on Malayan development and rubber policies by authors such as, inter alia, Bauer (1957; 1973) and Rudner (1970; 1972; 1975; 1976). White's account, as with his broader work (1996), focuses principally on relationships between government and business and argues that there was no collusion between the two, thereby rejecting an instrumentalist account of the state, which had been provided by Rudner (1976) that White (1996:119) characterises as an

"anti-development conspiracy" before 1955 (after which elections occurred in Malaya) to keep Asian producers of rubber and tin undeveloped compared with European producers, to whom the colonial state was subservient.

14. The capitalist purchases the labour time of the worker but the worker provides a greater labour power than his wage would suggest. For example, if a worker sells his labour for a wage of £20 per hour yet in that hour he produces £60 worth of finished commodities, the remainder (minus the cost of the means of production) is surplus value.

15. As discussed previously in this chapter, it is difficult at best and foolish at worst to break down the circuit of capital into its component phases, since they function together and cannot be understood separately. Indeed, it is only an analytical conceit that allows it to be divided at all. However, the circuit is still a series of transformations "as capital clothes itself in its different stages, alternately assuming them and casting them aside", and if a crisis occurs at any point in the cycle, then the whole circuit ceases to operate (Marx 1992b:133; Burnham 2006:78).

16. Clarke (1994:171) points out that these crises are merely proximate expressions of the most basic contradiction upon which capitalist production is founded, between the production of use values and the production of exchange value and the supremacy of the latter over the former.

17. One aspect of this is the tendency for the rate of profit to fall. As the capitalist seeks to increase overall production, the growth of constant capital will increase relative to the growth of variable capital. Since the only source of surplus value derives from labour, the rate of profit (understood as the ratio of surplus value to total capital expended) will fall (Marx 1992c:317).

18. This term is also used by Hilferding to refer to the crises that serve as the impetus for international capitalist expansion, and is used generally to refer to any kind of crisis. Indeed, it is intended to refer to the uneven development and progression of different circuits of capital that are still essentially interlinked, thus causing a general disproportionality (Clarke 1994:170).

19. Bieler and Morton write a great deal on the subject of open Marxism, more so than many open Marxists, and so spend many words characterising and describing the approach. I have used their accounts here as they are generally accurate and represent the basic ideas of open Marxism very well.

20. There is no particular reason to halt at this abstract "middle ground", that of the analysis and reification of "different forms of the state", such as the developmental state, the neoliberal state, and the absolutist state, as argued by Bieler et al. (2010). In fact, there is little critical analysis of this point in their work and therefore constitute an argumentum ad temperantiam.

21. While this point is not crucial to the argument presented in this chapter, it still remains relevant as an issue for the conceptualisation of social relations. If the organisation of the state takes ontological precedence over its function, then emphasis can be placed on the open and fluid nature of not just the state but also social relations more broadly (of which the state is a form). If a functionalist approach is adopted, then the nature of the state is delimited and closed, providing no conceptual room for class struggle within its formulation. Similarly, functionalist approaches are teleological in scope, providing a further aspect of closure to the approach. This point also has relevance in making a distinction between relational approaches to the state

and other approaches such as fractionalist or instrumentalist approaches, which focus on the function of the state.

22. Bradley's references to "states" here are not intended to refer to the national state but rather a condition of existence, or "state of reality".

23. For a more substantial assessment of this literature, see, for example, Brewer (1990), MacQueen (2002), Pradella (2012), Kettell and Sutton (2013), Sutton (2013).

24. See Lenin (1934), Bukharin (2003), Luxemburg (1963; 1972) and Kautsky (1916).

25. See, inter alia, Cohen (1973), Amin (1974), Wallerstein (1974; 1980; 1989), Frank (1978; 1980), Frank and Gills (1993) and Arrighi (1994).

26. See, inter alia, Harvey (1999; 2003), Hardt and Negri (2000) and Ignatieff (2003).

27. There is a lack of clarity in the literature over where the novelty of "new imperialism" actually lies: is it a description of a qualitatively different imperialism as it exists today, a new approach to the study of imperialism, or both? (Harvey 2007; Kettell and Sutton 2013; Sutton 2013).

28. See, for example, Ferguson (2003; 2004) and Ignatieff (2003).

29. For example, Lenin (1934), Wallerstein (1974) and Frank (1979).

30. To understand state competition in terms of states exploiting other states would be erroneous. While states seek to deprive other states of surplus value by attracting and immobilising capital within their own boundaries, this is not a fundamentally exploitative relationship despite the historically developed inequalities of the inter-state system. Indeed all states are fundamentally a part of the global capitalist mode of production. Without this mode of production, the national form of the state could not exist, nor without the state could the capitalist mode of production exist. The very nature of this competition ensures the existence of the circuit of capital (the reproduction and self-valorisation of capital) and thus the existence of the state; therefore, the notion of inter-state exploitation is difficult to reconcile with an open Marxist understanding of the state. As Holloway (1994:35) notes:

> exploitation is not the exploitation of poor countries by rich countries but of global labour by global capital, and the bipolarity is not a centre-periphery bipolarity but a bipolarity of class, a bipolarity in which all states, by virtue of their very existence as states dependent on the reproduction of capital, are located at the capitalist pole.

2 British Relative Economic Decline

1. The general consensus in the literature on British political economy takes British relative economic decline as a fact, with some variation. Specific literature on British decline includes Elbaum and Lazonick (1987), Dintenfass (1992), Coates (1994), Hobsbawm (1999) and many more. There are a number of authors who seek to refute the idea of decline, including Manser (1971), Edgerton (1991) and Bernstein (2004). For an excellent analysis of the historical origins and context of the notion of decline itself, see Tomlinson (1996).

2. By "negative", Coates means that unemployment has been caused not by improved production methods but through a loss of market share by British firms.

3. Both Dintenfass and Hobsbawm acknowledge that current accounts of British relative economic decline remain incomplete and unconvincing. Dintenfass (1992:71) himself states: "There is a great deal of work to be done". For further accounts of British political economy in this period, see, inter alia, Langan and Schwarz (1985), Elbaum and Lazonick (1987) and Youngson (1960).

4. While Nairn and Anderson can both be accused of exceptionalism, this also leads to a further accusation of idealism. That is, their arguments for British exceptionalism rest on an ideal-typical conception of the development of capitalism.

5. Poulantzas (1967) defends Nairn and Anderson's work from Thompson on this basis, as both historicist and subjectivist.

6. This measure was also intended to impose discipline on financial capital too, since the higher interest rates were intended to limit excessive lending, forcing the City to adopt more cautious practices (Kettell 2004:80).

7. There is some uncertainty about the term "disequilibrium" in this instance. If we consider the manifestation of this disequilibrium, or disproportionality, as a shortage of means of circulation, then we can comprehend the episode presented here as a crisis of overproduction. Given Clarke's (1994:40) notion that disproportionality is not simply an imbalance of production but, due to the contradictions between value and use value, it can be best presented and understood as a crisis, or burgeoning or developing crisis, of overproduction.

8. See Burnham (1990:16–25), Jessop (1992) inter alia for a more thorough description.

9. A further reason for the demand of US goods was the elasticity of output in the US and the relatively small fraction of output that exports represented to US producers. This meant that deliveries for orders were always very prompt (TNA T230/177, "World Supply of Dollars", 25 June 1952).

10. The price of gold to the dollar was significantly increased by the devaluation of the dollar in 1933 (TNA T230/177, "World Supply of Dollars", 25 June 1952).

11. An entire list of Sterling Area countries would be exhaustive. The Sterling Area, from its true inception in 1939, consisted of the UK, all dominions, save Canada, Newfoundland and Hong Kong (though Hong Kong joined in 1945) and the entire British Empire.

12. They had incentive therefore to peg their currencies to Sterling, to avoid depreciation (in terms of their own currencies) of their considerable holdings of Sterling.

13. This also led to an acceptance of Keynesian policies, as stated by the conference conclusions: "His Majesty's Government nevertheless recognizes that an ample supply of short-term money at low rates may have a valuable influence, and they are confident that the efforts which have successfully brought about the present favourable monetary conditions can and will, unless unforeseen difficulties arise, be continued" (cited in McKay 1932:881).

14. Indeed, this did happen; however, whether trade increased because of imperial preference or because of growing complementarity within the

Empire and dominions is not entirely clear (Scholte 1952; Thorbeck 1960; Eichengreen and Irwin 1995).

15. The legally defined Sterling Area (and its exchange controls) continued after the war; in 1947, the Exchange Control Act (ECA) gave the Defence (Finance) Regulations statutory form and the Treasury's powers in the Sterling Area (particularly over British holdings of foreign securities) were increased. However, the ECA actually made no mention of the Sterling Area; instead it refers to "the scheduled territories" (though this was actually the same thing).

16. However, under Regulation 6 of the Defence (Finance) Regulations, it was still illegal to make an issue of capital in the United Kingdom without the consent of the Treasury (TNA T266/53, Letter to CA Grossmith from M. T. Flett, 4 January 1940).

17. Even by 1950 these agreements were still "the principal legal basis of Sterling Area arrangements with non-dollar countries" (TNA FO371/82915, "The Sterling Area", 24 January 1950). Some countries did not conform to this; arrangements were then made on a bilateral basis.

18. As does Newton (1984:392): "Britain's position as banker to the sterling area did involve her in a world role after 1945 but there is no need to invoke antiquated imperial ambitions to explain it".

19. If the UK were not included in this calculation, the table would 47.4%. Furthermore, Malaya's gross exports to the US stood at US$164m p.a. on average over this period while her imports from the US stood at only US$7m (BE OV65/3, "Malaya's Contribution to Sterling Area Dollar Income", 15 January 1947).

20. Province Wellesley for M$10,000 p.a.

21. Negeri Sembilan, Pahang, Perak, Selangor.

22. Johan, Kedah, Kelantan, Perlis, Terengganu.

23. The term "Malaya" is generally taken to mean the entirety of the region today known as Malaysia, along with Singapore. However, officially, "Malaya" referred to only Penang, Malacca and the nine Malay states. However, archival documentation shows that both usages of the word are common throughout the 20th century, indiscriminately. This can be understood on the basis that British officials considered Malaya and Singapore both economically and politically inseparable (BE OV65/5, "Federation of Malaya: Sterling Assets, Trade and Balance of Payments", 24 January 1957).

24. Remittances to businesses were likely to be very high after reoccupation, and so the UK had to guard against large-scale capital outflows after the war: "The prohibition on the export of currency, gold, etc. to the sterling area, and also on dealings in securities, would be covered by a general prohibition as formerly. There would be no sterling area exemption" (BE OV65/3, "Malaya and Hongkong: Reoccupation problems – Exchange Control", 20 August 1942).

25. There was even a possibility of annexing a part of Thailand (then Siam) as a punishment for their actions during the war, and then including this territory as part of Malaya – there were many untouched and operational rubber plantations in Siam and this would have greatly eased the difficulty of restarting Malayan rubber production (BE OV65/3, "Malaya", 22 February 1943).

26. Straits regulations also made clear that residents of Malaya and Singapore were required to surrender gold and foreign currency to authorised dealers.

The Financial Secretary of the colony specified these dealers. Banks and authorised dealers needed special exemption to keep hold of them (BE OV65/3, "Malaya", 4 October 1943).

27. However, at this stage before reoccupation, it was uncertain exactly how stringent exchange controls would have to be. It was considered to be one of two possibilities: "maintain a complete ban on transfers outside the sterling area" or "to re-establish Exchange Control making transfers to non-sterling area countries subject to permission" (BE OV65/3, "Treasury Committee Minutes of Meeting", 23 November 1943).

3   The Dollar Drain and Colonial Import Policy (1945–1950)

1. The dollar area comprised: US, Philippines (and any territory under US sovereignty), Bolivia, Chile, Colombia, Costa Rica, Cuba, Dominican Republic, Ecuador, Guatemala, Haiti, Honduras, Mexico, Nicaragua, Panama, Peru, Salvador and Venezuela; Canada and Newfoundland (TNA T236/3995, "Import Control Order 1949, Southern Rhodesia", 5 March 1949).

2. *The Times, Financial Times, Telegraph, Express, Mail, Daily Graphic, Sunday Times* and *Bankers' magazine, Manchester Guardian, Economist, Banker* and *News Chronicle, Investors' Chronicle, Reuters, Exchange Telegraph, United Press of America.*

3. Those countries with whom Britain had entered into arrangements concerning the blocking of their accumulated sterling balances.

4. Since convertibility came into effect most countries had used this as an opportunity to convert their surplus sterling and so, from 21 August 1947, George Bolton, the Executive Director of the Bank of England, claimed, the world would be in a position where there was a shortage of sterling. Furthermore, the accumulated sterling balances had been resolved due to intense negotiations: £3.5bn of sterling was no longer a major concern as it had either been set aside or blocked by agreement or held by currency boards or by monetary authorities, or else was held in the Sterling Area (where mostly tacit agreements were held that this sterling was not for current account expenditure). As such, sterling was quite strong. Maintaining this depended on the adverse balance of payments, but HMG had already indicated action to be taken to resolve this (BE 3A38/1, "Press Conference at HM Treasury", 20 August 1947).

5. The blanket import licence ban imposed by the Colonial Secretary on the day of suspension, 20 August 1947.

6. However, the Korean War also was only a brief respite from the global dollar shortage and returned after the war had concluded.

7. Certainly Malaya was not a particularly violent colony; however, there had been a number of strikes and work stoppages prior to the outbreak of the emergency, but these had dropped precipitously before June 1948, with a decline in strikes from 49 in August 1947 to 19 in October, and the number of man-hours lost down from 97,052 to 19,988. This was mainly due to the increase in the price of rubber and employers deciding to restore a cut made in the rate for Chinese contractors (TNA CO1045/177, Visit of Labour

Adviser to Federation of Malaya, 13 December 1947). The declaration of the emergency was instead a "tipping point" on a spectrum of escalation of violent tactics used by the Malayan Communist Party (MCP), and a similar escalation of the suppression of radicalism by the colonial government in Malaya (Harper 2001:147). There seems to be no direct correlation between stoppages and strikes and the development of the communist insurgency (ibid.).

8. i.e. Colonial governments, the Colonial Development Corporation, the Overseas Food Corporation and also "private undertakings operating in the Colonies" would all seek International Bank loans (TNA T232/154, "Caine to Wilson-Smith", 2 July 1948).

9. Another possibility that was suggested by the Bank to the Treasury was for the ECA to distribute between all ERP recipients a sum of £150m in dollars earmarked specifically for purchases from the Sterling Area (BE OV46/5, "Sterling Area – Dollar Deficit", 21 July 1948). However, the US rejected this on the basis that it would lead to substantially enlarged sterling balances following the end of ERP (BE OV46/5, "Sterling Area", 28 July 1948).

10. If a colony wished to receive a portion of the ERP loan for reconstruction and development, they then had to provide a description of the project for funding, the estimated dollar and sterling cost and the duration of the project. With this information, the Colonial Office would approve or deny the funds, though this was only to begin in late 1949 at the earliest (TNA T232/154, "Circular Despatch to all Colonies from Arthur Creech-Jones", 20 September 1948).

11. The chancellor also sent a telegram to the Independent Sterling Area the same day, reiterating what Noel-Baker had already said and apologising for the sense of shock and disappointment they must be feeling, especially considering that the import targets were set at a finance ministers' meeting only three months earlier (TNA T236/3995, "Outward Telegram no.373 Dollar Import Programme" (Top Secret), 22 October 1949).

12. The import restrictions were extremely severe and even Independent Sterling Area members found them particularly difficult to implement. In a letter from the Government of Southern Rhodesia to the chancellor, Stafford Cripps is told how Rhodesia's surplus of US$12m in 1949/50 had led to serious strictures and could not be practicably maintained beyond mid-1950 due to the "real hardship" caused by limiting dollar imports. The letter is revealing in that it underlines that the purpose of these import restrictions is to rebuild the Sterling Area reserves (TNA T236/3995, Letter from Edgar Whitehead to Stafford Cripps, 21 November 1949).

13. Official UK and colonial financial policy had been to support the continuous improvement of standards of living and the resources of the colonies. A key element of this had been avoiding inflationary measures, such as spending financial resources that impeded development by multiplying the demand on limited goods. Provisions had also been made for colonial governments to borrow on London markets, as well as to borrow from the International Bank for Reconstruction and Development under the UK's guarantee (BE OV46/6, "General Memorandum for OEEC: United Kingdom Position in 1950–1951", December 1949).

14. See, for example, Schenk (1996), Hinds (2001) and Krozewski (2001).

4   The Dollar Deficit Continues (1950–1955)

1. Interestingly, these terms were previously "restore peace and order [in] the colony" though were changed since it suggested that Britain had lost control in Malaya, and also emphasised Britain's imperial status over Malaya.

2. In the report, Jim Griffiths, the Colonial Secretary, stated that 350 major economic projects were planned in 1950 for the colonies, with around £400m being spent. Furthermore, he re-emphasised the established view that the colonial territories were economically interdependent with Britain. While the UK provided a large, and growing, market for colonial goods (around 9.8% of UK imports in 1949 were from the colonies), the colonies remained vital as both dollar earners and dollar savers "and so made a further vital contribution to the economic recovery of the sterling area" (TNA T266/53, "Development in Colonies", 1 June 1950).

3. Poynton, during his visit, came under the impression that there was great fondness for the Colonial Office in Malaya, with the idea that when things went right it was because of the Colonial Office and when things went wrong, it was due to the interference of other departments, particularly the Treasury and the Bank.

4. This figure came from the London office of the CDC – the local office in Malaya seemed embarrassed by this rate, though this was due to the high rates at which the CDC was required to borrow money from the Treasury and other sources.

5. Tobacco was specifically mentioned as it was considered a good source of tax revenue.

6. There was no prioritisation made between the two: equal position was expected to mean there would be clashes on occasion but these would be settled on an ad hoc basis.

7. The Nitze Plan emerged from NSC-68 in 1950, and argued that the US needed to greatly increase defence spending and financial support to its allies to boost its own defence capabilities, in order to combat the supposed threat from the Soviet Union (Casey 2005).

8. This was certainly the case in certain "home essentials", like lard and sugar.

9. Chartered Bank of India, Australia and China; the Hong Kong and Shanghai Banking Corporation; the Mercantile Bank of India; and the Eastern Bank.

10. The Colombo Plan was an international organisation created after a Meeting of Commonwealth Foreign Ministers in Sri Lanka in 1950 for the purpose of cooperation in economic development and the raising of living standards in the Asia–Pacific region (Blackton 1951:27).

11. The Briggs Plan was a counter-insurgency strategy devised by Harold Briggs in 1950. The plan called for the forced resettlement of a large section of Malaya's rural population into so-called "New Villages". The purpose of this was to separate the communist insurgents, operating largely from the jungles, from their support among the rural population of Malaya, mainly Chinese "squatters" who practiced subsistence agriculture on the fringes of the jungle. Around 500,000 people were resettled into these villages, which were guarded around the clock by soldiers and police to prevent ingress or egress. Briggs left the post of Director of Operations in 1951 due to ill health and was replaced by Gerald Templer, who oversaw the full implementation

of the Briggs Plan. For further and more detailed accounts of the Briggs Plan and the prosecution of the counter-insurgency campaign see, inter alia, Clutterbuck (1967), Barber (1972), Short (1975), Carruthers (1995), Thompson (1996), Hack (1999, 2000).

12. Interestingly, Churchill recommended to Lyttleton that he also visit Rangoon, Jakarta and Saigon to better understand the problems in Malaya, though this eventually did not transpire (TNA PREM11/122, telegram from Prime Minister to Foreign Secretary, 25 November 1951). Furthermore, Lyttleton changed the initial reference from "terrorism" in his public statement in Malaya to "intestine strife" as, according to Churchill's advice, it made it sound like the "two races of Malaya were at each other's throats" (TNA PREM11/122, EG Cass to Barry G Smallman, 8 December 1951).

13. Montgomery had a particularly ambitious plan for South East Asia, wishing to combine the whole of British South East Asia into a single political unit (TNA PREM11/121, Letter from "Montgomery of Alamein" to Prime Minister, 4 January 1952).

14. Despite the Chancellor's hopes, total reserves did not reach the level of July 1951 (£1,338m) until after 1960, though they did reach similar and consistent levels (around £1,100m) towards the end of 1960 (Bank 1970:162).

15. Finished manufactures comprised a minute fraction of all imports. In 1952, all imported manufactures made up 0.2% of US GNP, and these were largely luxury gods such as pottery, whisky and watches. Devaluation did not significantly alter this and there were other factors to consider, including tariffs and "buy American" clauses (TNA T230/177, "World Supply of Dollars", 25 June 1952).

16. In those years, average rubber prices were (in chronological order) 50.84, 28.34, 19.91, 20.5 and 33.56 p/lb (Lim 1967:335). These figures correspond very closely to the figures for Malayan GDP.

5 Malayan Independence and the Sterling Area (1955–1960)

1. The Exchange Control Ordinances had come into force on 1 January 1954 for one year. They had then been extended by another one-year period and would expire on 31 December 1955 unless renewed. In Council, Saul Marshall suggested a renewal of only six months because the Ordinance operated unfairly against Singapore. The decision was postponed (TNA CO1030/100, "Exchange Control", 9 November 1955).

2. In this Bank document, the memo seems to be referring to Singapore by itself and not included with the rest of Malaya. The Colonial Office considers Singapore's threat dangerous simply by implication that it might lead all of Malaya to abandon exchange controls. However, it is also reasonable to think that the Bank was more committed to the Collective Approach than the Colonial Office and so were more apathetic about the desire of a small colony to, effectively, secede from the Sterling Area.

3. Furthermore, British West Africa was a collective term referring to a number of colonies including Gambia, parts of Nigeria, Sierra Leone and the Gold

Coast (which later became Ghana). As such, it was only collectively valuable and, unlike Malaya, its value was not concentrated in a single industry or territory.

4. However, in late 1955, the Bank was particularly disappointed that the autumn Budget provided no "psychological support" to the value of sterling, particularly since the threat of strikes caused by increased purchases taxation overshadowed the position of sterling. Sterling, at this time of the year with seasonal buying of Sterling Area raw materials, would be expected to strengthen and reserves grow, especially coupled with the highest base rate since the end of the Second World War at 5.5%; however, the Budget had entirely offset this and, by the end of December 1955, the foreign currency reserve had fallen to £38m, the lowest since January 1952. To resolve this, the Bank tried to push transferable sterling up to a rate of US$2.77.5 with a purchase of around US$15–20m of sterling. By the beginning of January 1956, foreign currency reserves had risen to £65m (BE C43/31, "Exchange Market Tactics", 1 November 1955).

5. Marshall made clear to Sir Robert Black, the Governor of Singapore, that he sought complete internal self-government for Singapore by 1959, and would accept British responsibility over external defence and external affairs even then. He also felt that, by then, Singapore's economic responsibility would be total apart from observing GATT, and Singapore would also remain in the Sterling Area (TNA CO1030/100, Telegram no.143, 9 November 1955).

6. A metaphor to which the Prime Minister, Anthony Eden, referred as "more blackmail" (TNA CO1030/100, Philip de Zulueta to J.B. Johnston, 10 November 1955).

7. Marshall was already posturing by this point, to both the Singaporean public and the political class, by seeking an economics adviser from the IMF to replace Loynes from the Bank. Marshall felt that Loynes could not divorce Malaya's interest from Britain's and the Bank of England's interests. It was widely believed in Malayan political circles that, while the Colonial Office had Malaya's best interests at heart, the Bank had sectional interests and was not committed to the development of the Malayan economy (BE OV65/4, "Malaya", 28 April 1950). However, Sir Robert Black, the Governor of Singapore, felt that, with this action, Marshall sought to present himself as a Malayan politician, independent of London (TNA CO1030/100, Telegram no.142, 8 November 1955).

8. Interestingly, Marshall approved the one-year renewal of the Control of Imports and Exports Ordinance, which was complementary to the Exchange Control Ordinance. Taking the same policy with the Im–Ex Ordinance would have made the issue even more pressing and strengthened his hand. This further convinced the Colonial Office that Marshall was not seriously interested in the economic implications or details of his policies (TNA CO1030/100, "Exchange Control", 9 November 1955).

9. However, MacGillivray reiterated that if the Federation did recommend the limited extension, he would refuse to accept it and, if they wished to make a public issue of it, he would have to make clear to the public the reason he did so was because of the disastrous effect it would have on the economy of the country. There would be no need to use reserve powers in the Federation (unlike Singapore), as it was by order of the High Commissioner,

not by bill of the Legislative Council, that the Exchange Control Ordinance is extended (TNA CO1030/100, Telegram no.745, "Exchange Control", 25 November 1955).

10. This seemed a peculiar thing to say since the Colonial Office's stated figure of 70,000 tons accounted for around 11% of Malaya's entire rubber crop in 1956 (calculated from Barlow 1978, Appendix 3.1). The figure then, while not representing an amount that would have a massive impact on the price of natural rubber, was an enormous quantity of rubber and, therefore, of great importance to the Malayan economy.

11. Cyprus was allowed to seek to satisfy its capital requirements in London, though very specific conditions came together to permit this allowance.

12. Indeed, a memo from the Colonial Office stresses the importance placed upon the needs of the colonies, which resonates well with Burnham's (2003:185) characterisation of the Collective Approach as moving "only as fast as the slowest and least-willing country":

> We consider that Colonial claims on the UK must be put in a special category of their own, since the Colonies are, so to speak a part of us, and constitute a first and direct responsibility of HMG. Failure to carry out these responsibilities must have repercussions on the internal position of the UK itself – probably more so than in the case of many of our other external commitments.
>
> (TNA CO1025/56, Memorandum on Overseas
> Expenditure by the Chancellor, 9 January 1956)

13. The Colonial Office realised that they were stuck between two difficult positions regarding end-use information concerning Malayan rubber exports to China. On the one hand, the government would be criticised for being inept, or naïve, by insisting on end-use information, and the trade would be lost since the Chinese would not agree. Alternatively, if Britain did permit the trade, there might be complaints from the US that the British were not enforcing controls on Chinese trade properly (TNA CO1029/112, Record of phone conversation between Eden and Rolleston, 5 October 1956).

14. While Treasury and Bank officials were unsure of how successful would be the Chancellor's statement on 4 December 1956 in boosting confidence in sterling, the reserves did see a boost. The Bank decided to hold sterling rates at their current levels but, in the event of a speculative attack, it was told to take no action in preventing a fall in quotations of forward sterling. However, there was greater concern about the domestic political situation and whether this would see the Conservative government collapse (BE C43/31, "Exchange Market Tactics", 3 December 1956).

15. Sir Robert Scott makes the argument that generous aid is, in a sense, "an insurance premium" to cover those investments since their protection depended on a stable, friendly and prosperous Malaya. He also points out that British military strength east of Suez relied on bases in Malaya. The Anglo-Malayan Defence Agreement legally permitted the UK to maintain forces in the Federation for the fulfilment of Commonwealth and international obligations, as well as to assist the Federation in defending its territory. An agreement with New Zealand and Australia also made available their forces "to continue to assist the Government of the Federation

in its campaign against the Communist terrorists". (TNA CO1030/627, "Federation of Malaya", 27 February 1958; TNA CO1030/903, Letter from Commissioner-General, SE Asia to Colonial Secretary, 6 December 1956).

16. The Malayans argued this was legitimate as the Emergency was not a "local war" but a major part of the worldwide battle against Communism (TNA CO1030/903, "Note for Prime Minister", 8 January 1957).

17. It was to be decided at the time whether the fund would take the form of a grant, a low-interest loan, or a split between the two (TNA CO1030/903, Telegram no.59, 10 January 1957).

18. Abdul Rahman went so far as to say that, considering the UK's financial position at the time, the terms were extremely generous (TNA CO1030/903, Telegram no.59, 10 January 1957).

19. The Malayan dollar was now at a parity of M$3.06122:US$1, and Abdul Rahman sought assurance from the Colonial Secretary, even after independence, that he would not intervene in the par value of the Malayan dollar, or commissions between exchanges of the two, unless he sought the approval of the Federation government (BE OV65/5, "Application by Malaya to IMF, IBRD, IFC", 19 November 1957; BE OV65/5, UK High Commissioner to PM of Malaya, 20 February 1958).

20. The letter makes the same argument made previously a number of times that there were no restrictions on the movement of British capital to Malaya due to Area membership:

> Her natural resources have been developed and her trade built up largely with British money and enterprise. Her plantations and tin mines are still largely financed by British concerns and her trade by British merchant banks. All this would be upset if she left the Sterling Area because the flow of capital from the UK would then be restricted.
>
> (BE OV65/5, "Malaya", 10 September 1957)

21. A currency reserve of £137m was shared with Singapore and British Borneo, with the Federation's share earmarked at £91m (BE OV65/5, "Malaya – London Market Borrowing", 24 January 1958).

22. There was even some discussion as to how far the UK would be willing to go to support the cost of the Emergency in Malaya even further. An inquiry to the Treasury was made by the Colonial Office concerning policy on British financial support for security operations in the Colonies (including Malaya). The Treasury responded that policy on financial responsibility for internal security operations was that the cost must be borne by the civil authority in that colony. This was also true of additional charges raised by British forces in aid of that authority. However, if it could be shown that it was in the interests of Britain that these forces be stationed there (e.g. in a cold war role) then Britain contributed to those costs. Britain would also meet those costs if the colony were shown unable to pay. In Malaya, no charge was raised, nor in Singapore. Therefore, Malaya could only receive further support if it lacked any available funds (TNA CO1030/657, William Russell Edmunds to John Hennings, 28 October 1958).

23. Which prompted the observation that "once ECGD is mentioned, the whole thing seems to look like Christmas to our overseas friends and the frequency

with which Rowan pulls out ECGD makes him look like Father Christmas."
(BE OV65/6, "Malaya", 20 August 1958).

24. Indeed, Malaya seemed very reticent to listen to the Bank's advice and
had become very disenchanted with the Bank's intransigence over a number of issues. When the Bank had suggested a candidate for the Governor
of Malaya's Central Bank, it had been turned down and the Federation
asked Australia for assistance (BE OV65/5, "Federation of Malaya", 14 April
1958).

25. Interestingly, Gould mentioned to Jenkyns that all dollar expenditures by
Malaya still had to pass through the Bank of England first: "Mr Gould said
that returns of authorisation for dollar expenditure all found their way eventually to the Bank of England. This was a surprise to me and I suppose that
it may be a relic of war-time and early post-war Colonial arrangements for
limiting dollar expenditure. It seems to me that unless these returns are of
real importance to the Bank of England we should drop them because of the
danger that they represent to newly-independent countries a symbol of continuing dependent status." (BE OV65/5, "Malayan Desire to Hold Dollars",
11 June 1958).

26. The US$6m figure was also so small that it was not worth worrying about,
according to Crawshaw. Further, If the UK made the situation difficult for the
Federation, it would be likely to invoice Singapore for the US dollars generated from the goods sold on to the US (BE OV65/5, "Federation of Malaya –
US Dollar Transactions", 19 June 1958).

27. Indeed, since independence, there had been substantial communication
between the Federation and Singapore governments, the Colonial Office, the
Treasury and the Bank about the legitimacy and consequences of banning
the Bank of China in Malaya. The Malayan governments were convinced,
though had no evidence, that the Bank of China was supporting communist
insurgents and acting as an "unofficial consulate" for the People's Republic
of China in Malaya, and therefore had to be shut down (BE OV65/5, "Bank
of China", 10 April 1957; BE OV65/6, "Bank of China in Malaya", 21 November 1958; BE OV65/6, Telegram no.129, "Bank of China", 21 November 1958;
BE OV65/6, "Banking Bill", 1 December 1958; BE OV65/6, Telegram no.99,
"The Bank of China", 19 December 1958).

28. The United Malays National Organisation (UMNO), the Malayan Chinese
Association (MCA) and the Malayan Indian Congress (MIC) were quite broad
parties in ideological terms – their names reveal the basis behind their constitution. The only real challenger to these parties was the Socialist Front party
as, though small, it was growing in size (BE OV65/6, "Federation of Malaya",
15 January 1959).

29. All figures shown at 1959 prices.

30. With population growth at 3–4% annually, at least this much growth was
required to maintain living standards in Malaya. The Federation had allocated to its development plan around $775m for the period 1955–1959, but
it was unlikely that this was going to improve the economy substantially in
the next couple of years, and a much greater effort would have been required
if the stated figure of 15% of national income to be used for investment
was to be achieved. This figure was based on an investment of three- to
fourfold the required addition to national income, so for a minimum 3–4%

growth, about 15% investment of national income was required (BE OV65/6, "Federation of Malaya: The Economy", 23 June 1959).

31. The Federation had made a loan agreement with the US Development Loan Fund, a US government agency, for US$10m to develop a port at the Klang Straits, and another US$10m loan for the rehabilitation of bridges and roads in the Federation (BE OV65/6, "Loan Agreement", 18 March 1959).

32. Haslam also felt that the Sterling Area offered something that Malaya from which Malaya specifically benefitted:

> In particular I should regard the unrestricted flow of short term credit and longer term capital as being of vital importance to a country in Malaya's position, faced with the task of maintaining its existing assets and of laying the foundation for further economic development on a large scale.
>
> (BE OV65/6, E. P. Haslam to W. H. Wilcock, 23 June 1959)

33. Colonel Lee was due to retire in 1959, to be replaced by Tan Siew Sin as Minister of Finance in the Malayan Cabinet. As with Colonel Lee, he was very wealthy with significant interests in the rubber industry: director of a number of rubber estates; President of the Malaccan Estate Owners Association; and member of the Rubber Producers Council and other rubber-planting associations. He had held a number of other business posts, and government positions, and was previously Minister of Commerce and Industry from August 1957. Colonel Lee went on to set up the Development and Commercial Bank, which became one of the largest banks in Malaysia (BE OV65/6, "Tan Siew Sin", 24 August 1959).

34. In a meeting with Tan Siew Sin, the new Finance Minister, and the Chancellor, Mr Tan echoed Colonel Lee's statement about building up an independent dollar reserve. The figure was still US$25m and it would be built up gradually. The Chancellor replied: "he hoped that Malaya would keep the figure down to the smallest possible level. The strength of sterling and of the Sterling Area depended to a large extent on the pooling of reserves by its members" (TNA T236/5151, "Malaya", 24 September 1959).

35. Singapore, as a major entrepôt port, bought a great deal of the Federation's rubber and then sold it to the dollar area, and it had always appeared as if Singapore was the major dollar earner in Malaya when, in actual fact, as noted already in this chapter, the instrument for this was the Federation's rubber supply difficulties (TNA T236/5151, "Note of a Meeting in the Chancellor's Room", 9 September 1959).

36. Lee also suggested the IBRD be given greater funds (though he was not as interested in increasing the funds available to the IMF as Malaya did not use their services as much). The Chancellor said he hoped to see an increase in resources for the IBRD (to further aid underdeveloped countries) and the IMF (because of its contribution to increasing world liquidity) (TNA T236/5151, "Note of a Meeting in the Chancellor's Room", 9 September 1959).

37. Present: Wilcock (Central Bank of Malaya, Governor), Denis Rickett (Bank) and Taylor and Jenkyns (Treasury).

38. Tan Siew Sin also said that the Central Bank had taken up IBRD bonds, and confirmed that "since the Federation was in the Sterling Area, a large part of

the Federation's reserves would continue to be invested in sterling securities" (TNA T236/5151, "Malayan Holdings of US Dollars", 27 November 1959.

39. Interestingly, the Treasury noted that the Bank of England was extremely reticent about providing figures on Malayan purchases of foreign currency (TNA T236/5151, "Malayan Dollar Purchases", 1 March 1960). As explanation, the Bank informed the Treasury that, as the Treasury's agents, the Bank was prepared to tell them the amount of a transaction but not the purpose. The Bank might not know officially, as either agents for the Treasury or as bankers for the Central Bank, why the purchase was made. The Treasury was entitled to receive information from the Bank in execution of the Bank's responsibility as the administrators of the Exchange Control Act, but passing it on further rested with the Treasury. Informing the Treasury of customer details followed the line set by Fisher in 1949: "information relating either to our own or other bankers' customers individually would not normally be passed to the Treasury except in so far as is necessary to determine Treasury liability". Furthermore, as advisers to the Treasury, the Bank was obliged to pass on information regarding the implementation of agreements between governments (BE OV65/6, "Federation of Malaya: Independent Dollar Reserves", 21 March 1960).

40. See, inter alia, Holland (1984; 1985), Darwin (1988; 2006), Schenk (1996), Krozewski (1997; 2001) and Hinds (2001).

Bibliography

Primary sources

The National Archives, Kew

CAB23 War Cabinet and Cabinet: Minutes
CAB24 War Cabinet and Cabinet: Memoranda
CAB128 Cabinet: Minutes
CAB129 Cabinet: Memoranda
CO537 Colonial Office and Predecessors: Confidential General and Confidential Original Correspondence
CO967 Colonial Office: Private Office Papers
CO1022 Colonial Office: South East Asia Department: Original Correspondence
CO1025 Economy in Government expenditure: Effect on emergency expenditure in Kenya and Malaya, and on Colonial services vote
CO1029 Colonial Office: Production and Marketing Department: Registered Files
CO1030 Colonial Office and Commonwealth Office: Far Eastern Department and successors: Registered Files
CO1045 Colonial Office and other departments: Papers of Sir Christopher Cox, Educational Adviser
FO371 Foreign Office: Political Departments: General Correspondence, 1906–1966
FCO141 Foreign and Commonwealth Office and predecessors: Records of Former Colonial Administrations: Migrated Archives
PREM8 Prime Minister's Office: Correspondence and Papers, 1945–1951
PREM11 Prime Minister's Office: Correspondence and Papers, 1951–1964
T220 Treasury: Imperial and Foreign Division: Registered Files
T230 Cabinet Office, Economic Section, and Treasury, Economic Advisory Section: Registered Files
T232 Treasury: European Economic Co-operation Committee (Rowan Committee): Registered Files
T236 Treasury: Overseas Finance Division: Registered Files
T266 Capital Issues Committee: Minutes and Papers

The Bank of England Archives, Threadneedle Street

3A38 Chief Cashier's Monetary Policy Files
C43 Gold and Foreign Exchange Files
G1 Governor's Files
OV44 Sterling and Sterling Area Policy
OV46 Post-War Reconstruction: OEEC, EPU, EMA
OV65 Malaya, Singapore and Borneo Territories – Papers

Statistical abstracts and other sources

Bank of England Statistical Abstract No.1 (1970)
British Labour Statistics Historical Abstract 1886–1968, HMSO, London (1971)
Financial Times
Hansard
HMSO; Board of Trade Statistical Abstract for the United Kingdom 83, 1924–1938; HMSO, London (1940)
HMSO; Central Statistical Office, Annual Abstract of Statistics 88, 1938–1950; HMSO, London (1950)
HMSO; Central Statistical Office, Annual Abstract of Statistics 97; HMSO, London (1960)
House of Commons Library; Research Paper 99/111: A Century of Change: Trends in UK Statistics since 1900 (1999)
International Bank for Reconstruction and Development; The Economic Development of Malaya; The Johns Hopkins Press, Baltimore (1955)
Mitchell, B. R. and H. G. Jones; Second Abstract of British Historical Statistics; Cambridge University Press, Cambridge (1971)
The Economist

Secondary sources

Anderson, Perry; The Figures of Descent; New Left Review 161 (1987).
Arrighi, Giovanni; *The Long Twentieth Century: Money, Power, and the Origins of Our Times*; Verso, London (1994).
Barber, Noel; *The War of the Running Dogs: Malaya, 1948–1960*; Fontana Books, London (1972).
Bauer, P. T.; Post War Malayan Rubber Policy: A Comment; *Journal of South East Asian Studies* 4 (1973).
Bauer, P. T.; Malayan Rubber Policy; *Political Science Quarterly* 72:1 (1957).
Bell, Philip; *The Sterling Area in the Postwar World: Internal Mechanism and Cohesion, 1946–1952*; Clarendon Press, Oxford (1958).
Bernstein, George L.; *The Myth of Decline: The Rise of Britain since 1945*; Pimlico, London (2004).
Bieler, Andreas, Ian Bruff and Andrew David Morton; Acorns and Fruit: From Totalisation to Periodisation in the Critique of Capitalism; *Capital and Class* 34:1 (2010).
Bieler, Andreas and Adam David Morton; A Critical Theory Route to Hegemony, World Order and Historical Change: Neo-Gramscian Perspectives in International Relations; *Capital and Class* 82 (2004).
Blackton, Charles S.; The Colombo Plan; *Far Eastern Survey* 20:3 (1951).
Block, Fred; *Revising State Theory*; Temple University Press, Philadelphia (1987).
Bonefeld, Werner, Richard Gunn, John Holloway and Kosmas Psychopedis (eds.); *Open Marxism Volume III: Emancipating Marx*; Pluto Press, London (1995).
Bonefeld, Werner, Richard Gunn and Kosmas Psychopedis (eds.); *Open Marxism Volume I: Dialectics and History*; Pluto Press, London (1992a).
Bradley, F. H.; *Appearance and Reality*; Oxford University Press, Oxford (1930).
Brewer, Anthony (ed.); *Marxist Theories of Imperialism: A Critical Survey*; Routledge, London (1990).

Bukharin, Nikolai; *Imperialism and World Economy*; Bookmarks, London (2003).

Burnham, Peter, Karen Gilland Lutz, Wyn Grant and Zyg Layton-Henry (eds.); Research Methods in Politics (2nd ed.); Palgrave Macmillan, London (2008).

Burnham, Peter; Marxism, the State, and British Politics; *British Politics* 1 (2006).

Burnham, Peter; *Remaking the Postwar World Economy: Robot and British Policy in the 1950s*; Palgrave Macmillan, London (2003).

Burnham, Peter; Marx, International Political Economy and Globalisation; *Capital and Class* 75 (2001).

Burnham, Peter and Jim Bulpitt; Operation Robot and the British Political Economy in the Early 1950s: The Politics of Market Strategies; *Contemporary British History*, 13:1 pp. 1–31 (1999).

Burnham, Peter; Rearming for the Korean War; *Contemporary Record* 9:2 (1995).

Burnham, Peter; The Organisational View of the State; *Politics* 14:1 (1994).

Burnham, Peter; Neo-Gramscian Hegemony and the International Order; *Capital and Class* 45 (1991).

Burnham, Peter; *The Political Economy of Postwar Reconstruction*; Macmillan, London (1990).

Cain, P. J. and A. G. Hopkins; *British Imperialism, 1688–2000*; Pearson, London (2002).

Cain, P. J. and A. G. Hopkins; *British Imperialism: Crisis and Deconstruction 1914–1990*; Longman, New York (1993).

Cain, P. J. and Hopkins, A. G.; The Political Economy of British Expansion Overseas, 1750–1914; *The Economic History Review*, 33:463–490 (1980)

Carruthers, Susan; *Winning Hearts and Minds: British Governments, the Media and Colonial Counter-Insurgency, 1944–1960*; Leicester University Press, London (1995).

Casey, Steven; Selling NSC-68: The Truman Administration, Public Opinion, and the Politics of Mobilization, 1950–1951; *Diplomatic History* 29:4 (2005).

de Cecco, Marcello; *Money and Empire: The International Gold Standard, 1890–1914*; Basil Blackwell, Oxford (1974).

Chakrabarty, Dipesh; *Rethinking Working-Class History: Bengal 1890–1940*; Princeton University Press, Princeton (1989).

Chibber, Vivek; *Postcolonial Theory and the Specter of Capital*; Verso, London (2013).

Childs, David; *Britain since 1945: A Political History*; Routledge, London (1997).

Clarke, Peter; *Hope and Glory: Britain, 1900–2000*; Penguin Books, London (2004).

Clarke, Simon; Capitalist Competition and the Tendency to Overproduction: Comments on Brenner's "Uneven Development and the Long Downturn"; *Historical Materialism* 4:1 (1999).

Clarke, Simon; *Marx's Theory of Crisis*; Macmillan, London (1994).

Clarke, Simon; The Global Accumulation of Capital and the Periodisation of the Capitalist State Form, in Bonefeld, Werner, Richard Gunn and Kosmas Psychopedis (eds.); *Open Marxism Volume I: Dialectics and History*; Pluto Press, London (1992).

Clarke, Simon (ed.); *The State Debate*; Macmillan, London (1991).

Clarke, Simon; *Keynesianism, Monetarism, and the Crisis of the State*; Edward Elgar, Hants (1988).

Clarke, Simon; Capital, Fractions of Capital, and the State: "Neo-Marxist" Analysis of the South African State; *Capital and Class* 5 (1978).

Clift, Ben and Jim Tomlinson; Whatever Happened to the Balance of Payments "Problem"? The Contingent (Re)Construction of British Economic Performance Assessment; *British Journal of Politics and International Relations* 10:4 (2008).

Clutterbuck, Richard; *The Long, Long War: The Emergency in Malaya, 1948–1960*; Cassell, London (1967).

Coates, David; *The Question of UK Decline: The Economy, State and Society*; Harvester Wheatsheaf, London (1994).

Coates, John; *Suppressing Insurgency: An Analysis of the Malayan Emergency, 1948–1954*; Westview Press, Colorado (1994).

Cohen, Benjamin J.; *The Question of Imperialism*; Basic Books, New York (1973).

Conan, A. R.; *The Rationale of the Sterling Area*; Macmillan, London (1961).

Cooper, Frederick; Colonialism in Question: Theory, Knowledge, History; Princeton University Press, Berkeley (2005).

Darwin, John; *The Empire Project*; Cambridge University Press, Cambridge (2009).

Darwin, John; *The End of the British Empire: The Historical Debate*; Wiley Blackwell, London (2006).

Darwin, John; *Britain and Decolonisation: The Retreat from Empire in the Post-War World*; Macmillan, London (1988).

Dintenfass, Michael; *The Decline of Industrial Britain, 1870–1980*; Routledge, London (1992).

Dumett, Raymond E. (ed.); *Gentlemanly Capitalism and British Imperialism: The New Debate on Empire*; Longman, London (1999).

Eagleton, Terry; *After Theory*; Basic Books, New York (2003).

Edgerton, D.; The Prophet Militant and the Industrial Peculiarities of Correlli Barnett; *Twentieth Century British History* 2 (1991).

Eichengreen, Barry and Douglas A. Irwin; Trade Blocs, Currency Blocs and the Reorientation of World Trade in the 1930s; *Journal of International Economics* 38 (1995).

Elbaum, Bernard and William Lazonick (eds.); *The Decline of the British Economy*; Clarendon Press, Oxford (1987).

Elbaum, Bernard and William Lazonick; The Decline of the British Economy: An Institutional Perspective; *The Journal of Economic History* 44:2 pp. 567–583 (1984).

Fforde, John; *The Bank of England and Public Policy 1941–1958*; Cambridge University Press, Cambridge (1992).

Frank, Andre Gunder; *Crisis in the World Economy*; Holmes and Meier, New York (1980).

Frank, Andre Gunder; *Dependent Accumulation and Underdevelopment*; Macmillan, London (1978).

Frank, Andre Gunder and Barry Gills (eds.); *The World System: Five Hundred Years of Five Thousand?* Routledge, London (1993).

Frankel, Joseph; *British Foreign Policy, 1945–1973*; Oxford University Press, London (1975).

Gallagher, J. and Robinson, R.; The Imperialism of Free Trade; *The Economic History Review* 6:1 (1953).

Gardner, Richard N.; *Sterling-Dollar Diplomacy: Anglo-American Collaboration in the Reconstruction of Multilateral Trade*; Clarendon Press, Oxford (1956).

Gilmartin, M; Colonialism/Imperialism, in C. Gallaher, C. Dahlman, M. Gilmartin, A. Mountz and P. Shirlow; *Key Concepts in Political Geography*; Sage, London (2009).

Greaves, Ida; Dollar Pooling in the Sterling Area: Comment; *The American Economic Review* 45:4 (1955).

Gunn, Richard; Against Historical Materialism: Marxism as First-Order Discourse, in Werner Bonefeld, Richard Gunn and Kosmos Psychopedis (eds.); *Open Marxism Volume II: Theory and Practice*; Pluto Press, London (1992).

Hack, Karl; *Defence and Decolonisation in South-East Asia: Britain, Malaya and Singapore 1941–1967*; Routledge, London (2000).

Hack, Karl; "Iron Claws on Malaya": The Historiography of the Malayan Emergency; *Journal of Southeast Asian Studies* 30:1 (1999).

Hall, C.; *At Home with the Empire: Metropolitan Culture and the Imperial World*; Cambridge University Press, Cambridge (2006).

Hardt, Michael and Antonio Negri; *Empire*; Harvard University Press, London (2000).

Harper, T. N.; *The End of Empire and the Making of Malaya*; Cambridge University Press, Cambridge (2001).

Harvey, David; In What Ways Is "The New Imperialism" Really New? *Historical Materialism* 15:3 (2007).

Harvey, David; *The New Imperialism*; Oxford University Press, Oxford (2003).

Harvey, David; *The Limits of Capital*; Verso Books, London (1999).

Hilferding, Rudolf; *Finance Capital: A Study of the Latest Phase in Capitalist Development*; Routledge, London (1981).

Hinds, Allister; *Britain's Sterling Colonial Policy and Decolonisation, 1939–1958*; Greenwood Press, London (2001).

Hinds, Allister; Sterling and Decolonisation in the British Empire, 1945–1958; *Social and Economic Studies* 48:4 (1999).

Hinds, Allister; Sterling and Imperial Policy, 1945–1951; *The Journal of Imperial and Commonwealth History* 15:2 (1987).

Hobsbawm, Eric; *Industry and Empire: From 1750 to the Present Day*; Penguin, London (1999).

Hobson, J. A.; *Imperialism – A Study*; Allen and Unwin, London (1968).

Holland, R. F.; *European Decolonisation 1918–1981: An Introductory Survey*; Macmillan, London (1985).

Holloway, John; *Change the World without Taking Power*; Pluto Press, London (2002).

Holloway, John; Global Capital and the State; *Capital and Class* 52 (1994).

Holloway, John and Sol Picciotto; Capital, Crisis and the State; *Capital and Class* 2 (1977).

Hollowell, Jonathan; *Britain since 1945*; Blackwell, Malden (2003).

Horne, Alistair; *Harold Macmillan, 1894–1956: Volume I of the Official Biography*; Macmillan, London (1988).

Howe, Stephen (ed.); *The New Imperial Histories Reader*; Routledge, London (2009).

Ignatieff, Michael; *Empire Lite: Nation-Building in Bosnia, Kosovo and Afghanistan*; Penguin, London (2003).

Jameson, Fredric; *Postmodernism, or the Cultural Logic of Late Capitalism*; Verso, London (1991).

Jen, Li Dun; *British Malaya: An Economic Analysis*; The American Press, New York (1955).

Jessop, Bob; Fordism and post-Fordism: A Critical Reformulation, in Storper, Michael and Scott, Allen John (eds.); *Pathways to Industrialisation and Regional Development*; Routledge, London (1992).

Jomo, K. S.; *A Question of Class: Capital, the State and Uneven Development in Malaya*; Monthly Review Press, New York (1988).

Kautsky, Karl; *The Social Revolution*. Chicago, IL: Charles H. Kerr (1916).

Kettell, Steven; Circuits of Capital and Overproduction: A Marxist Analysis of the Present World Economic Crisis; *Review of Radical Political Economics* 38:1 (2006).

Kettell, Steven; *The Political Economy of Exchange Rate Policy-Making: From the Gold Standard to the Euro*; Palgrave Macmillan, Hampshire (2004).

Kindleberger, Charles P.; *The Dollar Shortage*; Chapman and Hall, Ltd, London (1950).

Kolko, Gabriel; *The Limits of Power: The World and United States Foreign Policy, 1945–1954*; Harper and Row, London (1972).

Kolko, Gabriel; *The Roots of American Foreign Policy*; Beacon Press, Boston (1969).

Krozewski, Gerold; *Money and the End of Empire: British International Economic Policy and the Colonies, 1947–58*; Cambridge University Press, Cambridge (2001).

Krozewski, Gerold; Finance and Empire: A Note in Reply to Catherine R. Schenk; *The International History Review* 19:4 (1997).

Krozewski, Gerold; Finance and Empire: The Dilemma Facing Great Britain in the 1950s; *The International History Review* 18:1 (1996).

Krozewski, Gerold; Sterling, the "Minor" Territories, and the End of Formal Empire, 1939–1958; *The Economic History Review* 46:2 (1993).

Langan, M. and B. Schwarz (eds.); *Crises in the British State 1880–1930*; Hutchinson, London (1985).

Lenin, V. I.; *Imperialism: The Highest Stage of Capitalism*; International Publishers, New York (1934).

Lim, Chong-Yah; *Economic Development of Modern Malaya*; Oxford University Press, Kuala Lumpur (1967).

Ling, Tom; *The British State since 1945: An Introduction*; Polity Press, Oxford (1998).

Luxemburg, Rosa (translated by Agnes Schwarzchild); *The Accumulation of Capital*; Routledge, London (1963).

Luxemburg, Rosa and Nikolai Bukharin (translated by Rudolf Wichmann), in Kenneth J. Tarbuck (ed.); *Imperialism and the Accumulation of Capital*; Allen Lane, London (1972).

Macqueen, Norrie; *Colonialism*; Pearson Longman, London (2007).

Mandel, Ernest and Johannes Agnoli; *Offener Marxismus: ein Gespräch über Dogmen, Orthodoxie und die Häresien der Realität*; Frankfurt/New York (1980).

Manser, W; *Britain in Balance*; Prentice Hall, London (1971).

Marx, Karl; *Capital: A Critique of Political Economy, Volume I* (translated by Ernest Mandel); Penguin Books, London (1992a).

Marx, Karl; *Capital: A Critique of Political Economy, Volume II* (translated by Ernest Mandel); Penguin Books, London (1992b).

Marx, Karl; *Capital: A Critique of Political Economy, Volume III* (translated by Ernest Mandel); Penguin Books, London (1992c).

Marx, Karl; *Grundrisse: Foundations of the Critique of Political Economy* (translated by Martin Nicholaus); Penguin, New York (1973).

Marx, Karl; *Theories of Surplus Value, Part 3* (translated by Jack Cohen and S. W. Ryazanskaya); Progress Publishers, Moscow (1971).

Marx, Karl and Friedrich Engels; *The Communist Manifesto*; Longman, London (2005).

Marx, Karl and Friedrich Engels; *The German Ideology*; Prometheus Books, London 1998 [1845].

Marx, Karl and Friedrich Engels (translated by Richard Dixon and Clemens Dutt); *The Holy Family, or Critique of Critical Criticism*; Progress Publishers, Moscow (1975).

McKay, Robert; Imperial Economics at Ottawa; *Pacific Affairs* 5:10 (1932).

McKenzie, J (ed.); *Imperialism and Popular Culture*; Manchester University Press, Manchester (1986).

Miliband, Ralph; *Class Power and State Power*; Verso, London (1983).

Miliband, Ralph; *Marxism and Politics*; Oxford University Press, Oxford (1977).

Miliband, Ralph; The Capitalist State: Reply to Nicos Poulantzas, in John Urry and John Wakeford (eds.); *Power in Britain*; Heinemann Education Books, London (1973a).

Miliband, Ralph; Poulantzas and the Capitalist State; *New Left Review* 82 (1973b).

Miliband, Ralph; The Capitalist State; *New Left Review* 59 (1970).

Miliband, Ralph; *The State in Capitalist Society*; Weidenfeld and Nicolson, London (1969).

Nairn, Tom; The British Political Elite; *New Left Review* 23 (1964).

Newton, C. S. S.; The Sterling Crisis of 1947 and the British Response to the Marshall Plan; *Economic History Review* 37:3 (1984).

Newton, Scott; Britain, the Sterling Area and European Integration, 1945–50; *Journal of Imperial and Commonwealth Studies* 13:3 (1985).

Offe, Claus; *Contradictions of the Welfare State*; Hutchinson, London (1984).

Offe, Claus; Structural Problems of the Capitalist State: Class Rule and the Political System. On the Selectiveness of Political Institutions, in von Beyme, Klaus (ed.); *German Political Studies: Volume I*; Sage, London (1974).

Ollman, Bertell; *Dance of the Dialectic: Steps in Marx's Method*; University of Illinois Press, Urbana (2003).

Pasuhkanis, Evgeny; *Law and Marxism: A General Theory* (translated by Barbara Einhorn); Ink Links, London (1978).

Pollard, Sidney; *Britain's Prime and Britain's Decline: The British Economy, 1870–1914*; Edward Arnold, London (1991).

Porter, A. N. and A. J. Stockwell; *British Imperial Policy and Decolonisation*; Macmillan, London (1987).

Porter, B; *The Absent-Minded Imperialists: Empire, Society and Culture in Britain*; Oxford University Press, Oxford (2005).

Poulantzas, Nicos; Marxist Political Theory in Britain; *New Left Review* 43:57–74 (1967).

Pozo, Luis M.; The Roots of Hegemony: The Mechanisms of Class Accommodation and the Emergence of the Nation-People; *Capital and Class* 91 (2007).

Przeworski, Adam and Michael Wallerstein; Structural Dependence of the State on Capital; *American Political Science Review* 82:1 (1988).

Puthucheary, James; *Ownership and Control in the Malayan Economy*; Eastern Universities Press, Singapore (1960).

Reynolds, David; *Britannia Overruled: British Policy & World Power in the 20th Century*; Longman, London (1991).

Rogers, Chris; *The IMF and European Economies: Crisis and Conditionality*; Palgrave Macmillan, Basingstoke (2012).

Rudner, Martin; Malayan Rubber Policy: Development and Anti-Development during the 1950s; *Journal of Southeast Asian Studies* 7:2 (1976).

Rudner, Martin; Financial Policies in Post-War Malaya: The Fiscal and Monetary Measures of Liberation and Reconstruction; *The Journal of Imperial and Commonwealth History* 3 (1975).

Rudner, Martin; The Draft Development Plan of the Federation of Malaya; *Journal of Southeast Asian Studies* 3:1 (1972).

Rudner, Martin; Rubber Strategy for Post-War Malaya: 1945–48; *Journal of Southeast Asian Studies* 1:1 (1970).

Said, Edward; Culture and Imperialism; Vintage Books, New York (1993).

Said, Edward; Orientalism; Penguin, London (1978).

Schenk, Catherine R.; *The Decline of Sterling Managing the Retreat of an International Currency*, 1945–1992; Cambridge University Press, Cambridge (2010).

Schenk, Catherine R.; Malaysia and the End of the Bretton Woods System, 1965–72: Disentangling from Sterling; *Journal of Imperial and Commonwealth History* 36:2 (2008).

Schenk, Catherine R.; Finance and Empire: Confusions and Complexities: A Note; *The International History Review* 18:4 (1996).

Schenk, Catherine R.; *Britain and the Sterling Area: From Devaluation to Convertibility in the 1950s*; Routledge, London (1994).

Schenk, Catherine R.; The Origins of a Central Bank in Malaya and the Transition to Independence, 1954–59; *Journal of Imperial and Commonwealth History* 21:2 (1993).

Scholte, Werner; British Overseas Trade from 1700 to the 1930s; Greenword Press, Westport (1952).

Short, Anthony; *The Communist Insurrection in Malaya, 1948–1960*; Frederick Muller, London (1975).

Stockwell, A. J.; Malaysia: The Making of a Neo-Colony? *Journal of Imperial and Commonwealth History* 26:2 (1998).

Stockwell, A. J.; British Imperial Policy and Decolonisation in Malaya, 1942–52; *Journal of Imperial and Commonwealth History* 13:1 (1984).

Strange, Susan; *Sterling and British Policy: A Political Study of an International Currency in Decline*; Oxford University Press, London (1971).

Stubbs, Richard; *Hearts and Minds in Guerrilla Warfare: The Malayan Emergency, 1948–1960*; Eastern Universities Press, Singapore (2004).

Sutton, Alex; Towards an Open Marxist Theory of Imperialism; *Capital and Class* 37:2 (2013).

Thompson, E. P.; The Peculiarities of the English; The Socialist Register (1965).

Thompson, Robert; *Defeating Communist Insurgency: Experiences from Malaya and Vietnam*; Chatto and Windus, London (1966).

Thorbeck, Erik; The Tendency towards Regionalisation in International Trade, 1928–1956; Martinus Nijhoff, The Hague (1960).

Tomlinson, B. R.; The Contraction of England: National Decline and the Loss of Empire; *The Journal of Imperial and Commonwealth History* 11:1 (1982).

Tomlinson, Jim; The Decline of the Empire and the Economic "Decline" of Britain; *Twentieth Century History Review* 14:3 (2003).

Tomlinson, Jim; Inventing Decline: The Falling behind of the British Economy in the Postwar Period; *Economic History Review* 49:9 (1996).

Tomlinson, Jim; The Attlee Government and the Balance of Payments, 1945–1951; *Twentieth Century History Review* 2:1 (1991).

Tsolakis, Andreas; Opening Up Open Marxist Theories of the State: A Historical Materialist Critique; *British Journal of Politics and International Relations* 12:3 (2010).

Wallerstein, Immanuel; *The Modern World-System, Volume Three: The Second Great Expansion of the Capitalist World-Economy, 1730–1840*; Academic Press, New York (1989).

Wallerstein, Immanuel; *The Modern World-System, Volume Two: Mercantilism and the Consolidation of the European World-Economy, 1600–1750*; Academic Press, New York (1980).

Wallerstein, Immanuel; *The Modern World-System, Volume One: Capitalist Agriculture and the Origins of the European World-Economy in the Sixteenth Century*; Academic Press, New York (1974).

White, Nicholas; Malaya and the Sterling Area Reconsidered: Continuity and Change in the 1950s, in Akita Shigeru and Nicholas (eds.); *The International Order of Asia in the 1930s and the 1950s*; Ashgate, Aldershot (2010).

White, Nicholas; *British Business in Post-Colonial Malaysia, 1957–70*; Routledge, London (2004).

White, Nicholas; The Survival, Revival and Decline of British Economic Influence in Malaysia, 1957–70; *Twentieth Century British History* 14:3 (2003).

White, Nicholas; British Business Groups and the Early Years of Malaysian Independence, 1957–65; *Asia Pacific Business Review* 7 (2000).

White, Nicholas; The Frustrations of Development: British Business and the Late Colonial State in Malaya, 1945–57; *Journal of Southeast Asian Studies* 28:1 (1997).

White, Nicholas; *Business, Government, and the End of Empire: Malaya, 1942–1957*; Oxford University Press, Oxford (1996).

Wilson, K.; *A New Imperial History: Culture, Identity and Modernity in Britain and the Empire, 1660–1840*; Cambridge University Press, Cambridge (2004).

Winstedt, R.; *Britain and Malaya, 1786–1941*; Longmans Green and Co, London (1944).

Wright, Kenneth M.; Dollar Pooling in the Sterling Area, 1939–1952; *The American Economic Review* 44:4 (1954).

Young, Hugo; *This Blessed Plot: Britain and Europe from Churchill to Blair*; Macmillan, London (1998).

Young, John W. and Tom Tomlinson; *Britain and the World in the 20th Century*; Hodder Arnold, London (1997).

Youngson, A. J.; *The British Economy: 1920–1957*; Harvard University Press, Harvard (1960).

Unpublished theses

Kaplan, Thomas; In the Front Line of the Cold War: Britain, Malaya and South-East Asian Security, 1948–1955; University of Oxford (1990).
Kettell, Steven; The Political Economy of Exchange Rate Policy-Making. A Re-Assessment of Britain's Return to the Gold Standard in 1925; University of Warwick (2001).
Pathak, Archana; British Foreign Policy towards Malaysia, 1957–1967; University of Hull (1988).

Index

Note: Locators followed by 'n' indicate notes section.

216

Printed and bound by CPI Group (UK) Ltd, Croydon, CR0 4YY